# Society *of the* Righteous

FRAMING THE GLOBAL
*Hilary E. Kahn and Deborah Piston-Hatlen, series editors*

# Society of the Righteous

*Ibadhi Muslim Identity and Transnationalism in Tanzania*

Kimberly T. Wortmann

INDIANA UNIVERSITY PRESS

This book is a publication of

Indiana University Press
Office of Scholarly Publishing
Herman B Wells Library 350
1320 East 10th Street
Bloomington, Indiana 47405 USA

iupress.org

© 2024 by Kimberly T. Wortmann

Parts of chapter 3 previously appeared in Kimberly T. Wortmann, "Ibadi Muslim Schools in Post-Revolutionary Zanzibar," *Africa: Journal of the International African Institute* 92 (2022): 249–64. © 2022 by the author, published by Cambridge University Press. Reprinted with permission.

All rights reserved
No part of this book may be reproduced or utilized in any form or by any means, electronic or mechanical, including photocopying and recording, or by any information storage and retrieval system, without permission in writing from the publisher.

First printing 2024

Cataloging information is available from the Library of Congress.
ISBN 978-0-253-07114-9 (hardback)
ISBN 978-0-253-07115-6 (paperback)
ISBN 978-0-253-07116-3 (ebook)

For My Parents and the Istiqaama Community of Tanzania

# CONTENTS

*Acknowledgments ix*
*Note on Transliteration xv*
*Acronyms xvii*

Introduction 1

1. Ibadhi Identity and Intra-Muslim Relations in Postrevolution Zanzibar 39
2. Building a Righteous Muslim Society 77
3. Ibadhi Schools and Their Transnational Networks 111
4. Ibadhi Students and Teachers between Tanzania and Algeria 131
5. Ibadhi Migrations, Religion, and Commerce in the Lake Region 161
6. Gendered Righteousness: Ibadhi Women and Their Local Networks 195

  Conclusion 217

*Glossary 221*
*Bibliography 227*
*List of Interviews 239*
*Index 241*

# ACKNOWLEDGMENTS

I would like to express my deep gratitude to the Istiqaama Muslim Community in mainland Tanzania, Zanzibar, and Oman, for welcoming me into their mosques, schools, offices, and homes during my research for this book. I am moved by the dedication of the Tanzanian, Omani, and Algerian teachers, students, administrators, and scholars I met at the branches of Istiqaama I visited. My best wishes to them in their educational endeavors. My appreciation extends to the many people who took the time to sit and speak with me at Ahlul Bayt Foundation, Madrasat al-Noor, and the Mufti's Office in Unguja and Pemba.

Special thanks to Said El-Gheithy, at the Princess Salme Gallery in Stone Town, for introducing me to the work of Istiqaama and facilitating my initial connections with the community and its leadership in Zanzibar. I am grateful to my dear friend Sabrina Zahor for helping me connect with Ibadhi communities in Dar es Salaam and Mwanza, and for her constant support throughout my research and writing. Without her insights and assistance in various aspects of the research process, this work would not have been possible.

I have great appreciation for Salim al-Mugheiry and family in Zanzibar, Bi Moza and family in Pemba, Shamsa al-Habsy and family in Dar es Salaam, and Bwana Nassor for the many connections he helped me make with Ibadhi communities in the rural northwest. I am beholden to Baba and Mama Sabrina in Mwanza for treating me like family and being so generous with their time.

I want to thank Bethany Mowry at the University of Indiana Press (IUP) for unreservedly acknowledging the value of my work and helping me bring this interdisciplinary project to life. To Lesley Bolton, my production editor at IUP, and Laura Abrams at Amnet, thank you for guiding me through the final stages of production. This book could not have been published without the generous feedback of the two blind reviewers and copy editor of my manuscript and the support of the board for the Framing the Global series at IUP. I appreciate the editorial insights of Lynn Everett throughout the manuscript and Sylvia Benvenuto's development of the index.

This book originally started as my doctoral dissertation at Harvard University, and I am thankful to have had the gift of time to expand on the ideas presented in it and to enhance its overall presentation. I would like to express my gratitude to my dissertation advisor, professor, and mentor Ousmane Kane, for consistently advocating for and guiding me in a challenging academic environment. I acknowledge the support and encouragement given by Professor Jacob Olupona in my study of religion in Africa. The mentorship and dedication of you both in centering African ways of knowing have truly made a difference in my academic pursuits. I am grateful to the late Professor Anne Monius for her tremendous investment in my success and to Professors Malika Zeghal and Kai Kresse for their valuable feedback on my dissertation.

I am also thankful for the various institutions and organizations that have provided me with funding for my research. At Wake Forest University, the Study of Religions, the Archie Fund for Faculty Research, the Provost's Travel Grant, and the Dean's Office Research and Publication Grant have all generously supported this work. Additionally, the Wake Forest Humanities Institute's Summer Writing Grant, Wabash Center's Workshop for Early Career Religion Faculty Teaching Undergraduates, and the African Studies Review Pipeline for Emerging African Studies Scholars Workshop have provided valuable resources for my professional development and research.

The Harvard Loeb Summer Research Fellowship, Fulbright Institute of International Education, and Harvard Sheldon Fellowship supported my year of research in Tanzania between 2015 and 2016, and several Foreign Language and Area Studies (FLAS) Fellowships in Arabic and Swahili, which have all contributed to my growth as a scholar and allowed me to pursue my research interests. In the end, my research in Tanzania would not have been possible without the permissions and assistance of the staff and administrators at the Tanzania Commission for Science and Technology (COSTECH), the Zanzibar National Archives (ZNA), and the Tanzanian National Archives (TNA). I am particularly grateful to Mussa Shehe of the U.S. Embassy in Tanzania and Sumait University and Vice Chancellor Hamed R.H. Hikmany for providing an institutional home for my project while in Zanzibar.

I am thankful to the Harvard Weatherhead Center for International Affairs for providing me with office space, funding, and a supportive community of faculty, student colleagues, and staff. I would also like to thank the University of North Carolina-Chapel Hill Moore Undergraduate Research Apprentice Program (MURAP) for identifying my potential as a scholar and for sparking my passion for research and setting me on this academic path.

I would like to recognize and thank the organizers and attendees of the various conferences and invited talks where I have presented my research on Ibadhi Muslim transnationalism, and Islam in East Africa and the Indian Ocean World. Among them are Farah El-Sharif, Kai Kresse, Mauro Nobili, Neelofer Qadir, Oludamini Ogunnaike, Scott Reese, Shankar Nair, Terje Østebø, and Zekeria Ould Ahmed Salem, Benjamin Pontzen, Benjamin Soares, Noah Solomon, and Macodou Fall. These opportunities have allowed me to engage in fruitful discussions and receive valuable feedback, significantly contributing to the development and refinement of my ideas for my book.

I am thankful for the support and funding from various conferences and institutions for some of these talks, such as the American Academy of Religion (AAR), the African Studies Association (ASA), the Middle East Studies Association (MESA), Swahili Studies Workshop at Columbia University, Institute for Islamic Thought in Africa at Northwestern University (ISITA), The Center for Global Islamic Studies at the University of Florida, Gainesville, Hamilton Lugar: School of Global and International Studies, Berlin, "Timbuktu Talks" at the University of Illinois, Urbana-Champaign, and Stanford University's Abbasi Program in Islamic Studies, among others.

The knowledge and insights gained from these forums have been crucial in shaping my understanding of Ibadhi society and have played a vital role in the writing of my book. I am particularly grateful for the invitations to participate in the annual international Ibadhi Studies conferences, which were made possible by scholars like Abdurrahman al-Salimi and Angeliki Ziaka. I fondly remember my experience learning from mentors in this small but vibrant sub-field of Islamic and religious studies, including Adam Gaiser, who spent countless hours reading my chapters and guiding me through the final stages of this book. I want to express my gratitude to Valerie Hoffman and Amal Ghazal whose works have been critical starting points for my own research. I am grateful for the guidance and feedback on selected chapters in this book from my respected colleagues in anthropology and the history of East Africa and the Arabian Peninsula specifically, Mandana Limbert, and Dodi McDow, whose work that imagines the Indian Ocean world as extending to Lake Victoria has been a great inspiration in my writing. The generous feedback and works of Augustin Jomier and Paul Love on chapter four helped me better understand and articulate the historical context of Ibadhi intellectual history and reform in North Africa. Richard Allen's thoughtful comments on the overall framing of the project have also been helpful.

Having the opportunity to conduct the research and writing for this book has been an immense privilege, as well as rewarding, and transformative, expanding my horizons and understanding of the life worlds I study and teach. However, this work can be a lonely endeavor which I could not have accomplished without the friendship and care of two colleagues, Drs. Neelam Khoja and Michal Hasson. The hours we spent discussing work and life over coffee, dinner, and at our regular stations in Widener library are some of fondest memories from writing this dissertation turned book.

I have enjoyed conversations about aspects of this book with Rabiat Akande, Lina Benabdallah, Deirdre DeBruyn Rubio, Alexander Fattal, Laura Goffman, Zachary Green, Sonia Hazard, Alisha Hines, Jieun Lee, Jodi Marshall, Nathaniel Mathews, Ryan Scroth, Ari Schriber, Matt Steele, and Lydia Walker, and thank them all for their camaraderie.

I deeply appreciate all my colleagues in the Study of Religions at Wake Forest University for their guidance, and support. I especially want to thank Lynn Neal, Mary Foskett, Segun Ilesanmi, Nelly van Doorn Harder, Tanisha Ramachandran, Annalise Glauz-Todrank, and Luke Johnston, for their mentorship, feedback, and encouragement in the most challenging stages of bringing this book to fruition.

To my parents, Dr. Charles and Tina Wortmann, to whom this book is dedicated, thank you for supporting my unconventional career path. I am grateful for your trust in my instincts, for reading my work, and affirming its importance and potential. To Chris, Joan, their partners, and Maya baby, thank you for expanding my vision of what is possible in life, and the memory of all my grandparents. I am thankful for my extended family in both the Southern and Northern Hemispheres, especially Mama Mkubwa and Shomari, Baba na Mama Wile, and Baba na Mama Joyce. Finally, thanks to Theodore (Teddy) Wooly Wortmann for being my delightful and playful muse in the final stages of the production of this book. I love you all and without your guidance, encouragement, and faith in me, I would not have been able to succeed on this journey to completion of *Society of the Righteous*.

While this work is the result of many conversations with numerous international interlocutors, the framing and narration of the events, figures, and histories in this book are ultimately mine. It is my hope that I have represented them with the nuance and care they deserve.

# NOTE ON TRANSLITERATION

The Arabic transliterations used in this study are based on the *International Journal of Middle Eastern Studies* (IJMES). This choice was made to maintain consistency and clarity when transliterating Islamic vocabulary and specific terms from Arabic sources. The IJMES transliteration system is widely recognized and used by various journals that focus on Islam or Arabic-speaking cultures and societies. For terms such as Sunni and Shiʿa, which are assumed to be familiar to most readers, diacritical marks are not retained. Due to the centrality of Ibāḍī Muslims (also known as Al-Ibāḍiyya in Arabic) in this study, diacritical marks are omitted when using this term to facilitate ease of reading. Ibāḍī will be rendered as Ibadhi. I will also use the proper noun Ibadhism.

The Swahili transliterations in this study adhere to the common spellings of *Taasisi ya Uchunguzi wa Kiswahili* (TUKI), or the Institute for Kiswahili Studies, University of Dar es Salaam. The interviews conducted for this book were primarily in the Swahili language. Swahili is a Bantu language with influences from Arabic and other languages and has its own transliteration system. Certain conventions are followed in Swahili transliteration, such as replacing the Arabic letter "ع" with "aa," as in, "Shaaban" (the month proceeding Ramadan), and "ح" or "خ" with "h," as in "husuni" (fortress) or "hotuba" (sermon). However, the specific rules for Swahili transliteration may vary depending on the specific context or purpose, for example, whether the cited text is an Islamic religious tract or a newspaper article intended for a general audience.

In sentences or paragraphs where both languages are used and it is unclear which language is being referred to, I use the following system of differentiation: Islamic school of law (Ar., *madhab*; Sw., *madhehebu*). Non-English words will be italicized on first occurrence and then written without italics in subsequent occurrences.

Although both systems aim to represent Arabic and Swahili using the Latin alphabet for English-speaking readers, they differ because of the specific sounds and letters in each language. For more examples of how these transliteration systems are used as well as the translation of specific words in this study, please consult the glossary.

# ACRONYMS

**ABF**: Ahlul Bayt Foundation
**ASP**: Afro-Shirazi Party
**BAKWATA**: The National Muslim Council of Tanzania
**BMMT**: Bilal Muslim Mission of Tanzania
**CCM**: Chama cha Mapinduzi
**EAMWS**: East African Muslim Welfare Society
**FBO**: faith-based organization
**GMO**: Grand Mufti's Office (Zanzibar)
**ICT**: Information and Communication Technology Commission
**IMCOT**: Istiqaama Muslim Community of Tanzania
**MERA**: (or MARA) Ministry of Endowments and Religious Affairs (Sultanate of Oman)
**NGO**: nongovernmental organization
**SMZ**: Serikali ya Mapinduzi ya Zanzibar
**TANU**: Tanganyikan African Union
**TDCF**: The Table and Desk Foundation
**TOEFL**: Test of English as a Foreign Language
**UAE**: United Arab Emirates
**VETA**: Vocational Education and Training Authority
**ZNP**: Zanzibar Nationalist Party

# Society
*of the*
Righteous

# Introduction

In August 2016, the construction of a capacious and elaborate congregational mosque, located just outside historic Stone Town, Zanzibar, came to a much anticipated completion. The mosque, officially called in Arabic *Jāmiʿi Zinjibār*, had an interior capacity to accommodate around two thousand congregants at one time, separate prayer halls for men and women, and an additional room for 250 worshippers in the exterior chambers. A computer lab, library, and lecture rooms surrounded the mosque, all intended for use by students and teachers from the neighboring Zanzibar Muslim Academy. Though the mosque was built on the main island of Zanzibar, an archipelago in the western Indian Ocean and part of the United Republic of Tanzania,[1] its construction had begun at the initiative of Qaboos bin Said, the former sultan of the Arab Gulf state of Oman (r. 1970–2020).[2] Sultan Qaboos was a follower of Ibadhism, a branch of Islam that is neither Sunni nor Shiʿa, yet the mosque was to be non-denominational. In the spirit of diplomacy, Omani royal architects produced the plans for the complex incorporating African and Arabic design elements while a multinational contractor based in the mainland Tanzanian coastal city of Dar es Salaam carried out its construction.[3] The process of building the mosque apparently proceeded unobstructed. Oman presented the work as a collaboration, but at the end of the day, the funding came from the sultan's cabinet, or diwan, in Muscat, Oman's capital.

In many ways Jāmiʿi Zinjibār mirrored other mosque-building projects undertaken by Gulf countries elsewhere in the world. In its design, it fit art historian Rivzi Kishwar's description of "transnational mosques," architectural projects with a timeless quality that represent nostalgia while also using modern building materials and equipment to anticipate future needs. In this sense, Jāmiʿi Zinjibār indeed served as "simultaneously a memorial to the past and an aspiration toward what is to come. At the same time, their design and patronage reveal the multiple transnational agents involved, from foreign governments to local associations with international ties."[4] In contrast to most transnational mosques, Jāmiʿi Zinjibār was built atop a complex, deeply intertwined, and contested history between Oman and Zanzibar. This history presented challenges to the inauguration of the mosque, which did not open for more than a year after it was completed.

Rumors circulated in Zanzibar and online about an ongoing dispute over which government—Oman or Zanzibar—had jurisdiction over the mosque's affairs. The Revolutionary Government of Zanzibar or Serikali ya Mapinduziy Zanzibar (SMZ) initially welcomed this gift from the royal house of Oman, even though "revolutionary" in its name referred to the 1964 uprising that deposed a sultan from the same Omani royal family that had ruled Zanzibar for more than a century. For its part, the Omani government described the new religious structure as a symbol of the enduring fraternal ties between the two states and an example of Oman's continued support of education, religious patronage, and development in its former dominion. Indeed, at the official opening, September 22, 2017, the shared heritage (Ar., turāth; Sw., urithi) of both Oman and Zanzibar and their distinct national identities were on display. In his speech marking the occasion, His Excellency Habib al-Riyami, secretary-general of the sultan's Center for Culture and Science in Oman, described the mosque as a blessing from his sovereign that "embodies Oman's message to spread peace, and tolerance for all that concerns it."[5] The Zanzibari and Omani officials present at the opening all wore the traditional long white garments (Sw., kanzu; Gulf; Ar., dishdāsha) preferred by men in many Muslim-majority states. Yet where the Omanis wore theirs with turbans, the Zanzibaris added dark blazers on top of their kanzus and donned unturbaned round caps (Sw. kofia). Most, if not all, of the Omanis in attendance at the opening of Jāmiʿi Zinjibār were Ibadhis (Ar., al-Ibaḍiyya),[6] a historic branch of Islam with deep ties to Oman, while the Zanzibari representatives were overwhelmingly Sunni Muslims. Moreover, while the congregational mosque is nonsectarian, its patronage and resonance in Zanzibar is linked to Omani-Ibadhi ideas about religious tolerance and Islamic cosmopolitanism, ideas that undergird Oman's foreign policy in the Gulf and East Africa.[7]

The mosque exemplifies the role that religious institutions and actors play in reimagining Oman's role in Tanzania as a benevolent and pious patron

INTRODUCTION 3

**Figure 0.1**: *Jāmiʿi Zinjibār*, 2017. Officials from Zanzibar and the Sultanate of Oman at the opening of the "Sultan Qaboos Mosque" in Zanzibar. Photo by Othman Maulid, Zanzi News online.

of religious and cultural institutions. These institutions include the Ibadhi transnational, diaspora-run religious community called the Istiqaama Muslim Community of Tanzania, known in Swahili as *Jumuiya ya Kiislamu ya Istiqaama Tanzania* (IMCOT), which is at the heart of this book. Indeed, Istiqaama not only is actively involved in the conservation of Omani cultural and religious heritage across Tanzania but also plays a critical role in paving the way for diplomatic relations in the region. Similar to what anthropologist Nathalie Peutz observes in Yemen's Soqotra Archipelago, such grassroots claims to heritage can be a potent form of political engagement with the most imminent concerns of the present: human rights, globalization, democracy, and sustainability.[8] This is important in a diverse postcolonial African society that was once simultaneously ruled by both European and Omani powers, both of which continue to express interest in economic investment and tourism across the country, raising questions about how "post" the colonial really is.

For example, the Zanzibar mosque controversy indicates a lingering anxiety in Tanzanian leaders that suggests, although the Omani sultanate's political power in Zanzibar came to an official end more than fifty years ago, there are ways in which Oman's imperial legacy persists in Zanzibar today. It also shows how Oman's investment in various forms of religious patronage in Tanzania, generally, such as in mosques and schools, both alleviates and exacerbates existing tensions between the two states, providing much needed social services tied to an Omani vision for religious reform in the mainland and island regions. This tension is apparent in the popular way of referring to the mosque as "Masjid Sultan Qaboos." It is additionally evident in the growing influence of Ibadhi schools and charities that have ties to Oman and the influence of Omani religious authorities in Tanzania. The mosque is a high-profile example of transnational government collaboration and competition over a shared cultural heritage, and as anthropologist Clifford Geertz argues, it is a model *of* human behavior and a guide *for* developmental initiatives in the future.[9]

## Approaching a Transnational Muslim Community

With its unique focus on Istiqaama and drawing primarily on interviews, oral histories, and writings narrated by Ibadhis in Tanzania and Oman, *Society of the Righteous* documents the ways that Ibadhi identity has been understood in Tanzania since the 1980s. This period marked the end of Tanzanian socialism and the beginning of democratic and neoliberal reforms that gave rise to transnational religious organizations with ties to the Gulf. It was also a time when the country had begun to open its borders to foreign investment and travel, enabling a delegation of religious scholars from Oman to visit and propagate modern Ibadhi ideals centered on religious tolerance and intra-Muslim diplomacy. Throughout my research, I asked how these reforms have served to transform the public and private image of Ibadhism—which in Tanzania is understood as an ethnoreligious identity often conflated with being Omani or Arab—in the decades following the 1964 Zanzibar Revolution.

The origins of Ibadhism can be traced back to the contests over the caliphate and early Muslim rule at the battles of Siffin (657 CE) and Nahrawan (658 CE) and the Islamic movement entangled in both events known as the *Khawārij*. The Khawārij often clashed with Muslim authorities during the rule of the Sunni Umayyad (661 to 750 CE) and the Abbasid caliphates (750–1258). Ibadhis today try to distance themselves from the Khawārij, who are criticized by their modern detractors for their violent acts against other Muslims who disagreed with their strict beliefs.[10] Instead, Ibadhis emphasize that a conservative approach to the teachings of Islam need not preclude religious tolerance and moderation toward non-Ibadhis. However, one obvious connection that remains between the two groups is their shared rejection of the belief that the leader of the Muslim community (*umma*) must come from a specific lineage or dynasty. Instead, Ibadhism advocates for the election of this leader (known as the *imam*) through communal consultation (Ar., *al-shūrā*). This principle of just leadership is consistent in the writings of various figures across what historian Cyrille Aillet calls the "Ibadhi archipelago."[11] This region spans from Oman in the Arab or Persian Gulf to the coastal and interior regions of East Africa and extends as far west as Tunisia, Libya, and Algeria,[12] where thriving Ibadhi communities still exist, one of which will be discussed in chapter four.

The way Istiqaama refers to itself in Swahili, as an Ibadhi Jumuiya (community or association), is like the Arabic used in Oman *jamʿiyya* (society, organization, or association).[13] Istiqaama is a self-proclaimed nongovernmental organization headquartered in Muscat with over twenty-four branches in Tanzania run by male leaders of Omani heritage. It was formally established in 1995 through a joint effort between the Office of the Mufti in the sultanate of Oman, led by Sheikh Ahmad bin Hamad al-Khalili—the country's Ibadhi grand mufti or supreme legal authority who was born in Zanzibar in 1946—and Ibadhis in Tanzania. The term Istiqaama comes from the Ibadhi self-appellation "Ahl al-Haqq wa-l Istiqaama,"[14] or "the people of truth and righteousness." Relatedly, the various institutes and organizations established by Istiqaama and discussed herein are key to the self-representation of the Ibadhi community and serve as a model for religious tolerance (Ar., *al-tasāmuh*); what I term a Muslim *society of the righteous*. This righteous society, or the moral community that Istiqaama established in Tanzania, includes an innumerable network of mosques, schools, radio stations, orphanages, and charities that I argue are at the center of the Omani diaspora's efforts to reimagine and shape Ibadhi identity and sense of belonging in postcolonial and postrevolution Tanzania.

It should be noted, however, that this Ibadhi conception of tolerance does not imply that all religious beliefs or interpretations of Islam are equally valid, or that any given religious groups must agree with the teachings of all others. As historian Evan Haefali explains, "tolerance" and "toleration" are unstable categories that are historically contingent and "constantly in flux" due to changing social and political realities.[15] Tolerance should not be confused with religious freedom. The latter term, as political scientist Elizabeth Hurd argues, is an idealistic but misleading and moralizing endeavor for many modern nation states, particularly the United States and its western allies.[16] Rather the modern Ibadhi ideal of tolerance (Ar., *al-tasāmuḥ*) in Tanzania and Oman pertains more to maintaining an open-minded attitude and flexibility when encountering different ideas and beliefs. It means coexisting peacefully with others despite differences in opinion or backgrounds.

I further argue that in a more understated—but nevertheless apparent—way, Istiqaama also plays a critical role as a symbol of Omani soft power[17] and religious diplomacy in Tanzania. As I demonstrate throughout the book, it does so in three distinctive ways. First, by strengthening familial and religious ties between Tanzanians of Omani descent and their Ibadhi brethren in Oman. Second, by creating a public image that ties Ibadhi and Omani associational life with Muslim philanthropy. Third, by enabling Oman's distinctive Ibadhi religious identity to take shape outside of the Gulf region, where it was underplayed in the modernization efforts of the former sultan Qaboos bin Said in favor of an Omani foreign policy centered on nonsectarianism and political neutrality. While Ibadhis tend to downplay their sectarian identity in Oman, Istiqaama in Tanzania enables the public expression of a global Ibadhi identity, which is heavily influenced by religious authorities in Oman. Istiqaama has introduced a new form of Ibadhi institutions inspired by over two centuries of transnational Ibadhi reformist efforts that center on righteous living through religious education and just leadership.[18] This book offers a new perspective on Ibadhism and Oman-Zanzibar relations since the Zanzibar Revolution (Mapinduzi ya Zanzibar) of 1964, beginning specifically in the 1980s, when nonstate actors began to play a major role in providing social services and support for religious institutions and heritage conservation. It considers how religious actors work in real time and across ever-shifting social and political boundaries in the Indian Ocean world;[19] this work binds communities of people together across this wide geography.

## Istiqaama and the Ibadhi-Omani Diaspora in Tanzania

The Tanzanian branches of Istiqaama are located across the country in towns and cities where Omanis settled in large numbers. Many of these are major urban areas like Zanzibar Town, Tanga, Tabora, and Kigoma, which grew to prominence in the historical record through interactions between African, Asian, and Arab trading communities, demonstrating that the history of Ibadhism and Istiqaama in East Africa cannot be separated from the history of the Omani diaspora and its migrations. So, while there is an Istiqaama presence in Oman, this book is about the Tanzanian branches of the organization, including

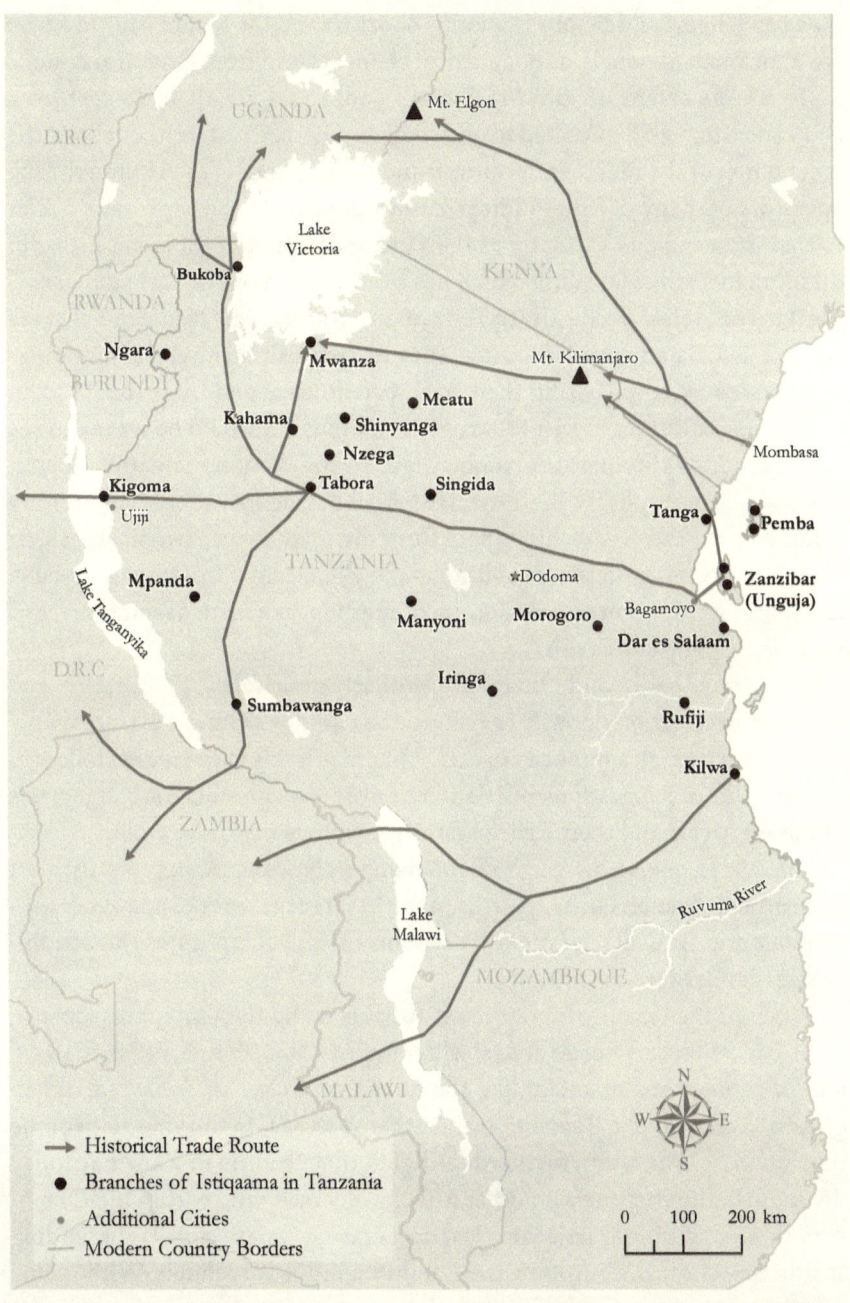

**Map 0.1**: Istiqaama Branches in Tanzania and Historical Trade Routes, 2023. Map by Zach Sherman and Jeff Blossom, Center for Geographic Analysis, Harvard University.

those on Unguja and Pemba islands in Zanzibar and the Ibadhi Muslims who are Tanzanian nationals, although most claim descent from Omani ancestors.

To a large extent, Ibadhi Muslims in Tanzania trace their descent from Arab ancestors who migrated to and settled in East Africa from Oman in the second half of the nineteenth century and the first half of the twentieth. The ancestors of many of those I interviewed were part of the later wave. I refer to their descendants variously as the Omani diaspora or the Omani-Ibadhi diaspora in Tanzania. While much has been written on the term *diaspora*, I use it here to refer specifically to Tanzanian nationals who reside in Tanzania and are associated with Istiqaama. They distinguish themselves from other Tanzanians by emphasizing their Arab patrilineage and their Ibadhi identity. Yet, as cultural theorist Stuart Hall cautions, "it would be wrong to see these trends as singular or unambiguous. In the diaspora situation, identities become multiple."[20] The Tanzanian national identity of this community is important in distinguishing them from the mixed-race, Swahili-speaking diaspora in Oman, here referred to as the *Zinjibāris*.[21] In Oman, the label Zinjibāri can function as an outgroup or ingroup, as a mark of solidarity, as a term of prestige, or as a slur.[22]

The terms Ibadhi and Omani are similarly multivalent in Tanzania and are often used synonymously to refer to the country's Omani diaspora. This is true even though a minority of early Omani arrivals in the region followed non-Ibadhi interpretations of Islam and even though non-Arab associates of these arrivals and their African family members may have embraced Ibadhi beliefs. Likewise, although membership in Istiqaama has typically been determined through Omani patrilineage, the large presence of non-Arab worshippers and students in Istiqaama schools further complicates this Ibadhi-Omani conflation.

Much of the existing literature on Ibadhism and the Omani diaspora in Zanzibar centers on stories of Arab elites under sultanate rule, of Zinjibāris,[23] and of contentious practices like the forced marriages of Arab and Indian girls to "leaders of the Revolution and other Africans" in the aftermath of the revolution.[24] This study further highlights that Ibadhis in Zanzibar today distinguish themselves from other Muslims by marrying within the Omani community, serving as Istiqaama leaders, wearing Omani clothing, attending Ibadhi mosques, and enrolling their children in Ibadhi schools. While some members of Istiqaama do trace their descent to longstanding and prominent Omani families who had extensive landholdings under the sultanate, many more are the descendants of poorer forebears who migrated to East Africa between the 1920s and 1940s as migrant workers, petty traders, shop owners, and small-scale farmers. The term that came to signify these newer migrants in Zanzibar, which the British colonial administration adopted to distinguish them from the Arab aristocracy, is *wamanga*. This Swahili term is still in use in Zanzibar, frequently framed in a derogatory manner in popular discourse.[25]

By projecting a righteous image, Omani Ibadhis affiliated with Istiqaama can gain influence in ways that appear benevolent and apolitical, even while they advance Omani economic interests in Tanzania and play a role in public diplomacy in their former African dominion. For example, as an organization defined by moral righteousness, Istiqaama works on educational and building projects at a grassroots level, relying on the extensive social and economic networks of pious businesspeople of Omani heritage who are locally grounded in Tanzania. Its active involvement in the conservation of tangible forms of Omani heritage across Tanzania also includes the renovation of family mosques in Zanzibar and the southern Lake Victoria region, which are now registered under the organization.[26]

Signaling Omani-Ibadhi identity through local heritage projects in Tanzania indicates the historical significance of mainland diaspora communities, which are often marginalized in discourses on conserving religious heritage.

## An Organization at Odds

In its earliest stages of formation, Istiqaama aimed to revive Ibadhi religious practice and group consciousness in Tanzania while promoting intra-Muslim cooperation and a policy of nondiscrimination in its mosques and schools. These aims, however, are sometimes at odds. Through their emphasis on creating inclusive educational institutions, charities, and mosques, they deemphasize communal boundaries in public. In private, however, they maintain identitarian boundaries in complex and sometimes controversial ways.

As one example: the basis of Istiqaama membership is one's ability to demonstrate Omani-Ibadhi patrilineage. This emphasis on "pure" Omani origins has led to the conflation of Omani and Ibadhi identities in Tanzania,[27] recalling colonial-era ethnic hierarchies that placed those who could prove origins from an Arab ancestor above the majority non-Arab African population.

The emphasis on constructing Omani-Ibadhi identity along lines of descent in the diaspora further relates to a larger process of Arabization in the Gulf states, where one's claims to citizenship are also dependent on an ability to demonstrate indigeneity, speak Arabic, and adopt certain modes of dress and behavior considered representative of a righteous Muslim society. Indeed, one's proximity to Oman through marriage or citizenship is a status marker among Ibadhis in Tanzania and impacts the role one plays within Istiqaama as either a leader, a general member, or simply (as in the case of most non-Arab affiliates) a recipient of charity. To demonstrate the point further, within this exclusivist imaginary, even someone who has a Yemeni Arab father but a Sukuma African mother is outside the imagined parameters of belonging. This does not preclude their acceptance and participation in Ibadhi schools, mosques, or public events, but it does prevent them (with few exceptions) from participating in communal leadership and decision-making or, in some cases, prevents eligibility for marriage within the community.[28]

Debates about purity of descent through marriage play a critical role in the social relations among Ibadhi Muslims in Oman and the diaspora. The matter is of particular concern among Ibadhi youth in Tanzania who identify as mixed race (Afro-Arab). These youth appear more in tune than previous generations to global discourses around racial justice and anti-Black racism, commonly following social media debates on these topics and reflecting on how racial discrimination operates within their own communities.[29]

As an organization, Istiqaama struggles to reconcile its mission to project an inclusive public image in its mosques and schools while also relying on Ibadhi identity to delineate Arabness in Tanzania and Omani identity to define Ibadhiness. The current sultan of Oman Haitham bin Tarik's 2023 royal decree allowed citizens to marry foreigners without the approval of the Ministry of the Interior provided the marriage does not "violate provisions of the Shariʿa law or the public order in Oman."[30] The decree has the potential to alleviate some of these tensions around citizenship and purity of descent, but its effects are yet to be seen.

## Approaching a Layered History of Empire

Peeling apart Tanzania's complex history of imperialism and postcolonial governance and its specific relationship to Oman is a daunting task for any researcher interested in tracing religious or economic networks across the union. Still, understanding these political dynamics, especially those that precipitated the rise and fall of the sultanate in Zanzibar and the rise of neoliberal institutions in the 1980s, are critical for understanding how Ibadhis, and other religious minorities in Tanzania, have weathered changing political tides and adapted to ever-evolving social environments. Moreover, it shows the continuity of Ibadhi migrations between Oman and Tanzania and between Zanzibar and the mainland, during more than a century and a half of dramatic changes. Zanzibar has been and remains a key connecting point, though not the sole center, of these migrations and evolving expressions of a living Ibadhism.

To fully appreciate the role that Istiqaama has played in the lives of Omani-Ibadhi Muslims, we must first understand the history at play in East Africa. Ibadhi Muslims from Oman began to settle in greater numbers all over this area of the Western Indian Ocean following the founding of the Zanzibar sultanate in the 1830s. The sultanate was established under the leadership of the Ibadhi leader Sayyid Said bin Sultan (1791–1856), who had moved his capital there from Muscat. Over time, cities that were home to substantial Arab and South Asian diasporic communities developed along the region's historic trade routes, expanding their presence and influence as far as central Africa. While the sultan was still alive, Oman and Zanzibar were considered one country under the domain of the Busaidi dynasty (al-Bū Saʿīdī), which remains in power in Oman today. After Sayyid Said died while at sea on a return trip to Zanzibar from Muscat, a dispute emerged over who should rule the two parts of his dominion. This resulted in a settlement imposed by the then British viceroy of India, Lord Charles Canning, who would divide the two territories between the sultan's sons, Majid bin Said (Zanzibar) and Thuwaini bin Said (Muscat), in 1861.

The division, called the Canning Award, fragmented the lucrative Indian Ocean Omani empire that Sayyid Said had built through painstaking political alliances, including the British East India Company. It also caused tensions within the Omani ruling family and opened the door for greater British colonial interference in governance in both sides of what historian Abdul Sheriff has called, the "Commercial Empire" based on "a twin foundation of commerce and a plantation economy on Zanzibar."[31] By 1873 the acting British consul of Zanzibar had convinced another of Majid's brothers and his successor to the sultanate, Barghash bin Said (r. 1870–1888), to sign a treaty that would end the export of enslaved persons to Zanzibar and other locations overseas. The colonial government's interest in ending regional slavery had more to do with its own commercial designs than a moral imperative. While slavery was formally abolished on the islands in 1897, the trade in human beings continued illegally. Following these events and other restrictions that preceded them, historian Saada Omar Wahab writes, "The sultans of Zanzibar began to lose their independence and influence over the East African coast and started to act as British puppets in East Africa."[32] Their legitimacy as rulers faded in the eyes of slave-dealing plantation owners and merchants, many of whom were from the upper crust of Omani society in Zanzibar.

The formal period of British colonial rule extended from 1890 until independence in 1963. During this time efforts were made to "rationalize" systems of rule from the court system to religious endowments and schools to centralize and capitalize on local resources and skill sets. Another side effect of colonial rule was the creation of ethnic associations, most notably the Arab, Indian, and African, roughly ranked in that order by the colonial administrators who encouraged the associations as part of a broader strategy of divide and rule, especially in colonies where they had few officers on the ground. Preexisting but previously more fluid understandings of race and racial identities had begun to crystallize under British colonialism, which served as a basis for later discourses around difference that would be adopted and elaborated on by leading Zanzibari intellectuals of the preindependence era.

Historian Jonathan Glassman describes two opposing groups in Zanzibar politics during that time. One group, the Afro-Shirazi Party (ASP), promoted explicit racial nationalism, while the other group, the Zanzibar National Party (ZNP), a mixed coalition of Zanzibaris led by elite Arabs, rejected the idea of Arab oppression and advocated for a multiracial society.[33] With these tensions already in the air in 1964, historian Amal Ghazal explains that "a coalition of communists, socialists and anti-Arabs led a successful insurrection against dynastic Al-Busaidi rule in Zanzibar, closing one chapter of Omani history on the East African coast."[34] Called the Zanzibar Revolution, "the coup was accompanied by the pogroms that took the lives of thousands of the islands' Arab minority"[35] and forced many others into exile. A few months later, Zanzibar under the new leadership of the ASP, joined in a rushed union with the government of the newly independent mainland territory of Tanganyika, which gave rise to the current African nationalist government and resulted in the two regions' union, now called the United Republic of Tanzania.

From its beginning, the union has been fraught with tension, and many in Zanzibar contend that it was imposed on them in the hasty aftermath of the revolution, when the island's first president, Abeid Amani Karume (r. 1964–1972), was looking for allies who would help consolidate his rule. From 1964 until the mid-1980s, Tanzania and Zanzibar both experimented with a failed policy of socialism that, although presented as an effort to unite the country's diverse populations under one unified Swahili-speaking African nationalist identity, resulted in stringent and unproductive economic policies that, among other things, viewed foreign investment with suspicion. It was not until the end of socialist governance in the mid-1980s, the introduction of multiparty elections in 1992, and liberalization of the economy that foreign trade and investment resumed on a broader scale, and religious institutions such as Istiqaama were allowed and encouraged to draw on international investors to advance their philanthropic and religious agendas. Assuming, of course, that their agendas supported, rather than challenged, government authority. While Tanzania was coming out of economic depression, an intensive modernization campaign called the Omani "renaissance" or "revival" (al-nahḍa) was already well underway in a newly oil-rich sultanate, led by Sultan Qaboos, who came to power in 1970 after overthrowing his father, Said bin Taimur (r. 1932–1970), in a coup. Whereas Omanis once traveled to Zanzibar and Tanganyika attracted by tales of prosperity under the Busaidi dynasty there, Tanzanians had now begun to look to Oman for new pathways to economic development.

## The Opposing Narratives of the Zanzibar Revolution

Supporters of the Zanzibar Revolution often describe it as an African fight for freedom against Arab imperialism, enslavement, and economic disenfranchisement. The official government version of the revolution depicts it as a revolt of the African working class, especially the descendants of slaves, against Zanzibar's former slave- and landowning Arab merchant class. They justify the violence as redress for the brutality of the slave trade and the forced labor of Africans on the island's plantations during much of the nineteenth and the early twentieth centuries. The revolution is further presented as a resistance against the stark class and social differences between Arabs, Indians, indigenous Africans and enslaved persons, which was a key justification for the violence and the removal of the sultanate.[36] By ultimately ending Arab landownership and class privilege in Zanzibar and calling for African sovereignty from Arab sultanate rule, the revolution brought the injustices of slavery and the slave trade into high relief.

On the other hand, opponents contest the revolution as an anti-Arab, anti-Asian violent coup. Indeed, the revolution engendered a highly controversial series of events that included the indiscriminate killing, imprisonment, and forced exile of Arabs and South Asians, along with the rise to power of an authoritarian regime that called for the seizure of property and the nationalization of the extensive landholdings of former elites. This narrative is particularly espoused by intellectuals from Zanzibar whose families were forced into exile in the 1960s. They posit instead that the "revolution" was a genocide of ethnic minorities perpetrated primarily by African mainlanders.[37]

Compounding these differing views, although the proportions of Christian and Muslim populations in Tanzania are now roughly even, Muslims—particularly in the areas of the coast once under sultanate rule—have long felt marginalized by the Christian majority government on the mainland.[38] This sense of marginalization goes back to British colonial rule in Tanganyika and the rise of English-speaking mission schools, which trained the first generations of African teachers and ministers and those who would become the country's first leaders after independence.

The net result of these events and dynamics is a palpable narrative of decline among Ibadhis in Tanzania today—a narrative that says the revolution targeted Arab residents for massacre and exile and resulted not only in the loss of sultanate power and Omani economic enterprise but also in a deficit of the religious scholars, texts, and institutions that served as the community's moral guides and collective memory. In response to this discourse of loss, which tends to idealize the prerevolutionary past in Zanzibar as a time of great religious, cultural, and economic flourishing, the Omani-Ibadhi diaspora has developed strategies to ensure the longevity of its religious practices and communal institutions under the aegis of Istiqaama.

## The Role of the Collective Memory in Understanding the Present

The drastically different interpretations of the events of 1964 and their aftermath are part of the reason the sultanate era remains a controversial memory in Tanzania today, especially in Zanzibar. It is variously viewed nostalgically, by Omanis with East African heritage, as the height of Islamic civilization on the coast and in East Africa, and by many non-Arabs as what historian Eve Troutt-Powell calls, in another context, "a different shade of colonialism"[39] of the European variety, as it is at once local and foreign.

Thus, like Indian settlers in Africa, Arab diaspora communities are caught in what historian Shobana Shankar calls "an uneasy embrace"[40] with the majority populations, despite having lived in these communities and spoken their local languages for generations. This is due, in part, to their relative economic successes and privileges under colonial rule, which inspire the perception of them "as avatars of alien dominance or occupation," like the

European powers.⁴¹ However, mere phenotypical differences between so-called Africans and Asians do little to explain the tensions between the two groups, and the "divide and rule" policy often associated with British colonial rule is not adequate either.⁴²

The task here is not to determine which of these narratives about the revolution is objectively true. However, I am convinced by anthropologist Michel-Rolph Trouillot's proposition that stories and memories of traumatic events are constructed through power plays, with each side of a debate operating according to its own formula of historicity.⁴³ Neither is it my intention to give a full account of the politics of the revolution as such accounts can be found elsewhere.⁴⁴ Rather, I posit that the collective memory of the revolution is critical for understanding Tanzania-Oman relations since the 1960s and elaborating how Ibadhis reimagine their communal identity in a postcolonial African society. Indeed, how Zanzibaris, in particular, remember the violent pasts of slavery and revolution influences even minute details of their social relationships, including who they break bread with and marry.⁴⁵

In this book I am interested in how collective memory associated with the violence of the Zanzibar Revolution, and the complex political assemblages—in particular, how national identities came to be shaped by social processes and structures⁴⁶—that endured in its aftermath have paved the way for novel expressions of Ibadhi identity in the postcolonial and postrevolution period. In the case of Omanis in Tanzania and the Swahili-speaking diaspora in Oman, for many who had family members killed in the Zanzibar Revolution, the time before the revolution is imagined as one of righteous guidance under the scholars of old and one of prosperity under the sultanate.⁴⁷ Rarely are the less savory elements of this past, such as the enslavement of Africans, included in these glossy narratives. The time after the revolution, on the other hand, is remembered as one of moral decline and loss, a reality that persisted until the celebrated return of Mufti Al-Khalili. He is credited with the transnational Ibadhi reform movement in Tanzania, which would eventually result in the formation of Istiqaama.

The tension is best explained by this shared memory of colonial rule and Arab imperialism, which is incidentally also encapsulated by the name and slogan of the current ruling political party in Zanzibar. Although Tanzania and Zanzibar both adopted multiparty elections in 1992, the as yet undefeated African socialist party, which represents both the islands and the mainland, has continued to rule both governments in the country since 1977. Its name, Chama cha Mapinduzi (Party of the Revolution), or CCM, signifies the enduring legacy of the revolution in the political consciousness of the country's leaders and citizenry. Likewise, its slogan, *"Mapinduzi Daima!"* ("Revolution Forever!"), has become a pervasive imprint on the political merchandise worn during annual celebrations of the event and during elections every five years,[48] keeping the collective memory of the struggle for independence—both from European colonial and sultanate rule—alive in the popular imagination.

This collective memory of the revolution—as evidenced in the name of both the ruling party and the ways in which controversial events of the past are celebrated and justified as a fight for African liberation—is reflected in the subtle power struggle and tensions that undergird postcolonial collaborations between countries of the Global South. Combined with the competing visions of the past, this memory further indicates the necessity of nongovernmental diaspora networks to develop alternative pathways forward. It also belies the heritage projects and shared visions for the future that now exist between Tanzania and Oman.

### The Politics of Nostalgia and Ibadhism: (In)Tangible Aspects of Omani Heritage

Since the sultanate era, the successive governments of Zanzibar have invoked Islam, religious pluralism, and its own mercantile tradition in diplomatic relations with the broader Indian Ocean world as a way of signaling the cosmopolitanism and harmony within the islands' diverse communities. Similarly, the Sultanate of Oman has established what anthropologist Amal Sachedina calls following Hady Geimar, different "heritage regimes" in Oman and Zanzibar, which are "processes at work to discipline the past through reconfiguring its contours,"[49] in this case to commemorate the cosmopolitan and mercantile brilliance of the sultanate's former trading empire in Zanzibar. This is done to assert its connection and belonging to Africa in the current era. However, the Zanzibar government tactfully uses the same artifacts and narratives to validate its authority and assert its ownership of a majestic and diverse Afro-Islamic history. In short, it is contested heritage, imbued with sentiments of oppression and loss for Omanis and Tanzanians alike, and representatives from both countries frequently draw on this shared heritage when engaging in diplomatic negotiations—for example, over the plans for the construction of the Oman- and China-funded port in Bagamoyo, which now also remains stalled.[50] As religion scholar Russell T. McCutcheon points out, these contested narratives become "domesticated" in such a way that they can be deployed as an expression of group identities.[51]

Moreover, Jāmiʻi Zinjibār, as a shared symbol and model of righteousness produced by actors with competing national interests, is a contested site of mobile meaning[52] defined by the various authorizing discourses and practices that take place in and around it.[53] Zanzibari religious authorities and governmental officials face difficulties in finding a middle ground in order to maintain the image of religious and economic independence for their small, yet strong-willed, islands. They also aim to benefit from the material resources and religious support provided by wealthy Oman. However, they find themselves in an uncertain alliance with the government of mainland Tanzania. As Jāmiʻi Zinjibār shows, the work of transnational religious institutions and actors do not just have implications for Omanis and their kin in Tanzania, many of whom are Ibadhi in confession; they also have real implications for transnational diplomacy and Omani soft power in East Africa.

Anthropologist Ahmed Skounti writes that intangible heritage—in distinguishing it from examples of tangible heritage, like built monuments and artifacts[54]—is insulated from destruction as it is transgenerational and constantly being reformulated to meet the exigencies of the present. He argues that intangible heritage "is transformed, adapted, hidden (sometimes to reappear with more vigor), it retracts or expands depending on circumstances, it scatters the micro-elements that make up this heritage to be incorporated into new, emerging cultural traits, and so forth."[55]

Ibadhism is part of the intangible cultural heritage of Omanis in the Gulf and East Africa. This is a heritage and identity that is both fragile and in constant threat of extinction due to the minority status of its members and their struggle to compete with more popular Salafi movements.[56] Yet it is also resilient. Its history is one of complex actors—some wealthy, some aristocrats, many impoverished, and many from low-caste origins in Oman—but all enterprising enough to survive the everchanging political and economic landscapes of East Africa from the time of most of their ancestors' arrivals in the late nineteenth and early twentieth centuries.

It is also evolving in that its followers are constantly redefining what it means to be Ibadhi in the present. Faced with the conflation of Omani and Ibadhi identity and the enduring local and governmental suspicions of Omani and Arab neoimperial designs, the Afro-Arab Swahili-speaking diaspora in Tanzania is caught in a quandary of how to distance itself from its imperial past while also reviving and reforming Ibadhi institutions of worship and learning. As such, Ibadhi reformist discourse and practice in Tanzania today are steeped in an acute sense of nostalgia. It is a nostalgia intimately connected to the experience of the Omani diaspora in the second half of the twentieth century and onward, following the fall of the sultanate, the exile of the Zanzibari elites, and the economic strictures faced by all under the post-independence socialist regime. The politics of nostalgia emerging from these contested histories invokes a particular vision of the past that is selected and authorized. This contested image of the past is, ironically, a powerful weapon both for Omani and Tanzanian nationalist efforts and state building.[57]

This sense of nostalgia and loss are evident in the stories of Istiqaama leaders who explain the reasons for the Ibadhi revival in East Africa that started in the 1980s. They also express this sentiment when they frame their pious works as an attempt to salvage the knowledge lost in the Zanzibar Revolution. They recall that during the revolution there were violent acts against religion and Arab people, which led to the burning of manuscripts were closure of religious schools and institutions associated with the Arab elite. They also mention that promising Muslim students and scholars, such as Mufti al-Khalili fled the islands in the 1960s leaving a vacuum in moral leadership. My interlocutors in Zanzibar, especially, speak of the high level of Islamic and Arabic knowledge found in local mosques during the sultanate era, such as that of reformer sultans like Barghash bin Said, who patronized and hosted Ibadhi scholars from as far as away as Algeria. In their imaginations, the intellectual fervor of the late nineteenth and early twentieth centuries gradually declined under British colonial rule, when government schools attended by the children of Arab elites introduced curricular reforms aimed at imparting "marketable" rather than "social" skills.[58] Colonial administrators disparaged the culture of memorization and repetition, which served as a foundation for more advanced knowledge in Qur'an and mosque schools, as irrational or impractical.[59] To address the abandonment of Ibadhi education and the loss of religious identity following the revolution and exile of learned members of the community, Istiqaama has developed educational initiatives that reintroduce the rigorous study of the Qur'an and Arabic into their mosque classes and their K–12 schools, which teach both secular and religious subjects.

This revival of the Omani-Ibadhi diaspora's intangible heritage also largely operates in the construction of new Friday congregational mosques, the restoration of small community mosques, the support of Ibadhi schools, the sponsorship of Tanzanian students who study abroad in religious institutions in Oman and Algeria, and the training of Ibadhi imams (prayer leaders) and teachers.

Unfortunately, while the proponents of these reforms perceive their work as acts of piety driven by righteous intentions, sometimes their focus on heritage conservation has the effect of obscuring the tangible needs of the communities they serve in Tanzania, whether Ibadhi or non-Ibadhi. For example, while Omani donors may be keen on maintaining the original architectural character of the mosque where their grandparents used to worship, the community that frequents the mosque may be more interested in assistance with updating the existing architecture and creating vernacular learning materials. Notwithstanding, Omani philanthropy is evident in Tanzania, and, notably, its reach is arguably most visible through the work of the diaspora-run Istiqaama organization.

## Diasporas and Religious Transnationalism in Africa

Global Muslim diasporas have been the focus of recent scholarship on religious transnationalism. This is due in part to the extensive international support networks of these groups, which help fund their various developmental initiatives and in part to missionary work and scholarship programs for youth.[60] It is also due to the idea that studying transnationalism is helpful for explaining the religious practices of African, Asian, and Arab religious diasporas that have found themselves caught between two or more homelands and two or more ethnic or national identities. As scholar of religion Ousmane Kane shows, drawing on the example of Senegalese immigrants in New York City, transnational religious networks serve as bridges that facilitate the flow of ideas, resources, and identities between Muslim communities and the world.[61]

I am often asked how the Ibadhi-Omani diaspora differs from other transnational religious communities on the African continent, such as various Muslim communities. In my research I identify four general ways that the Ibadhi-Omani diaspora differs. First, while the economic histories of the Lebanese Shiʿa in Senegal and the Khoja Shiʿa in East Africa are traceable to French and British imperial networks, none of these groups themselves ever held the reins of political power in the lands in which they settled—although their merchant capital may have been key to the survival of empire. Therefore, while indigenous communities may suspiciously view these diasporas as having a hand in the economic subjugation of Africans under colonial rule, they do not appear as a potential threat to African sovereignty in the way Oman might.

Second, the legacy of the Omani empire and landownership in East Africa raises complicated questions about current rights to land, citizenship, and a shared Afro-Arab material culture of texts, monuments, and ritual spaces. The Zanzibar and Omani governments, for example, have both developed state archives and museums dedicated to their own interpretations of Zanzibar's past under Omani rule. In some cases, this has led to conflicts over stolen archival documents and clashes over who has the rights to patronage of new and old mosques in Zanzibar Town.[62]

Third, Ibadhis are like other Muslim diasporas and minorities in Tanzania, such as the South Asian Nizari and Bohora Ismaili Shiʿa, in that they migrated to and settled in East Africa earlier and in great numbers in the nineteenth and twentieth centuries. While there is socioeconomic diversity within both groups, Ibadhis and Ismailis are often associated with business and relative economic success in Tanzania. In postcolonial Tanzania, all have developed transnational networks that unite their communities within the diaspora while also providing educational opportunities, health care, and other support to religious outsiders. However, Nizari Ismailis draw a clear distinction between the religious institutions that are reserved exclusively for the global Ismaili community (known as the *Jamaʿat*) and the secular institutions that serve non-Ismailis and non-Muslims, such as the Aga Khan hospital, university, and school in Dar es Salaam. In contrast Istiqaama maintains no clear distinction between institutions that serve Ibadhis and non-Ibadhis.[63]

Fourth, although Istiqaama does invest in rental properties, shops, and land for building and revenue purposes, it would be a mistake to view such Gulf-based institutions in East Africa as examples of mere economic opportunism. Its members, like those of the other Muslim groups discussed, are deeply religious men and women who view their interpretation of Islam as the path that all pious Muslims are expected to tread—one that leads to the righteousness that will ensure their salvation.

## Methodology

During my preliminary research trip to Zanzibar in 2014, I came to know the dedicated curator and founder of the Princess Salme Gallery in the island's historic Stone Town, Said El-Gheithy. The princess was the daughter of the first sultan of Zanzibar, Sayyid Said, and perhaps best known for having scandalously eloped with a German officer based in Zanzibar, converting to Christianity, and living in exile in Germany. She was later widowed, following the tragic death of her husband in a carriage accident, and to make money to support herself and her two children, she wrote and published her now widely translated memoirs, detailing her upbringing in the Omani-Zanzibari royal household and her observations on life in her father's large and diverse harem.[64] Though some parts of the memoir were clearly written to regale a European Orientalist audience who had an appetite for stories of the decadent lives of Eastern court cultures,[65] the diary, as the nostalgic reflections of a former princess in exile from her homeland, is perhaps the best account available of the intimate lives of Omani-Ibadhi elites under sultanate rule, and it is the only written account from a woman that I am aware of.

For some within the Omani diaspora, and for Omanis visiting from abroad, the gallery in the princess's name, which contains reproductions of court life, is both an embarrassing display of the royal family's dirty laundry and a blemish on the image of Ibadhi moral integrity; for others, it is an intriguing window into island court life and part of the sultanate's tangible heritage in Zanzibar. Princess Salme's story relates to the methodology of this book because it shows that the real sites of "heritage work" in postcolonial African societies tend to exist outside of the well-manicured displays of national museums. Rather, they are found in the practice of everyday life,[66] in family and community libraries and collections, where "ideas about tradition, patrimony, and authenticity are debated and defined."[67] For Ibadhis in Tanzania, Istiqaama is the space where these debates occur.

Scholarly work on Ibadhism and the Omani diaspora also focuses exclusively on the nineteenth century and the first half of the twentieth.[68] The primary source for these works is Ibadhi religious texts and manuscripts, colonial administrative files, and deeds of sale that connected Muslim merchants—all contributions of Ibadhi Islam to Zanzibar's intellectual history in the prerevolution period, during which the Omani diaspora benefited from tenuous association with the ruling elite.

As such, it is important to recognize the limitations of the written archive of legal documents. This is especially true when, in the case of religious institutions like Istiqaama, money and resources often flow through informal networks and hands of trusted family members rather than through a tangible trail of legal documents or contracts such as deeds of sale.[69] Such informality is often necessary as it enables Omani remissions to arrive more rapidly in the hands of struggling relatives and dependents in Tanzania; it also allows the building of second homes and charitable projects to continue, unobstructed by the formal procedures of customs and taxation.

I also, however, engage written sources, such as local and international newspapers, Ibadhi legal texts, memoirs, Istiqaama textbooks, and the writings of contemporary Omani and Zanzibari religious scholars and activists. The Omani government and private publishers in Oman, including Istiqaama's now closed publishing house in Muscat, Maktabat Istiqaama, were active in the preservation and documentation of the historical relationship between Oman and East Africa. Their texts provide useful insights on the recent history of Istiqaama, but they are often also tinged with a paternalistic nostalgia for Omani civilization and empire in East Africa.[70] They articulate how Zinjibāris in Oman grapple with being a "double diaspora"[71] or with the feeling of inhabiting two different homelands but never fully belonging to one or the other. These same works also capture the ongoing contestations over Zanzibar and Oman's shared archives and tangible and intangible heritages.

In the absence of public reporting on the number of members, institutions, and beneficiaries in Istiqaama, it is difficult to quantify the organization's impact in Tanzania. To my knowledge, Istiqaama does not publish annual reports for public review, and the leaders are generally unwilling to share information regarding sources of funding or the amounts of its annual cash donations. I therefore assessed the impact of Istiqaama on religious education and social welfare at its various branches across Tanzania by combining qualitative research methods with the sparse institutional data I found online.

Similar difficulties attended the gathering of information about the ethnic and religious breakdown of the Tanzania and Zanzibar populations. Tanzania is a country that prides itself on religious pluralism, national unity, and relative political stability. If the government were to publish data that highlighted the very real sociocultural differences between citizens or recognized Zanzibari autonomy, it would only disrupt this ideal.

Finally, the circulation of reformist newspapers, theological texts, and credit networks were especially important from the time of Barghash's rule through the 1940s, when pan-Islamic fervor and the Ibadhi naḥḍa,[72] reached its apex in Oman and Zanzibar.[73] Building on earlier works interested in documenting Ibadhi-Omani reformist and economic networks across the Western Indian Ocean, I am, perhaps ironically, led back toward the necessity of firsthand accounts of what it means to be Ibadhi in Tanzania today. I propose, following Sachedina, that we consider Ibadhism a critical part of the construction of modern Omani identity.[74] Unlike Sachedina, however, I am interested in the transnational character of Omani heritage regimes and how Ibadhism, as represented by Istiqaama, is at the center of efforts to construct a unified Omani identity in the diaspora. It is an identity that is at once exclusivist in its emphasis on purity of descent and inclusive in its efforts to bring the *madhab* (pl. *madhāhib*) more in line with mainstream Sunni Islam. Maybe more important, however, it is a diasporic religious identity that is *lived*[75] and *performed* through individual and collective practices such as learning and speaking Arabic, performing Friday congregational prayers, attending community events at Ibadhi mosques, reading literature, and wearing clothing imported from Oman.

## Research in a "United" Republic

Through El-Gheithy, who was himself raised in an Ibadhi family in Zanzibar, I became acquainted with a branch leader of the Istiqaama Muslim Society in Zanzibar Town, who I will refer to as Sheikh Ayman. Ayman introduced me to other Ibadhis in Zanzibar, and I began my research by interviewing teachers at the Istiqaama Institute in the Tungu village on the island's east coast.

My research process consisted primarily of following preexisting kinship and economic networks of the Omani diaspora, from the coast to the islands. My travels and interactions with Ibadhi leaders at the different branches of Istiqaama in Zanzibar and Tanzania revealed that, while all seemed invested in preserving Omani-Ibadhi identity in Tanzania and developing the resources of their communities, tensions and divisions existed between the branches. For example, in Zanzibar and Pemba, the Istiqaama community split into northern and southern branches, reflecting the regional diversity of the islands and the contestations over religious authority within local Ibadhi communities. Tracing the network in real time and across the country enabled me to assess how regional, cultural, and even linguistic differences influenced the ways in which urban and rural, coastal and mainland Ibadhis of Omani descent have responded to Istiqaama's role in shaping Ibadhi identity and institutions in postcolonial Tanzania.

To underscore the complexity of understanding the diversity of the region, the Zanzibar islands lie about forty nautical miles from the mainland Tanzanian port city of Dar es Salaam. Unguja is the seat of power on Zanzibar, and the island state has its own president, vice president, and house of representatives. The population of Unguja is 897,000; Pemba Island is the second largest in the archipelago, with a population of approximately 362,000. In 2010 the Pew Templeton Religious Futures Project estimated Tanzania's population to be 35.2 percent Muslims and 61.4 percent Christians but other estimates vary widely and are locally contested. About 98 percent of the inhabitants on Zanzibar are Muslim, but no figures exist detailing the number of Sunnis, Ibadhis, and Shiʿa Muslims within this population. My estimation is that Ibadhis form less than 5 percent of Zanzibar's Muslim population and an even smaller percentage of the Muslim population on the mainland. In a 2006 article on religion and society in Oman, religion scholar Valerie Hoffman wrote that Ibadhis made up 75 percent of Oman's 2.5 million people. Her study's estimate for the number of Ibadhi followers globally was 1,873,000.[76] The controversial Religious Freedom Report conducted by the US government on Oman in 2016 suggests that the Omani government estimates Ibadhis make up 75 percent, while nongovernmental sources place the number of Ibadhis in Oman at 45 percent.[77] In considering these figures, it is important to remember that religious people cannot be boxed into such neat categories of identity and belonging, and a study of material culture or architectures within a religious community, for example, often reveals diverse ways of belonging and asserting social and political influence.[78]

While diasporic religious networks such as Istiqaama transcend national boundaries and enable more fluid and extraterritorial identities among their members, the character of these institutions and networks remains affected by national and international politics and intracommunity tensions. During my research on mainland Tanzania (*bara*) and Zanzibar (*visiwani*), which included the strenuous process of securing separate permits to study both regions, I came to understand more intimately the intricacies of union politics and the competing visions of sovereignty and national identity held by these two regions of the same country. In my experience, Zanzibaris on Unguja rarely refer to themselves as Tanzanians, distinguishing themselves from mainlanders (Sw. *watu wa bara*). Similarly, though Pemba is considered a part of Zanzibar, island residents there do not typically self-identify as Zanzibari but rather call themselves Pembans.

When I returned to Tanzania for eleven months of research between 2015 and 2016, I depended on my initial contacts at Istiqaama in Zanzibar to arrange more formal interviews and informal meetings with members of the community. I conducted my interviews in Swahili, Arabic, and English, depending on the preferences of my interlocutors. My work included two research trips to Pemba Island and the mainland cities of Dar es Salaam, Tanga, Tabora,

Mwanza, and Shinyanga. Only occasionally did my interviewees permit me to use a tape recorder. I have used pseudonyms to protect their identities, except in the case of public officials and those who gave me permission to use their given names. My contacts in Zanzibar directed me to branches of Istiqaama across Tanzania.

In 2016 and 2017, I traveled to Muscat, Oman, where I interviewed members of Istiqaama affiliated with the Sultan Qaboos Mosque's Islamic Information Center. I also met individuals and families affected by the revolution of 1964—and Omanis whose families had fled Zanzibar during the revolution—though not all were Ibadhi. My conversations with Afro-Omanis there was a reminder of the enduring significance of the revolution and the precariousness of using oral histories mired with memory of violence, loss, and displacement in understanding the identity politics of the present.

In 2019, I carried out an extra two months of interviews and site visits in Zanzibar. During this time, I found that the Zanzibari community in Oman, which is racially and linguistically diverse, closely monitored political and economic developments in Tanzania. They were against perceiving the revolution as a conflict solely based on social class, led by non-Arab Africans, and addressing the discrimination and social stigma faced by descendants of those who were once enslaved on the islands.[79]

Being an outsider to the Istiqaama community and an unmarried woman meant that my access to certain religious and male-dominated spaces (such as most mosques and male study circles) was limited. On the other hand, being a foreigner sometimes afforded me greater opportunity to interview Istiqaama's all-male leadership and government officials in Zanzibar, mainland Tanzania, and Oman. Being a woman also gave me opportunities to enter women-only spaces and learn about the alliances and collaborations Ibadhi women build with other charities in their locales, a form of gendered networking that is largely unaddressed in the study of Islamic institutions across the Indian Ocean and East Africa. Moreover, being Tanzanian-American, with my own family ties to the region that borders southern Lake Victoria and a proficient speaker of Swahili and Arabic, offered me opportunities to connect with my interlocutors.

## Contributions to the Study of Islam

This book contributes to the extensive interdisciplinary scholarship in Islamic studies not only with its focus on Ibadhism, a minority *madhab*, poorly understood and documented only by a few specialists in this broader field of study, but also with its focus on a living Ibadhi community and their transnational networks. In so doing, it shows how Muslim minorities such as some Tanzanians of Ibadhi-Omani heritage who were perceived to hold great political and economic power continue to have influence in their former dominions through various forms of religious philanthropy. These include Omani-state-funded heritage projects in Zanzibar and elsewhere on the East African coast and smaller-scale, though wider reaching, initiatives, such as the schools, community mosques, and health care centers established with locally rooted, nonstate actors of Omani descent, such as the members of Istiqaama in Tanzania. While the lines of state-funded and local or privately funded initiatives sometimes appear blurred in the work of Istiqaama, what is clear is that both forms of philanthropy work together to present an image of Oman and Omani institutions in Tanzania as benevolent efforts to restore goodwill between the two countries in a postindependence and postrevolution era. What Istiqaama reveals is that transnational diaspora organizations play a critical role in paving the way for other forms of diplomacy and international investment in Africa. They are distinct from larger-scale Saudi Arabian-funded initiatives, whose financial resources may be unmatched, but whose benefactors do not typically claim or benefit from familial, linguistic, or ethnic bonds.

This work is important for scholars, policymakers, and students who are interested in the development of Ibadhism outside of Oman. In Oman, sectarian identities are suppressed and religious communities are closely monitored to maintain the sultanate's public image as a peaceful, tolerant, and neutral bastion in a Gulf region and Middle East otherwise plagued by sectarian conflict. Although the ruling class and sultan of Oman are primarily Ibadhi, references to Ibadhi Islam can only be detected through the discussions on religious tolerance. These discussions draw from modern Ibadhi writings about association (*walāya*) with religious insiders and nonviolent dissociation (*barā'a*) from religious outsiders. These ideas align with Istiqaama's practices of promoting inclusivity and diversity in public institutions while maintaining a leadership that is mainly Omani and Ibadhi in patrilineage.

Additionally, the global studies on Ibadhi thought and practice often overlook East Africa. For instance, the Ministry of Endowment and Religious Affairs (MARA) in Oman has annually funded and hosted Ibadhi Studies conferences for nearly a decade and published the proceeds covering various topics such as law, theology, hermeneutics, and archeology.[80] However, these works seldom include studies on the historical or current Ibadhi communities in Africa. This book aims to fill that gap by exploring a neglected area in Ibadhi Studies: East Africa, which houses one of the fastest growing Ibadhi communities worldwide. Furthermore, scholars of Africa who read this book will gain a better understanding of the Omani diaspora and the influence of Ibadhis on the religious landscape in Tanzania. The study of Islam in postindependence Tanzania has primarily focused on popular Sufi networks and Salafist organizations, often neglecting other well-established Muslim institutions and practices like Ibadhism. Past scholarship has assumed that Ibadhism had minimal impact on mainland African Muslim communities due to Omani prioritization of commerce over religious conversion. However, chapter 5, which specifically concentrates on the area around southern Lake Victoria in Tanzania, complicates this viewpoint, and suggests that the study of Islam in Africa should expand beyond the Sufi/Salafi framework to develop a more comprehensive understanding of the complex interactions among religion, politics, and economic life in Tanzania's recent history.

## Organization of the Chapters

Chapter 1 examines how Ibadhi identity is socially constructed in diverse East African contexts. This is achieved by analyzing conversations with current representatives of Ibadhi, Shiʿa, and Sunni communities in Zanzibar Town. The focus of the discussion is on the centrality of intra-Muslim hospitality and unity in local religious discourse, seen as crucial aspects of life on the coast and islands. The idea of a pluralistic Zanzibari society is explored, along with the Ibadhi community's rhetoric of religious tolerance. These policies prioritized economic success rather than imposing their religious traditions on the Sunni majority population. In contrast to the Euro-centric belief that doctrinal conservatism and religious tolerance are incompatible, the Ibadhi belief in moral righteousness enables them to be tolerant toward other religious doctrines. It is important to note, however, that this tolerance is limited and mitigated by numerous other factors, such as race, ethnicity, caste, and gender.

Chapter 2 tells the story of how, in the mid-1980s, the grand mufti of Oman, Sheikh Ahmad bin Hamad al-Khalili, visited Tanzania with a delegation from his office. They traveled to various sites across the country where Omanis had settled. During his visit, the grand mufti urged the Ibadhi communities to return to the teachings and practices of their traditional madhab to avoid religious extremism and come together with the common goals of socioeconomic development. In Sunni mosques, where Muslim men are required to listen to the weekly sermon and participate in special Friday prayers led by an imam from the community, the delegation delivered lectures to both Ibadhi and non-Ibadhi Muslim audiences. These lectures focused on the importance of Muslim unity and intra-Muslim cooperation. Omanis in East Africa had long refrained from attending Friday prayers and building congregational mosques because they lived outside the realm of the Ibadhi imam in Nizwa, Oman. They also saw the rulers of Zanzibar as illegitimate as they had not been elected to power by an Ibadhi council. Therefore, their abstention from prayers was a form of protest that some saw as the illegitimate religious authority of the rulers in Zanzibar, though they generally supported the rule of Oman on the coast.

The Zanzibari sultans supported Ibadhi institutions but did not try to impose Ibadhi teachings on the wider community. The grand mufti emphasized the necessity of congregational prayers for Ibadhis and encouraged the construction of mosques that could serve as places for intra-Muslim prayer, learning, and meeting places for local Ibadhi communities. I argue that this visit of the grand mufti and the Friday prayer movement sparked a revival of Ibadhi practices after the revolution, leading to the establishment of the Istiqaama Muslim community. Many of the new Ibadhi mosques built by the Istiqaama community are named after the grand mufti, symbolizing the inclusion of the East African community in an international moral community. This community is guided by religious authorities in Oman and aims to be a righteous society.

Chapters 3 and 4 focus on the Istiqaama schools in Zanzibar and their connections to Ibadhi communities and institutions in Oman and Algeria. The origins of this pipeline can be traced back to the Istiqaama Institute (*ma'had*) in the Zanzibari town of Tunguu and its sister institution in Chake Chake, Pemba. The Istiqaama ma'had serves as a K–12 school, offering both secular and religious education and a higher learning institution that focuses on Islamic sciences and Arabic language education. The institute attracts students from various backgrounds, including both Ibadhi and non-Ibadhi, and draws students from all over East Africa. Many of the students come from mixed-race or non-Arab backgrounds. Some graduates receive scholarships to study abroad in Muscat or Ibadhi-run schools in Algeria. East African students who complete their studies abroad benefit from increased respectability and credibility when they return to their home cities and towns across the region. Their learning experiences in Arabic-speaking cultures and practices make them valuable scholars and teachers in local Muslim communities in Tanzania. The language and cultural skills they acquire also open up greater opportunities in teaching and doing business in places like Dubai and Muscat.

However, the students' foreign certificates have little impact on their professional aspirations in fields such as government or law within Tanzania. This is because the emphasis on religious education in their studies poses a challenge for those seeking employment beyond the mosque or madrasa. The Arabic and Islamic Studies diplomas they obtain from colleges in Oman do not qualify them to pursue graduate studies in Tanzanian universities or seek government jobs, where English proficiency is valued instead of Arabic. Additionally, while they are away in the Gulf, they miss out on the opportunities to build social networks in Tanzania, which are increasingly crucial for finding meaningful employment.

The focus of chapter 5 is how Ibadhis in mainland Tanzania's urban and rural places maintain connections with Oman during the postindependence era. It also discusses how the prosperity of the community on the mainland has allowed them to seek donations from overseas for various projects led by Istiqaama. The growth of the Istiqaama community in Tanzania was made possible by the commercial success of some Omani families and the economic ties between the Ibadhi community and the Gulf. The most prominent Ibadhi families in the Lake Victoria region initially started their careers as small-scale traders, farmers, and miners of gold and diamonds. Later, they invested their capital in the transportation industry, specifically trucking, to move cotton harvests to ginneries that were either opened by the colonial powers or South Asian economic actors. When the cotton industry faced difficulties under socialist governance in the 1970s, the remaining Omani families in Tanzania switched from trucking to long-distance buses. These buses became the primary mode of affordable travel within the region and across northwest Tanzania. The leaders of Istiqaama mostly come from successful business backgrounds, having transformed the capital gained from their previous enterprises into juice factories, construction companies, fisheries, and manufacturing firms. The male members of these families play significant roles as regional leaders within the Istiqaama community. Many of them hold dual citizenship, allowing them to freely move between Oman and the other Gulf states for business, trade, family matters, and religious holidays.

Chapter 6 explores how the women's Istiqaama group in Mwanza, an important port town on the southern shores of Lake Victoria, has developed self-help and mutual aid societies. This group operates independently from, but in collaboration with, the national male-run organization. The day-to-day functioning of Istiqaam's branches relied on trust, which is built through family and communal bonds formed through marriage. The women use their social, professional, and family connections to provide care form Muslim families, children, the sick, the deceased, and neighbors. In Mwanza, they have established a separate organization that sustains itself through monthly membership fees, community fundraising events, periodic donations from other Muslim charities and schools—mainly those founded by Sunni women's groups—and the support of male leaders within Istiqaama. Like the male leadership, the women's organization is predominantly made up of women who have ties to well-known Ibadhi families. While they may not be the public face of Istiqaama, they are very active in Ibadhi religious life behind the scenes.

## Conclusion

As the first book-length study of the postcolonial Indian Ocean Ibadhi networks between Oman, mainland Tanzania, and Zanzibar, *Society of the Righteous* offers a new perspective on Ibadhism and Oman-Zanzibar relations since the 1980s, when nonstate religious actors like Istiqaama began to play a major role in providing social services and heritage conservation. While the population of Ibadhis in Tanzania is very small, the many branches of Istiqaama across the country suggest it is a community with wide reach and significant economic resources. At its core, Istiqaama is a transnational organization that depends greatly on preexisting transregional Ibadhi scholarship, kinship, and trade networks in connecting its schools, mosques, religious authorities, and students. The building of new Ibadhi Friday mosques and the introduction of Friday prayers in local Ibadhi communities under the leadership of Istiqaama has resulted in the increased visibility of the Omani diaspora in mainland Tanzania—a visibility that contrasts with the absence of Ibadhi institutions and practices in northwest Tanzania in written histories of the region.

### Notes

1. The United Republic of Tanzania is an East African nation-state formed in 1964 following the union of the country's mainland territories (formerly called

Tanganyika under German and then British colonial rule) and the semiautonomous Zanzibar archipelago, which includes the two main islands of Unguja, the capital, and Pemba. Locally, the term *Zanzibar* refers to Unguja.

2. The current sultan of Oman is Sultan Qaboos's cousin, Haitham bin Tarik, formerly the minister of heritage and culture. Much speculation preceded the succession, as the former sultan had no known heirs and had not publicly designated a successor, causing much anxiety in a country that had depended on his singular political leadership for fifty years.

3. Estim Construction Company Limited: accessed March 15, 2024, https://estimconstruction.co.tz/portfolio/jaameh-zinjbaar-zanzibar-mosque/.

4. Rizvi Kishwar, *The Transnational Mosque: Architecture and Historical Memory in the Contemporary Middle East* (Chapel Hill: The University of North Carolina Press, 2015), 4.

5. Iftitāḥ Jāmiʿ Zinjibār ʿalā Nafaqa Jalālat al-Sulṭān, "Opening of the Zanzibar Mosque at the Expense of His Majesty the Sultan," accessed October 9, 2023, https://sqhccs.gov.om/news/details/11?scrollto=start.

6. The term Ibadhi is transliterated from the Arabic in various ways, moret precisely as "Ibāḍī," but also as "Ibadi," "Ibathi," and "Ibaadhi." For greater readability I have chosen to use "Ibadhi," except when quoting from another source.

7. Sultan Qaboos commissioned the construction of numerous Friday congregational mosques across the Sultanate of Oman, including one in Muscat that bears his name. The Ministry of Tourism in Oman describes the Sultan Qaboos Grand Mosque using the same vocabularies of multiculturalism, religious tolerance, and Islamic civilization used by Al-Riyami in his remarks at the opening of Jāmiʿi Zinjibār. See my discussion on the role the Istiqaama Women's Group in Muscat plays in cultural tourism, public diplomacy, and Islamic education at the Grand Mosque: Kimberly Wortmann, "Daʿwa at the Sultan's Mosque: An Example of Ibāḍī Women's Activism in Muscat," in *Local and Global Ibadi Identities*, eds. Yohei Kondo and Angeliki Ziaka, Studies on Ibadhism and Oman 13 (Hildesheim, Germany: Georg Olms, 2020), 367–73.

8. Quote drawn from the blurb of the book *Islands of Heritage* on Stanford University Press's website. For a fuller discussion on this topic read Nathalie Peutz, *Islands of Heritage: Conservation and Transformation in Yemen* (Stanford: Stanford University Press, 2018).

9. See a discussion on religious symbols as "models of and for" in Clifford Geertz, *The Interpretation of Cultures: Selected Essays by Clifford Geertz* (New York: Basic, 1973), 93.

10. Including the assassination of the cousin and son-in-law of the prophet Muhammad, Ali ibn Abi Talib whom Sunnis considered to be the fourth of the Rightly Guided successors to the prophet and whom so-called Twelver Shiʿa Muslims consider to be the first of the Shiʿa imams.

11. Cyrille Aillet, "L'ibâḍisme, une minorité au cœur de l'islam," *Revue des mondes Musulmans et de la Méditerranée*, 2012, 13–36. Cited in Augustin Jomier, "Les réseaux étendus d'un Archipel Saharien. Les circulations de lettrés Ibadites (XVIIe Siècle-Années 1950)," *Revue d'histoire moderne & contemporaine* 2 (2016): 17.

12. Specifically, the island of Jerba in Tunisia, the Nafusa mountains in Libya, and the Mzab valley in Algeria (the subject of chapter four).

13. The full name of Istiqaama in Oman is *Jam ʿīya al-istiqāma al-khayriyya al-islamiyya al-ʿālamiyya* (International Istiqama Muslim Charitable Association); the web address for Istiqaama in Oman is located at https://istiqama.om/ar/home.

14. See Majʾmūʿa min al-bāhithīn, "Ahl Al-Ḥaqq Wa-l Istiqāma (Ḥaḍāra, Madhāhib)," in *Muʿjam Muṣṭalihāt Al-Ibāḍiyya* (Sulṭanate ʿUmān: Wizārat al-Awqāf wa-l Shuʾūn al-Dīniyya, 2011), 79–80; Muḥammad ibn Saʿīd Kadamī, *Al-Istiqāmah* (Muscat, Sulṭanat ʿUmān: Wizārat al-Turāth al-Qawmī wa-al-Thaqāfah, 1985).

15. Evan Haefali. "The Problem with the History of Toleration." In *Politics of Religious Freedom*, 105–1 (Chicago: University of Chicago Press, 2015), 108.

16. Elizabeth Shakman Hurd. *Beyond Religious Freedom* (Princeton: Princeton University Press, 2016.), 37–64.

17. Joseph S. Nye "Public Diplomacy and Soft Power." *The Annals of the American Academy of Political and Social Science*, no. 616 (2008): 94–109.

18. See chapters three and four of Augustin Jomier's *Islam, réforme, et colonization: Une Histoire de L'Ibadisme en Algérie (1882-1862)*. Paris, Bibliothèque Historique des Pays d'Islam, 2020, for an analysis of how such associations have played a central role in the Algerian Ibadhi community's efforts to "re-imagine and shape" Mozabite Ibadhi identity during colonial Algeria and in the years following independence in the early 1960s.

19. I follow recent scholarship in the use of the term "Indian Ocean world" following historians Michael Pearson, Gwyn Campbell and more recently, Phillip Gooding who describes it "as a macro-region spanning eastern Africa, the Middle East and South, Southeast, and East Asia," see: Phillip Gooding, On the Frontiers of the Indian Ocean World: A History of Lake Tanganyika C. 1830–1890 (Cambridge, Cambridge University Press, 2022), 3.

20. Stuart Hall and David Morley, *Essential Essays. Volume 2* (Durham: Duke University Press, 2019), 207.

21. I draw on Nafla Kharusi's explanation of the term as those who arrived in their ancestral homeland as refugees following the Zanzibar Revolution in 1964, which led to the persecution of island residents of Arab and Indian descent. See Nafla S. Kharusi, "The Ethnic Label Zinjibari: Politics and Language Choice Implications among Swahili Speakers in Oman," *Ethnicities* 12, no. 3 (2012): 335–53.

22. Ibid., 335.

23. Nafla S. Kharusi, "Identity and Belonging among Ethnic Return Migrants of Oman," *Nationalism and Ethnic Politics* 19, no. 4 (2013).

24. Akbar Keshodkar, "Marriage as the Means to Preserve 'Asian-Ness': The Post-Revolutionary Experience of the Asians of Zanzibar," *Journal of Asian and African Studies* 45, no. 2 (2010): 229.

25. Mandana E. Limbert, "Caste, Ethnicity, and the Politics of Arabness in Southern Arabia," *Comparative Studies of South Asia, Africa, and the Middle East* 34, no. 3 (2014): 590–98.

26. See Kimberly T. Wortmann, "Reading Ibāḍī Women's Legacies through Stone Town's Built Environment," *Islamic Africa* 12, no. 1 (2021): 1–28.

27. For a study of this discourse on purity of descent in the context of the modern sultanate of Oman, see Irtefa Binte-Farid, "'True' Sons of Oman: National Narratives, Genealogical Purity and Transnational Connections in Modern Oman," in *Gulfization of the Arab World*, eds. Marc Owen Jones, Ross Porter, and Marc Valeri, vol. 1 (Berlin: Gerlach, 2018), 41–56.

28. Khaled al-'Azri explains this tension between traditionalism and the desire for change in modern Oman in his discussion of the institution of *kafa'a*, or the idea that a woman can marry a man only of equal or superior socioeconomic and religious status. See Khalid Al-Azri, "Change and Conflict in Contemporary Omani Society: The Case of Kafa'a in Marriage," *British Journal of Middle Eastern Studies* 37, no. 3 (2010): 121–37. For more historical discussion of *kafa'a* and its relevance to defining Arab identity in East Africa, see Limbert, "Caste, Ethnicity, and the Politics of Arabness," 2014; Nathaniel Mathews, "Imagining Arab Communities: Colonialism, Islamic Reform, and Arab Identity in Mombasa, Kenya, 1897–1933," *Islamic Africa* 4, no. 2 (2013): 135–63; and Thomas F. McDow, *Buying Time: Debt and Mobility in the Western Indian Ocean* (Athens: Ohio University Press, 2018).

29. Interestingly, while older generations of the diaspora in Tanzania rarely discussed these issues openly in my presence, the matter appeared to cause deep concern for their children, who expressed frustration in the difficulty they experienced—despite having the requisite parentage—in obtaining Omani citizenship.

30. "Oman Announces New Marriage Laws for Foreigners," *Arabian Business*, April 18, 2023, accessed March 15, 2024, https://www.arabianbusiness.com/culture-society/oman-announces-new-marriage-laws-for-foreigners.

31. Abdul Sheriff, "Race and Class in the Politics of Zanzibar," *Africa Spectrum* 36, no. 3 (2001): 301.

32. Saada Omar Wahab, "Emancipation and Post-Emancipation in Zanzibar," in *Transition from Slavery in Zanzibar and Mauritius*, eds. Vijayalakshmi Teelock and Satyendra Peerthum (DakAr. CODESRIA, 2016), 48.

33. Jonathon Glassman, *War of Words, War of Stones: Racial Thought and Violence in Colonial Zanzibar* (Bloomington: Indiana University Press, 2011), 4.

34. Amal N. Ghazal, "The Other 'Andalus': The Omani Elite in Zanzibar and the Making of an Identity, 1880s–1930s," *MIT Electronic Journal of Middle East Studies* 5 (2005): 43–4.

35. Glassman, *War of Words, War of Stones*, 3.

36. In 1873, Barghash signed a treaty under British influence to end the slave trade within his territories; however, the trade continued covertly, and slavery itself remained legal in Zanzibar until 1897. Moreover, as historian Frederick Cooper explains, even after abolition, Arab and Swahili slaveholders continued to try to assert their dominance over the formerly enslaved, many of whom became squatters or found other ways to acquire land of their own. See Frederick Cooper, *From Slaves to Squatters: Plantation Labor and Agriculture in Zanzibar and Coastal Kenya, 1890–1925* (New Haven, CT: Yale University Press, 1980).

37. Abdullahi Ali Ibrahim, "The 1964 Zanzibar Genocide: The Politics of Denial," in *Africa and the Gulf Region: Blurred Boundaries and Shifting Ties*, eds. Rogaia Mustafa Abusharaf and Dale F. Eickelman (Berlin: Gerlach, 2015), 55–73; Rogaia Mustafa Abusharaf, "The Omani-Zanzibari Family: Between Politics and Pedigree in an Empire on the Rim," *Journal of Women of the Middle East and the Islamic World*, no. 16 (2018): 60–89; Ibrahim Noor Shariff, *Tanzania Na Propaganda Za Udini* (self-pub., 2014).

38. See Roman Loimeier, "Perceptions of Marginalization: Muslims in Contemporary Tanzania," in *Islam and Muslim Politics in Africa*, eds. Benjamin Soares and René Otayek (London: Palgrave MacMillan, 2007), 137–56.

39. Eve Troutt-Powell, *A Different Shade of Colonialism: Egypt, Great Britain, and the Mastery of the Sudan* (Berkeley: University of California Press, 2003).

40. Shobana Shankar, *An Uneasy Embrace: Africa, India and the Spectre of Race* (Oxford: Oxford University Press, 2021).

41. Shankar, *An Uneasy Embrace*, ix.

42. For more on these issues, see Mahmood Mamdani, *Citizen and Subject: Contemporary Africa and the Legacy of Late Colonialism* (Princeton: Princeton University Press, 1996); Mahmood Mamdani, *Neither Settler nor Native* (Cambridge, MA: The Belknap Press of Harvard University Press, 2020).

43. Michel-Rolph Trouillot, *Silencing the Past: Power and the Production of History* (Boston: Beacon, 1995), 4 and 28.

44. Abdul Sheriff, "Race and Class in the Politics of Zanzibar," *Africa Spectrum* 36, no. 3 (2001): 301–18; Issa Shivji, "Race, Class and Politics on the Eve of the Revolution," in *Pan-Africanism or Pragmatism* (Dar es Salaam: Mkuki na Nyota, 2008), 16–40; Jonathon Glassman, *War of Words, War of Stones: Racial Thought and Violence in Colonial Zanzibar* (Bloomington: Indiana University Press, 2011).

45. G. Thomas Burgess, *Race, Revolution, and the Struggle for Human Rights in Zanzibar* (Athens: Ohio University Press, 2009), 2.

46. For more on how diverse social actors and objects come together to shape nationalist ideologies and practices see: Saskia Sassen. *Territory, Authority, Rights from Medieval to Global Assemblages*. Updated ed. (Princeton, N.J: Princeton University Press, 2006).

47. I use the term "imagined" in this book following political scientist Benedict Anderson's concept of "imagined communities" that highlights the role of shared cultural symbols, myths, memories, and narratives in creating a sense of common identity among people, even if they have never met. See: Benedict Anderson. *Imagined Communities: Reflections on the Origin and Spread of Nationalism*. Revised edition. London; Verso, 2006.

48. In an edited volume where the authors examine symbols, memories, and media representations of the revolution in more recent times, scholars of Zanzibar history explain how this slogan was used by the ruling Party of the Revolution (CCM) as a rallying call during the 2015 election period. During the same period, I witnessed followers of the party wearing T-shirts and kanga cloths with the slogan. See William Cunningham Bissell, *Social Memory, Silenced Voices, and Political Struggle: Remembering the Revolution in Zanzibar* (Dar es Salaam: Mkuki na Nyota in association with French Institute for Research in Africa, 2018), 11.

49. Amal Sachedina, *Cultivating the Past, Living the Modern: The Politics of Time in the Sultanate of Oman* (Ithaca: Cornell University Press, 2021), 5.

50. The deal for the port project was initially signed in 2013, with support from Oman and China, under Tanzanian president Jakaya Kikwete, but it has since been stalled. China has recently pushed to restart the project. See Njiraini Muchira, "China Pushes for Implementation of Tanzania's Bagamoyo Port," *Maritime Executive*, April 29, 2022, accessed March 15, 2024, https://maritime-executive.com/article/china-pushing-for-implementation-of-tanzania-s-bagamoyo-port.

51. Russell T. McCutcheon, *Religion and the Domestication of Dissent or, How to Live in a Less Than Perfect Nation* (London: Equinox, 2005).

52. Kishwar, *Transnational Mosque*, 4.

53. See Talal Asad, *Genealogies of Religion: Discipline and Reasons of Power in Christianity and Islam* (Baltimore and London: Johns Hopkins University Press, 1992), 37.

54. Monuments and artifacts (such as forts, coffee pots, and weaponry) are the focus of Sachedina's work on heritage in modern Oman; Sachedina, "Nizwa Fort," 2019.

55. Ahmed Skounti, "The Authentic Illusion: Humanity's Intangible Cultural Heritage, the Moroccan Experience," in *Intangible Heritage* (New York: Routledge, 2009), 77.

56. As also stated in the glossary, Salafism is a global Islamic interpretive tradition that aims to purify the faith by following the pious ancestors of Islam and rejecting unlawful innovations, Islamic revivalism.

57. For more about how narratives and memories of the revolution influence nation-building in Oman and Zanzibar, see: Nathaniel Mathews. *Zanzibar Was a Country: Exile and Citizenship between East Africa and the Gulf*. (Oakland: University of California Press, 2024).

58. Roman Loimeier, *Between Social Skills and Marketable Skills: The Politics of Islamic Education in 20th Century Zanzibar* (Leiden, Netherlands: Brill, 2009).

59. See Rudolph Ware's discussion of the impact of colonial thinking on African Muslim epistemologies and education in: Rudolph T. Ware. *The Walking Qur'an: Islamic Education, Embodied Knowledge, and History in West Africa*. 1st ed. (Chapel Hill: The University of North Carolina Press, 2014).

60. Marloes Janson, *Islam, Youth, and Modernity in the Gambia: The Tablighi Jama'at* (New York: Cambridge University Press, 2014); Mara A. Leichtman, *Shi'i Cosmopolitanisms in Africa: Lebanese Migration and Religious Conversion in Senegal* (Bloomington: Indiana University Press, 2015); Ezgi Guner, "NGOization of Islamic Education: The Post-Coup Turkish State and Sufi Orders in Africa South of the Sahara," *Religions* 12, no. 1 (2021).

61. See: Ousmane Kane. *The Homeland Is the Arena Religion, Transnationalism, and the Integration of Senegalese Immigrants in America*. New York; Oxford University Press, 2011.

62. In 2012 there was a controversy involving the alleged theft of some of Arabic manuscripts from the Zanzibar National Archives (ZNA) by an Omani diplomat working for the sultanate's consulate in Zanzibar. The suspect came to the islands as part of an Omani delegation tasked with the renovations of the then deteriorating, and now partially collapsed "House of Wonders" that the post-revolutionary government had turned into a museum. According to a government report on the theft, the diplomat had previously frequented the ZNA with gifts and other enticements including monetary bribes with the aim of coaxing certain low-level, and likely underpaid employees with access to the collections, to sell him any manuscripts related to the rule of the sultans. See: Baraza la Wawakilisshi Zanzibar, "Ripoti Ya Kamati Teule Ya Kuchungwa Upotevu Wa Nyaraka Uliotokea Katika Taasisi Ya Nyaraka Na Kumbukumu Za Taifa Zanzibar," accessed March 28, 2024, https://testing.zanzibarassembly.go.tz/files/documents/select_report/RIPOTI_KAMATI_TEULE_NYARAKA.pdf.

63. Many other transnational diaspora organizations exist in Tanzania. For example, China has established at least sixty-one cultural centers called Confucius Institutes, along with forty-eight Confucius classrooms across the African continents. Meanwhile, Turkish schools and cultural centers affiliated with the Gülen movement have fast proliferated across the African continent in the last two decades, appealing to students and parents with their international educational programs and opportunities for study abroad. What distinguishes Istiqaama from these groups is the Omani diaspora's longstanding ties to local communities and the fact that most of the members in Tanzania have been citizens of the country for generations.

64. Emilie Ruete, *Memoirs of an Arabian Princess from Zanzibar* (Mineola, NY: Dover, 2009).

65. Edward W. Said, *Orientalism* (New York: Vintage Books, 1979).

66. Michel De Certeau, *The Practice of Everyday Life* (Berkeley and Los Angeles: University of California Press, 1984).

67. Derek R. Petersen, "Introduction: Heritage Management in Colonial and Contemporary Africa," in *The Politics of Heritage in Africa: Economies, Histories, and Infrastructures* (Cambridge: Cambridge University Press, 2015), 2.

68. Anne K. Bang and Knut S. Vikør, "A Tale of Three Shambas Shāfiʿī-Ibāḍī Legal Cooperation in the Zanzibar Protectorate: Part I," *Sudanic Africa* 10 (1999): 1–26; Valerie Hoffman, "The Articulation of Ibadi Identity in Modern Oman and Zanzibar," *Muslim World*, 2004; McDow, *Buying Time*.

69. For a discussion on the importance of contracts in creating networks of obligation and trust in the precolonial and colonial Indian Ocean world, see Fahad Ahmad Bishara, *A Sea of Debt: Law and Economic Life in the Western Indian Ocean, 1780–1950* (Cambridge: Cambridge University Press, 2017).

70. Lina Benabdallah has observed how President Xi Jinping of China has used "nostalgic borrowings from the Ancient Silk Road" as part of his "New Silk Road" grand strategy to emphasize ideas about "inclusivity and prosperity" in the present. This strategy depends on the glorification of the maritime exploits of "fifteenth-century Chinese admiral Zheng He." See Lina Benabdallah, "Spanning Thousands of Miles and Years: Political Nostalgia and China's Revival of the Silk Road," *International Studies Quarterly* 65 (2021): 294.

71. In an undergraduate thesis on Oman-Tanzania economic networks, Junius O. Williams aptly adopts this term used by diaspora scholars to describe the experience of those who emigrated out of and then returned to their homeland. This term is more nuanced than the more common Zinjibāri, which I argue overlooks the experience of mainland Tanzanian Omani returnees. See Junius Onome Williams, "Ties of the Past, Deals of the Future: Oman's Contemporary Economic Relationship with East Africa" (undergraduate thesis, Harvard College, 2018); Shibao Guo, "From International Migration to Transnational Diaspora: Theorizing Double Diaspora from the Experience of Chinese Canadians in Beijing," *International Migration & Integration* 17 (2016): 153–71.

72. This term, often also translated as "renaissance," has many meanings in Arabic and Islamic political thought generally and in the history of Oman and Ibadhism more specifically. Until the state-building reforms of Sultan Qaboos in the second half of the twentieth century, the term was used primarily in reference to the "rise and fall of the imamate" and, in the descriptions of John C. Wilkinson, meant "a modern renaissance in Ibadi scholarship"; Wilkinson, *The Arabs and the Scramble for Africa*. See also Anna Rita Coppola, "Oman and Omani Identity during the 'Nahḍahs': A Comparison of Three Modern Historiographic Works," *Orienta Moderno* 94, no. 1 (2014): 55–78.

73. An entire conference dedicated to the *naḥḍa* period, attended by Ibadhi Studies scholars from around the world, was held in St. Petersburg in 2015. It was funded largely by the Ministry of Endowments and Religious Affairs in Oman. This was part of the annual International Conferences on Ibadi Studies, which is held in various global locations and features different themes of study every summer.

74. Amal Sachedina, "Nizwa Fort: Transforming Ibadi Religion through Heritage Discourse in Oman," *Comparative Studies of South Asia, Africa and the Middle East* 39, no. 2 (2019): 328–43.

75. Following ethnographer of religion Robert Orsi, this term refers to the ways in which individuals and communities practice and experience religion in their everyday lives. Moreover, it concerns "embodied practice and imagination, as men, women, and children exist in and move through their built and found environments" (xxi) See: Robert A. Orsi, *The Madonna of 115th Street: Faith and Community in Italian Harlem, 1880–1950*. Second edition. (New Haven; Yale University Press, 2002).

76. Valerie Hoffman, "Oman: Country Overview," in *World Encyclopedia of Religious Practices*, vol. 3 (Thomson Gale, 2006), 172–78.

77. US Department of State: Office of International Religious Freedom, *2021 Report on International Religious Freedom: Oman*, June 2, 2022, accessed March 15, 2024, https://www.state.gov/reports/2021-report-on-international-religious-freedom/.

78. Email correspondence with religion scholar Lucas Johnston. See also Graham Harvey, *Food, Sex and Strangers: Understanding Religion as Everyday Life / Graham Harvey* (Durham, NC: Acumen, 2013).

79. For more on the history of slavery and the plantation economy in Zanzibar, see Cooper, *From Slaves to Squatters: Plantation Labor and Agriculture in Zanzibar and Coastal Kenya, 1890–1925*; Shane Doyle, *Slavery in the Great Lakes Region of East Africa*, Eastern African Studies (Athens, n.d.); Abdul Sheriff, *Slaves, Spices, & Ivory in Zanzibar. Integration of an East African Commercial Empire into the World Economy, 1770–1873*, East African Studies (London: J. Currey, 1987).

80. J. Spencer Trimingham, *Islam in East Africa* (Oxford: Clarendon, 1964); August H. Nimtz Jr., *Islam and Politics in East Africa: The Sufi Order in Tanzania* (Minneapolis: University of Minnesota Press, 1980); Felicitas Becker, *Becoming Muslim in Mainland Tanzania, 1890–2000* (Oxford: Oxford British Academy, 2008).

# 1

## Ibadhi Identity and Intra-Muslim Relations in Postrevolution Zanzibar

During the early stages of my research, I met a young Tanzanian woman in her midtwenties who had recently returned from doing collegiate studies in the United Arab Emirates (UAE). Mariam showed a keen interest in my research on Ibadhi history and institutions in Tanzania. Her father's paternal ancestors, who migrated to Zanzibar from Oman in the early twentieth century, were from the city of Adem and Ibadhi. Her paternal grandmother was Sukuma, from the largest African ethnolinguistic community in the region around southern Lake Victoria. Her mother, Shireen, is of Yemeni and Shafi'i Sunni heritage and is the head of the Istiqaama women's organization in the lake city of Mwanza—representing an exceptional case of a Sunni leading an Ibadhi community (see chap. 6). Mariam's father and uncle were also on the board of the Ibadhi Istiqaama Muslim Society in Mwanza and active members of the congregational mosque built in the city center in 1995. She later introduced me to the men and women who drive Istiqaama's educational and charitable efforts in the Lake Region.

When we met, Mariam explained that today, Istiqaama is very active in the lives of youth, eager to spread knowledge about Ibadhi Islam within the local Omani community; her religious education during childhood, however, came predominantly from a Sunni perspective. She initially learned to pray the five daily prayers under the supervision of her Sunni mother, with her hands crossed at the chest, until later when her uncle sternly advised her to pray in the Ibadhi way, keeping her hands at her sides. Apart from these differences in prayer, which Tanzanian Muslims typically explain as minor issues and not cause for dispute, Mariam had learned little growing up in Mwanza about what distinguished Ibadhis from other Muslims. It wasn't until many years later, while living and studying in the UAE, that her interest in Ibadhism was sparked.[1]

One day, Mariam and her sisters attended congregational prayers at a neighborhood mosque in Abu Dhabi. After prayers, they noticed another group of women whispering and looking in their direction. They eventually approached the sisters and confronted them about the madhab they followed while speaking Arabic. The sisters had only lived in the Gulf for a few years and their knowledge of Arabic was limited, so Mariam waited for one of the women's companions to translate: "Are you ladies Shi'a?" When she explained that they were Ibadhi, one of the women accused the sisters of not being "real" Muslims and blindly following a "false" sheikh from Oman.[2] The woman then commented on the way the sisters had placed their hands during prayer, reprimanding them for not raising the index finger when pronouncing the Islamic statement of faith (shahada)[3] according to the Sunnah, or custom of Prophet Muhammad.[4]

Mariam said the woman continued to share her unsolicited and disparaging views of Ibadhi ritual practice. "She also told us that we are false claimers who believe the Quran was created and not the true word of God. When we tried to explain ourselves, they laughed and just made gestures at us, calling us *majnoons* [mad people]. We were disheartened, and we never returned to that mosque again."[5] What agitated Mariam the most about the experience was the woman's comment about Ibadhis not believing in the *ru'ya*. The ru'ya is the belief that Muslims will come face-to-face with God in the afterlife, on the Day of Resurrection or Judgement (*Yawm al-Qiyama* or *Yawm al-Din*). Mariam had not heard this theological position in association with Ibadhism before. She was visibly distressed as she recounted the realization that the woman was convinced that she and her sisters would not experience the divine encounter that drives the faith of many Muslims.[6]

The arguments against Ibadhis deployed by the Sunni women at the mosque are part of what anthropologist Dale Eickelman has referred to as "an overall pattern of competing Muslim discourses shaped by discursive texts,"[7] such as the pamphlets and cassette tapes of national religious authorities that became popular among Muslim youth in Arab countries in the 1970s and 1980s. Indeed, in this particular instance, the women were likely drawing on the authority of the late cleric of neighboring Saudi Arabia Sheikh Abdullah b. Baz (1912–1999), who in 1986 "issued a fatwa (authoritative religious interpretation) that was interpreted as hostile to the Ibadhiyya."[8] In a rare show of international publicity, the grand mufti of Oman (the "false sheikh" mentioned above), Mufti Al-Khalili, challenged his Saudi counterpart to a debate on live television where he addressed criticisms and clarified the Ibadhi positions on key theological issues, like the ru'ya. His responses, which included citations drawn from a wide range of Sunni and Ibadhi authorities, appeared in *Al-Haqq al-Dāmigh (The Overwhelming Truth)*,[9] which has become the paradigmatic guide for modern Ibadhi youth in Oman in defending their madhab against critics. It has also been an important reference for Ibadhi youth and educators who are in the process of reimagining what it means to be Muslim, and specifically Ibadhi, in a modern world marked by nation states, capitalist economies, sectarian and ethnic conflicts, and public diplomacy.

Why do Mariam and other Ibadhis face such hostile responses to their madhab and the way they pray? How do leaders in the Ibadhi community address such hostility? What are the historical figures and events they invoke, and how do they navigate negative perceptions and discourses related to religious extremism in association with the global Muslim community (umma)? Finally, what parallels, if any, can we draw between the cosmopolitanism of port cities like Zanzibar and the vision of religious pluralism and tolerance (Ar., al-tasāmuḥ; Sw., uvamilifu) propagated by Muslim leaders in Tanzania today? To begin to answer these questions, I draw on three conversations about identity I had with male representatives of the Ibadhi, Shafi'i, and Twelver Shi'a communities in Zanzibar Town. These men are among the first generation of postrevolution educated elites in Zanzibar who, starting in the 1990s, began to push for greater Muslim representation in education and public life there. Together with compatriots, in Zanzibar and abroad, they established Muslim private schools aimed at reforming the local madrasa curriculum to integrate religious and secular studies. The public face of Islamic organizations and schools in Zanzibar is usually male. However, as later chapters will reveal, Muslim women in East Africa are very active behind the scenes in charitable work and education.

In this chapter, I show how Muslim leaders in Zanzibar understand the relationship between different Muslim groups on the islands but also what it means for their communities and neighbors to navigate multiple Muslim identities, demonstrating the practical and rhetorical strategies used by various Muslim groups in Zanzibar to present their communities as devout and morally upright, guided by the teachings of the Qur'an, the Sunnah, and/or the example of their religious leaders and scholars. They all emphasize the importance of religious tolerance and hospitality within Zanzibar's Muslim community, which is attributed to the islands' past as a haven for religious pluralism and cosmopolitanism going back to the sultanate (the 1830s to 1964). In contrast to the hecklers Mariam encountered at the mosque in Abu Dhabi, the public position of Muslim leaders in Zanzibar is that religious difference should not be a source of tension or conflict. Instead, they distinguish between shared tenets (Ar., *uṣūl*) among all Muslims, such as the concept of the oneness of God (Ar., *tawḥīd*), and the secondary aspects (Ar., furu'; Sw., matawi) of the religion. These secondary aspects include variations in ritual practices and creeds that are characteristic of different Muslim legal schools (madhab; madhabs in plural). The responses of Muslim authorities in Zanzibar regarding Islamic sectarianism—or, rather, interpretive differences—differed from those of the women in Abu Dhabi, possibly because they were aware they were discussing intra-Muslim relations with an outsider and wanted to minimize religious differences and tensions.[10] The following section provides a brief biographical sketch of the community representatives (here referred to using pseudonyms and the honorific sheikh at first mention).

I approach my conversations with the three Muslim scholars as someone who has studied Islam in a Western academic and religious studies setting. My main interest was understanding how religious discourse, including myths, rituals, sacred spaces, and symbols, influences society and how social structures and limits shape religious identity. In line with anthropologist Abdul Hamid El-Zein's study on the relationship between religion and everyday life in Lamu, Kenya, I argue that religion gives meaning and value to the lives of followers.[11] Religions are not static; they are always evolving in response to social realities. Therefore, they should be seen as interpreting and understanding these realities rather than solely a conservative form of force or power, as commonly perceived.[12] Similarly, as Stuart Hall argues inspired by Michel Foucault, articulations of identity or "identification" is an indeterminate and discursive "process" that cannot preclude difference and indeed "are more than productive of the marking of difference and exclusion, than they are the sign of an identical, naturally-constituted unity—an identity in its traditional meaning. . ."[13] As my interviews revealed, even the most conservative expressions of Ibadhism are not fixed and unchanging but rather constantly in the process of development. Nevertheless, like all forms of religious discourse, Ibadhi rhetoric about enacting religious tolerance, for example, is a form of persuasion that is supported by Omani state power, past and present.[14] The perspectives of Muslim leaders on intra-Muslim relations and Ibadhism in Tanzania are greatly influenced by a broader discourse on Zanzibari and

Omani Muslim cosmopolitanism and civilization. They reconstruct an idealized vision of a prosperous and harmonious Zanzibari past, patronized by the deposed Afro-Arab sultanate, which promoted religious tolerance and pluralism within its dominion. This vision is supported by their own lived experiences of coexistence and collaboration within their religious communities. These three perspectives illuminate the ideal of "Istiqaama" as steadfastness or righteousness, and its relationship to Ibadhism and the Omani imperial history in Zanzibar. In my engagement with them, I argue that Ibadhi, Sunni, and Shi'a Muslims in Zanzibar today construct real and imagined boundaries between their own communities and other Muslims groups, while also advocating for intra-Muslim cooperation.[15] Moreover, ethnoreligious boundaries in coastal East Africa are not static, but constantly negotiated and performed through social interactions.[16]

The discourse on tolerance in the Ibadhi community is present both locally in East Africa and nationally in Oman. However, there are certain restrictions influenced by a variety of factors. People living in port cities previously under the rule of Ibadhi sultans, have been celebrated for embracing the religious and ethnic diversity of these places as proof of Ibadhi tolerance toward those different religions. An example of this is seen in a 1963 stamp commissioned by Zanzibar's last Afro-Arab sultan, Jamshid bin Abdullah (r. 1963–1964), which commemorates the islands' independence from British colonial rule. This stamp features the steeple of an Anglican cathedral, the minarets of two different mosques, and the *sikharas*, symbolizing mountain peaks, of a Hindu temple in Stone Town, epitomizing the sultan's patronage of religious tolerance and pluralism.

However, there have been instances of dissociation from religious outsiders and uprisings that have disrupted this ideal, like the Zanzibar Revolution, which deposed the same Sultan Jamshid. The revolutionaries were not convinced of the sultan's capacity to fairly accommodate other forms of difference, including the stigma of slavery and the lack of representation of the descendants of slaves and non-Arab Africans in the sultan's government. Additionally, under the rule of Sultan Qaboos in Oman, writer Ahmad al-Ismailiy notes that religious tolerance did not prevent social discrimination against certain influential non-Arab minority groups, such as the Baluchi community originally from Balochistan in Pakistan. Similarly, the merchant classes of the Luwati Shi'a in both Muscat and Zanzibar often feel unwelcome in Omani-Ibadhi and Sunni mosques and live in relative seclusion.[17]

**Figure 1.1**: Zanzibar Independence Stamp, 1963. Jamshid bin Abudllah, the last sultan of Zanzibar presented as a patron of religious tolerance. From the collection of Adam Gaiser.

## Approaching Religious Difference in Islam: The Meaning of the *Madhab*

Ibadhism is a madhab "based on five legislative sources: the Koran, the Sunna (tradition), *al-ijmā'* (consensus), *al-qiyās* (reasoning by analogy), and *al-istidlāl* (induction)."[18] The term *madhab* literally means a "path" or a "way out"; and, in addition to its usual meaning as a school of law, the term *dhehebu* in Swahili often refers simply to a "sect" or "denomination." A related term, *tariqa*, also means "path" or "way" but refers more specifically to the "Sufi way" or the order of the Sufi brethren. Finally, the term Shari'a, which often connotes Islamic law or divine law, also carries a more literal sense in Arabic as "the clear path" or "the way," as in "the way to Truth."

These terms all convey the idea that the pursuit of Truth is both an individual and collective responsibility. Scholar of Islam Shahab Ahmed explains, "Even the legal *madhhab* is a discursive rather than an institutional entity: it has no physical or spatial corporate headquarters or salaried office-bearers—its statements are not formalized in a mosque council or a *madrasah* community, and its applied authority is entirely contingent on the willingness of the state and community to go its way—that is, to proceed in the *madhhab*."[19]

Ibadhis in Zanzibar today imagine their school's strict interpretation of Islam and Omani cultural distinctiveness as the *basis* for their unique culture of religious tolerance. They are at pains to project this ideal. However, this ideal is in tension with a history of dynastic descent in the selection of Ibadhi imams; the importance of kinship and genealogy to the construction of modern Ibadhi identity; and the uncomfortable connection between Ibadhism, Arab imperial rule, and cultural dominance (Sw., *ustaarabu*) in nineteenth- and twentieth-century East Africa.

## An Ibadhi, a Sunni, and a Shi'a Leader in Urban Zanzibar

Sheikh Ayman is a member of the Istiqaama education board and the main representative person for the organization with whom I maintained contact when I began my research in 2014. He worked out of his second-floor office in a school building outside Stone Town, where we met again two years later in 2016 for a full interview. Ayman was recruited by Mufti Al-Khalili in the late 1980s to study abroad at the Sharia College in Muscat. After returning to Zanzibar, he became one of the biggest advocates for Ibadhi youth education in Unguja. He now oversees the operation and expansion of the Istiqaama K–12 school and institute (ma'had) for advanced Arabic and Islamic Studies in the East Coast village of Tungu. Ayman later facilitated my introductions at the ma'had, helping me establish trust among Ibadhi teachers and former students on the island.

I was introduced to Sheikh Ibrahim, a Sunni teacher and administrator at Madrasat al-Noor, by a friend and one of his former female students. The meeting was held at the madrasa's administrative office in the Ukutani neighborhood of Stone Town. The office has an exterior staircase that ascends from the classrooms and a paved courtyard below, where students spend their recess. The courtyard is a valued and rare open space for chance encounters and children's pickup games in the heart of Stone Town, surrounded by tall buildings, mosques, schools, and businesses, many dating back to the late nineteenth century.

Sheikhs Ayman and Ibrahim agreed that the Ibadhi and Shafi'i scholars of the past in Zanzibar shared a special bond that dated back at least to prerevolutionary Islamic learning circles frequented by Ibadhi and Sunni scholars alike. This is perhaps due in part to the common origins of many students and scholars of the past on the Arabian Peninsula, specifically Yemen and Oman, and their shared cultural and linguistic heritages.

Sheikh Ibrahim described their relationships with the diverse Shi'a communities of Zanzibar as civil and cooperative, collectively referring to Shi'a Muslims as "wahindi" or Indians.[20] To assist me in seeking out Sh'ia perspectives, Ibrahim referred me to a prominent member of the Ahlul Bayt Foundation (ABF), which is the largest organization of the Ithnaashari Shi'a community of Zanzibar. The Shi'a leader, Sheikh Zayd, relocated to Zanzibar from his hometown in India in the 1990s. He was attracted by the opportunity of serving the growing Shi'a community in East Africa, which is now a majority African population though it began as South Asian. Zayd agreed to an interview in the ABF's office near its school in the Kiponda neighborhood, in Stone Town.

### Discourses on Difference: Politics, Law, and Creed

Zayd's office is filled with volumes of books by Shi'a scholars, a wall adorned with photographs from community events like the annual Hussein Day[21] celebration, and portraits of prominent bearded and turbaned Shi'a scholars from Iran and South Asia. He explained that while the Shi'a communities in Zanzibar rarely pray with their Ibadhi and Sunni neighbors, they often invite one another to take part in their community events. He believes that all the various madhabs share the fundamental concept of tawhid and the prophecy of Muhammad, expressed in the Shahada. "Islam is saying the phrase: *la ilaha ila allah wa Muhammadun rasul allah*. There is no God except God of the universe [and Muhammad is the messenger of God], so it is our faith, it is the *root*. We say the *oneness* of Allah, may He be praised and exalted (*subhana wa taala*)."[22]

He further elucidated that the divisions between the madhabs arose from conflicts over authority after the passing of Prophet Muhammad in 632 CE. Disagreements among Muslim leaders over who should become the successor or caliph (*khalīfa*) of the prophet serve as the origin of the predominant Sunni opinion that four rightly guided caliphs (the Rashidun) succeeded the Prophet Muhammad, while mainstream Shi'a recognized twelve imams and the Isma'ili Shi'a six.[23] For Zayd, early Muslim conceptualizations of political authority eventually gave rise to distinctive sectarian identities with their own legal and theological traditions.

Speaking from an Ibadhi perspective, Ayman, agreed that the differences were minor and proposed that they existed in three categories of analysis: politics (*siyāsa*), legal practice (*fiqh*), and ideology (*'itiqād*). He proceeded to explain what distinguished Ibadhis in these areas. Impeccably dressed in an Omani dishdasha, he spoke primarily in Swahili but resorted to classical Arabic when explaining religious concepts or citing verses from the Qur'an.

He specifically mentioned the Battle of Siffin in 657 CE following the death of the unpopular third Muslim caliph, or successor, 'Uthman b. Affan. The battle was fought between the cousin and son-in-law of the Prophet Muhammad, 'Ali b. Abi Talib and Mu'awiyya b. Abi Sufyan, who was the governor of Syria at the time. According to the story, when Mu'awiyya realized that his defeat was imminent, he called for arbitration, to which 'Ali eventually agreed. Objecting to the arbitration, members of 'Ali's ranks, later called the *khawārij* (Kharijites) or "those who went out," broke rank with his forces in protest. They were those who "held pious action to be the main criterion for accepting a person as a true Muslim, and who rejected the exclusive claims to the caliphate of the Quraysh, the tribe of Muhammad, as well as the claims of the 'Alids [supporters of 'Ali]."[24] The Kharijites became famous for their slogan *la ḥukm illā lillāh* (there is no judgment but that of God)[25] and infamous for their practice of excommunicating fellow Muslims who did not live by their strict interpretation of Islam.[26] Over time, splinter groups emerged within the movement. The more moderate groups, to escape religious dissimulation (Ar., *taqiyya*) and the persecution of state authorities, migrated away from the key cities of the Islamic caliphate, such as Basra and Kufa, settling in regions in North Africa and the Arabian Peninsula. By the time of the Abbasid Caliphate (750–1258) most Kharijite groups had disappeared, and today, only the Ibadhis remain.[27]

Though modern Ibadhis tend to reject any association with the Kharijites and other groups such as the Wahhabis, who excommunicate Muslims they view as heretics,[28] they share the Kharijite ideal, which centers on a quest for righteous leadership over the Muslim community.[29] Scholar of religion Valerie Hoffman explains, "Sinning Ibadi Muslims and non-Ibadi Muslims are considered not *kuffar shirk*, or unbelieving polytheists, but *kuffar nima*, people who are ungrateful for God's blessings."[30] Over time, Ibadhi scholars developed an elaborate doctrine on association (*walāya*) and nonhostile dissociation or avoidance (*barā'a*) in regard to *kuffār bil-ni'ma*.[31]

For the Kharijites, and for the Ibadhis descended from them, the imam, or caliph, did not have to come from a particular family, and the early community would establish a shūrā council made up of learned members of society who would "democratically" select the imam according to his piety and leadership abilities.[32] In practice, this ideal did not endure in the regions of the Ibadhi imamates of North Africa and Oman, where imams were often elected for their lineage and systems of dynastic rule developed.[33] Though the eponym of Ibadhiyya is 'Abd Allāh b. Ibāḍ, most Ibadhis consider Abū al-Sha'thā" Jābir bin Zayd (died before 722) to be the founding father and first imam of the school.[34] He was among the second-generation followers (tābi'īn) of Prophet Muhammad, was said to have died in his hometown of Nizwa, Oman, in about 711 CE.

Ayman echoed the traditional Kharijite view of the righteous imam and provided examples of how Ibadhis demonstrated these principles in the selection of their imams.

> When it comes to political matters, Ibadhis believe that the leaders of Islam can come from any tribe (kabila), as long as they have the necessary ability (uwezo). Whereas others, the Shafi'i say that he must come from the Quraysh.[35] The Shi'a say he must be among the descendants of the Prophet (ahlul bayt). You see, now Ibadhis have opened a great door, they reckon, because a Muslim can come from any tribe. [For example] when you consider some of the Ibadhi imams after Imam Zayd, there were figures like Abu 'Ubayda. Abu 'Ubayda was not an Arab. Abu 'Ubayda was an Abyssinian (alikuwa mtu wa Habasha) who was raised as an Ibadhi and took hold of the opportunity of leadership. [In the case of] Imam Abdurrahman bin Rustam, he was of mixed ancestry, perhaps Persian and Arab. He came from a tribe of Afghanistan—that is, he was a Persian person, but he studied under Ibadhis, and he was the leader of the North African dynasty called the Rustamids (al-Dawla al-Rustamiyya).[36]

The election of the Ibadhi imam occurs ideally through consultation among learned members of the community. The imam should be both a religious and secular authority trained in Islamic law and demonstrating exceptional piety. By contrasting Sunni and Shi'a traditions of dynastic rule with the Ibadhi ideal of an imamate as one who does not discriminate based on race or family origins, Ayman echoes the language of moderation and religious tolerance. He suggests that acceptance of outsiders is a cornerstone of Ibadhi thought and practice and that this foundational principle serves as a clear example of the meritorious nature of the Ibadhi imamate. He justifies these claims by drawing attention to the ancestry of two early Ibadhi imams: Abdurrahman bin Rustam, the Persian founder of the Rustamid dynasty and the Ibadhi imamate of North Africa,[37] and Abu ʿUbayda bin Muslim bin Abi Karima al-Tamimi, a poor but free basket weaver (*al-qaffāf*) from Basra and *mawlā*, or client, of the Yemeni tribe of the Banu Tamima from the Red Sea region of the Tihama.[38] Ibadhi sources claim that Abu ʿUbayda was Imam Zayd's successor—a teacher and guide to the emergent Ibadhi community who lived under the scrutiny of the Abbasid caliphs who were wary of their nonconformism.

Ibadhis credit Abu ʿUbayda with the spread of Ibadhi teachings and outreach (*da'wa*) while in concealment (*kitmān*), a practice that is like *taqiyya* in that it aims "to hide many of the practices of Ibādism in order to preserve it from enemies who might threaten or suppress it."[39] He is also said to have trained the missionaries who would transmit Ibadhi teachings in peripheral regions of the Islamic empire in North Africa, Yemen, and Oman, there "harnessing the discontent of the largely 'Yamani' tribes of Southern Arabia from Yemen through Hadramawt to Oman."[40] These efforts resulted in the establishment of one short-lived imamate in Hadramawt and another in Oman, both of which were defeated in attacks by the Abbasids. Various attempts were made to restore the imamate in Oman over the next centuries, but it wasn't until the seventeenth century, under the Yaʿariba Dynasty, that a line of strong imams was established, chasing "foreign Arab dynasties out of the interior and the Portuguese from the Omani and East African coasts." This marked the beginning of the modern imamate, which would survive in Oman until its overthrow in 1959.[41]

At its height, the imamate experienced a naḥḍa that mimicked trends in the diverse Salafi reformist movements of the time in their emphasis on following the example of pious predecessors as a way of showing the adaptability of Islam to life in a modern age.[42] The movement was concerned with rediscovering the "pure" origins of Islam by returning to the Qur'an and the foundational Ibadhi texts while also emphasizing areas of convergence between Ibadhism and modern life. This move served to defend the madhab against increasingly hostile outsiders, such as European colonizers in Muslim lands, and establish the authority and authenticity of Ibadhi writers. Ibadhi writings in the modern period tend to idealize the imams and early Ibadhi thinkers, along with their movements, such as that of Abu ʿUbayda.[43]

While the Arabic sources provide only vague information about Abu ʿUbayda's family history, some refer to the imam as *zanj*,[44] from which the term *zinjibār*, or Zanzibar, originated. The term *zanj* is typically a collective noun, sometimes employed as a toponym and frequently as an ethnonym in Arabic historical and geographic writings to refer to dark-complexioned people from the African continent or the lands in which they reside.⁴⁵ Ayman's decision to highlight it serves his point about Ibadhi nondiscrimination in leadership and tolerance of non-Arabs. Yet Ayman's comments about Abu ʿUbayda also hint at a parallel narrative about the African roots of early Ibadhi thought, which challenges scholarly assumptions that the Ibadhi madhab is originally or inherently Arab. This is akin to the "remapped Islamization" or indigenization that enables diasporic communities to appropriate "various Islamic figures, place names, texts, events, and themes in crafting black Islamic historical narratives."⁴⁶ The Afro-Arab Istiqaama leadership in Zanzibar is particularly wary of perceptions that they are an Arab organization and often emphasize that most of the students who attend their schools are African or Swahili.

The emphasis on African-Muslim indigeneity and inclusivity is a central component of the postcolonial (re)formation of Muslim-minority identity in East Africa, especially in communities where religious identity often historically corresponded to privileged ethnicities, such as Arabs or Indians. A Shiʿi nonprofit and nongovernmental organization (NGO) founded in 1963 by Indian Muslims, called the Bilal Muslim Mission of Tanzania (BMMT),⁴⁷ takes its name from Bilal b. Rabah. Bilal, scholar of religion Edward E. Curtis explains, was "a former black slave" and "companion of the Prophet Muhammad, and the first muezzin, or the one who calls Muslims to prayer."⁴⁸ Similar to the Ahlul Bayt Foundation and Istiqaama, the BMMT focuses on poverty reduction, education, and the provision of social services within local communities, in addition to "the spread of Twelver Shiʿism in East Africa and beyond."⁴⁹ By invoking the Muslim hero Bilal, the Shiʿa organization makes a clear statement about the African roots of Islamic social and racial justice work, a strategy integral to its missionizing efforts within East Africa and beyond the Asian Shiʿa community. Given the constant struggle for legitimation that Ibadhis and Shiʿa face as minority communities in most Muslim societies, the efforts (however subtle or explicit) of charities and NGOs to indigenize the madhab by emphasizing the African origins of early Muslim figures are even more critical for the survival and longevity of their communities. This is perhaps even more so for Ibadhis who are a religious and (usually) ethnic minority in every place but Oman.⁵⁰

As the earlier example of Mariam's encounter with the Emirati women at the mosque reveals, such critiques generated by state and religious authorities in Muslim-majority countries has a trickle-down effect, creating discomfort or hostility toward Ibadhis among Wahhabi reformist Muslim groups. Moreover, as the Abu Dhabi mosque anecdote reveals, Ibadhis are frequently mistaken for Shi'a Muslims due to their obscure and poorly understood origins and the similarities in their prayer practices. For their part, Ibadhis also present what they perceive as Wahhabi-influenced fanaticism (Ar., *al-ta'aṣṣub*) as the counterpoint to the Ibadhi culture of tolerance, al-tasāmuh. Ayman adopted a similar strategy in his explanation of Ibadhi ideas about nonviolence:

> For example, there is a difference between the Ibadhis and those Wahhabi [types] ... you know, what I mean is, in Ibadhi law and creed, spilling the blood of a Muslim is something called the "red line" ... if you meet a community of Ibadhis, they are always a calm people who live with their associates in a state of mutual listening. In history, if you read history, from the time of the imams in those past years, if they entered a place, they were able to live with people well. Different from other groups who, when they enter a place ... they visualize their opposition. So, it is different for the Ibadhis, just as their creed [is different], because to live with any person is to live with him in good spirits, whether he is Muslim or non-Muslim.[51]

The example of Ibadhi leaders of old evokes Ibadhi hospitality and tolerance. Ayman suggests that the imams would work to adapt to local conditions and establish a culture of coexistence (Ar., *ta'āyush*) rather than viewing conquered populations as adversaries to their rule. Ayman's explanation does two things: first, it distinguishes Wahhabi practice from how he imagines Ibadhi tolerance and second, following a typical strategy of modern Ibadhis, it attempts to distance Ibadhis from the violent reputation of their Kharijite forebears.[52]

Having established a historical basis for an Ibadhi ethic of nonviolence, Ayman shared a more contemporary example:

> If you study the influence of Ibadhism, you will not find even one person ... involved in these [extremist] groups, Daesh[53] and whoever. You will not find a single Ibadhi [among them]. If you look at Algeria, there are many Ibadhis; [an Ibadhi there] could not be affected because his mind forbade him [from doing these things]. [Same thing] if you go to Mali, or over there near Algeria ... I have heard there is a person, for example, from Mali who is involved with Boko Haram. People come [to join Boko Haram] from the East African countries along with people from other places. Among them, you cannot find Ibadhis ... because Ibadhis are very *strict*[54] about bloodshed and taking property that does not belong to them. So, this is the idea of [Mufti] Al-Khalili or someone else, that even young children understand.[55]

Though he appeared uncertain about the origins of contemporary Ibadhi policies regarding Islamic extremist organizations, Ayman suggests that the Ibadhi community in Zanzibar takes its queue on religious matters from authorities in Oman. In both Oman and Zanzibar, I found that the idea of school strictness and conservatism was a recurrent and translocal theme Ibadhis would draw on when making distinctions between themselves and their religious non-Ibadhi neighbors. Both terms recall how they identify as *Ahl al-Haqq wa al-Istiqāma* (the people of truth and righteousness), which implies a community defined by its righteousness and its avoidance of forbidden behavior, such as killing or stealing. Ayman presented the international terror networks established by the Islamic State and Boko Haram as the antithesis of Muslim values—values taught to and embodied by Ibadhi youth from Tanzania to Algeria. In this view, Ibadhi children embody righteous behavior from an early age so that by the time they are adults, they are *incapable* of committing grave sins. Ayman's comments also reveal anxieties of local and international governments and human rights groups about the ongoing marginalization and surveillance of Muslim communities and organizations in coastal East Africa.

Modern Ibadhi scholars in Oman also frequently draw on the example of self-restraint in the spilling of blood as a strategy to delineate between Ibadhi tolerance and the extremist rhetoric propagated by Saudi Salafi figures like the late Sheikh Bin Baz. Scholar of religion Emily Goshey points out how this issue frequently emerges in contemporary Ibadhi discussions about sin and eternal punishment. From the point of view of Ibadhis, it is precisely the fear of punishment that prevents them from committing grave sins like murder. However, Goshey writes, "The other side of this assertion is the sometimes explicit, sometimes implicit view that Sunnis, especially Salafis, are more likely to commit major sins because of their belief that being a Muslim will save them from eternal hellfire no matter their behavior."[56] The absence of fear for divine punishment in the Salafi religious imagination is the key factor "leading them to divide the Muslim community and commit acts of violence."[57] The Ibadhi self-identification as pacifist has even been picked up (with some skepticism) by security analysts "documenting the global jihad," who note that participants in online jihadist networks are confounded that "jihadis come from every country of the world except Oman," the homeland of the Ibadhis in the Arabian Peninsula.[58] The efforts of these global jihadis to recruit Omani youth to join their ranks are in vain, despite the presence of "authoritarian rule, no civil rights, a revolutionary and misanthropic ideology, and a U.S. [military] presence."[59] They attribute this failure to the majority of the Omani population's strict adherence to Ibadhi Islam and the interest in Sufism among non-Ibadhis.

Outside observers use similar language of strictness when referring to Ibadhi Islam. European and Christian visitors to Oman and Zanzibar in the first half of the twentieth century frequently commented on Ibadhis' strict adherence to Islamic traditions, describing it in their writings as a kind of "puritanism." The use of this term was perhaps a way for those writers to convey their observations about Ibadhi practices in a manner that their European Christian audiences would understand, and this term continues to be used in scholarship. In the 1930s, W. H. Ingrams noted that Ibadhis in Zanzibar[60] were as religiously conservative as the puritanical Christian groups he encountered in Europe, but unlike them, were exceptionally tolerant toward other religious communities. In his classic history and ethnology, *Zanzibar: Its History and Its People*, Ingrams states,

> Having lived for a year in a country of Baptists and Methodists, and for eight in a country of Ibathis [sic], would lead me to choose the Ibathis as being the most *tolerant*[61] people in the matter of religion I have known. In almost any town in Zanzibar there are Sunnis, Ibathis, Ithnasheries, Bohoras, Memons, Khoja, Banyans, Quakers, Church of England, Roman Catholics, and Parsees. This may not be remarkable in these days when religious tolerance is insisted on, but it has been the case for years before such a state was reached. Ibathis [sic] consider others mistaken, as who does not, but they mix freely with all, and eat with even an infidel like me. They acknowledge that the one God other people worship is the same as theirs, though the method of worship is irregular. Such a thing as *intolerance* I cannot conceive in relation to them.[62]

Ingrams here describes Ibadhis as the most tolerant people he had come across when it came to matters of religion, despite considering others to be mistaken in their beliefs. He pointed out that they freely interacted with individuals from different religious backgrounds and displayed an openness towards others' religious practices.

Although other British writers of his time held a critical view toward Ibadhi Islam, and Islam in general,[63] Burton's words appear remarkably progressive for his time. Through his observations of Zanzibar's religious diversity and his portrayal of Ibadhi practice, he inadvertently managed to reconcile the seemingly contradictory concepts of puritanism and religious tolerance within the Anglo-Christian worldview. This focus on strict religious observance and a culture of hospitality is deeply ingrained in modern Ibadhism and remains a fundamental principle of the postcolonial Omani nation state and sultanate as built under the leadership of the late Sultan Qaboos. Religious institutions in Oman actively promote a nationalist narrative of political neutrality and openness towards foreigners, asserting that these values are deeply rooted in Ibadhi and Omani society and culture, as observed by writers like Ingrams.

Another often-cited example of the Ibadhi rulers' tolerance is their practice of appointing advisors and aides from various religious backgrounds, as well as religious authorities of Comorian and Yemeni descent. Indeed, though he alone among the Busaidi sultans in Zanzibar bore the title of imam of Muscat and Zanzibar, Sayyid Said bin Sultan did not establish an imamate there, apparently opting for the more secular identification of sultan, a title also held by his successor sons. Scholar of Islam B. G. Martin comments on the relationships among key figures and groups within "learned classes of Zanzibar and East Africa," stating, "In matters of religion, closely associated with politics in Zanzibar as in any Islamic state, there is a maximum *tolerance*[64] of the Sunni Shāfiʿīs by the Ibāḍī rulers. This was reflected in the good relations between Ibāḍī and Shāfiʿī jurists and religious personnel, all of whom appeared on the same footing in the daily or weekly *barazas* (levées) of the Sayyids of Zanzibar."[65] He continues to say that Shafiʿis formed the scholarly (*ulama*) "class," which he refers to as the "flywheel" of the Busaidi state in Zanzibar.[66]

Historians Anne Bang and Vikør Knut further support this view of the scholars' central role in the state bureaucracy, citing numerous court cases demonstrating the ways in which sultan-appointed Ibadhi and Shafiʿi judges (*qadis*) would consult each other's texts and opinions on matters of Islamic law.[67] Anthropologist John Middleton, however, offered a more critical view of this relationship, claiming that the Shafiʿi judges viewed their Ibadhi colleagues with ambivalence due to their "strictness and exclusiveness as well as for holding much of the Shafiʿi behavior as unorthodox, although in fact the Ibadhi sultans showed great *tolerance*."[68] Middleton noted though, that Ibadhis were not interested in spreading their beliefs, as their unique religious identity enabled them to maintain local perceptions of Omani exclusivism and social and political superiority.[69]

## Components of Ibadhi Fiqh and Ritual Practice

Ibadhis in Zanzibar are keen to emphasize their proximity to mainstream Shafi'i Islam and insist that any discussion of *identity* distinguish between the religious fundamentals agreed on by all Muslims. Ayman explained,

> But on a basic level, they [the followers of the madhab] have no difference ... people agree on the five prayers, they agree that God is one. They do not differ on the religious basics; they differ in the branches, to close the hands, not to close the hands, things that are not the basics of religion. We say Amen, they do not say Amen, it is something that is not the basics of religion and madhabs differ from each other within the branches. They do not differ in the basics. In the basics of religion, all agree, everyone is on equal footing (*sawa sawa*). The prayers are five, they fast for the whole of Ramadan, there is Hajj, all [of the basics] they agree on, they differ in many things that we call branches.[70]

While Ayman does not explicitly state that followers of other madhabs are correct in their interpretations of Islam, he appears to suggest that the five pillars are what enable mutual tolerance among them. The five pillars begin with the Shahada, or the proclamation of faith. Embedded within this core statement, which marks a Muslim's lifecycle from birth to death and serves as a basis for conversion to Islam, is the idea of monotheism, or the oneness of God (*tawhid*). The second pillar consists of the five daily prayers (*salat*), performed by Muslims at dawn (*fajr*), at midday (*dhuhr*), in the afternoon (*'asr*), at sunset (*maghrib*), and before bed (*'isha*). Each prayer is made up of a prescribed number of prayer cycles (*raka'as*), and, from Ayman's point of view, the only real differences among the schools concern minor details like the positioning of the hands; the utterance, or lack thereof, of emphatics; and the use of closing statements like "amen" during the ritual. Almsgiving (*zakat*) and fasting during the holy month of Ramadan make up the third and fourth pillars. The fifth pillar is the *hajj* pilgrimage to the Ka'ba in Mecca, which all able-bodied and financially capable Muslims must perform at least once in their lifetimes.

Mosque-goers in Tanzania typically identify Ibadhis by their Arab ancestry and ritual practices. Like the Sunni women who approached Mariam, almost all my Ibadhi and non-Ibadhi interlocutors would focus on where Ibadhis placed their hands when performing the daily prayers. Like Shi'a

Muslims and followers of the Maliki madhab, which is the predominant Sunni school of law in West Africa and the Maghreb, Ibadhis leave their hands at their sides when praying. This differs from other Sunni groups that make up most Muslims in East Africa, South Arabia, and the Indian subcontinent, who cross their hands at the navel or chest during the raka'as.

In addition to his administrative responsibilities at Madrasat al-Noor, Ibrahim is also a Sunni imam at the affiliated Jibreel Mosque in the Ukutani neighborhood of Stone Town. He is a follower of the Shafi'i Sunni and Afro-Yemeni heritage, and his ancestors migrated to the east coast of Africa from the region of Hadramout in southern Arabia. Ibrahim was a student of a legendary community of scholars affiliated with the Baraza Mosque in Zanzibar, founded by a scholar from the northern island of Lamu (now part of Kenya) named Sheikh Abd Allah bin Ba Kathir Al-Kindy. Ba Kathir was a student of the nineteenth-century Zanzibari scholar and teacher from Hadramawt, Sheikh Ahmad bin Sumayt, who is credited with driving the development of Islamic education in Zanzibar during the sultanate era and early colonial period. The builder of the Jibreel Mosque was a benefactor from Abu Dhabi who, on viewing the conditions of the neighboring school, provided funding for its renovation.[71] The school and mosque community in Ukutani are not like Istiqaama part of a unified network of Shafi'i institutions that maintains ties to the religious institutions in the Gulf. Therefore, they concentrate their work in Stone Town and depend on the intermittent contributions of the local community and international sponsors.

Like his Ibadhi counterpart, Ibrahim cited prayer as a key distinguishing factor between Ibadhis and Sunnis:

> Eh, for example. In prayer. They [the Ibadhis] do not close their hands.... They do not pronounce "Amen" after finishing the recitation of the Opening Prayer [the *Fātiha*]. And if they give salaams, they give one salaam; these are the Ibadhis. Sunnis or Shafi'i Muslims close their hands; they pronounce "*Amen*," and they give both salaams. Now we say these things are *branches*.[72] Concerning prayer, whether it be the noon prayer or the *Asr* prayer, they do not differ on this. What they differ on is inside the prayer itself. Whether to close the hands or leave them.

Another example of this "strictness," which Ibadhis often cite, concerns extramarital affairs. Different from the Sunni schools of law, according to Ayman, "If a man commits adultery with a woman, it is not suitable for him to marry her. It is *haram*."[73] This statement is consistent with the prevailing Ibadhi legal opinion prohibiting marriage between a man and woman after they have had sexual intercourse.[74] Much earlier, W. H. Ingrams heard about this and other practices, comparing Ibadhi and Sunni traditions from another "Arab gentleman, learned in the Sheria."[75] Ibadhis also reject the practice upheld by Shi'a Muslims that recognizes temporary (*mut'a*) marriage.

Eventually, my discussion with Ayman turned to matters of Ibadhi creed ('*aqīda, i'tiqād*) and a famous debate that circulated in Muslim theological circles concerning the createdness of the Qur'an beginning in the eighth century. The debate might be summarized by Richard C. Martin in the following statement: "The controversy was over the claim of some dialectical theologians (*mutakkalimūn*) that the Qur'an, which is known to humans in its oral and written forms, was created (*makhlūq*) by God."[76] This claim, upheld by modern Ibadhis, is the position generally associated with the Mu'tazilite theological school of Islam. Ayman, however, says "another issue that is not a big thing is—whether the Qur'an was created (*imeumbwa*) or whether it was uncreated (*haikumbwi*). We say that the Qur'an was created; they say no, the Quran was not created. This is a small issue that is not a fundamental thing. It is not a big deal."[77]

Mufti al-Khalili explains and defends this position in *Al-Haqq al-Damigh*. Here he argues that the early Muslim community had reached a "consensus on the point that Allah is the Creator of everything, and that whatever is other than Him is created, and the Qur'an—like other revealed Books—is Allah's speech, His Revelation and sending down."[78] While North African Ibadhis continue to maintain this position, Al-Khalili suggests that earlier scholars of Oman created confusion and doubt on the issue, leading to a longstanding and (in his view) erroneous belief in the country that the Qur'an is uncreated.[79] The Ibadhi positions on both the ru'ya and the createdness/uncreatedness of the Qur'an are remnants of the madhab's earlier affinities to Mu'tazili— or so-called rationalist, theological doctrines that are in opposition to more mainstream Shafi'i-Ashari traditions followed by Sunni Muslims in Tanzania. Modern Ibadhis are more concerned with emphasizing their similarities to Shafi'i traditions and view these age-old theological debates as the domain of the 'ulama'; they maintain the debate has little bearing on how they conduct their day-to-day lives and hold that all will be resolved by Allah on the Day of Resurrection.[80] As Mariam's experience in the mosque in Abu Dhabi reveals, however, Ibadhi scholarly opinion does trickle down to the wider Muslim public and is sometimes used to discredit Ibadhis as "false" Muslims and heretics. Moreover, by relegating theological concerns to the scholarly establishment, we miss the very real ways in which these concepts impact the formation of distinctive communal identities like Ibadhism—including their ritual practices, styles of dress, and other observable differences. A focus on the lived experiences of Ibadhi Muslims also provides an alternative perspective on the madhab from the ideological writings of modern Ibadhi scholars and the heresiography of non-Ibadhi writers bent on discrediting the them.[81]

Indeed, Ayman's explanation of creedal differences between Ibadhis and non-Ibadhi Muslims sounded like a summary of Al-Khalili's manual, which addresses another issue he raised concerning intercession (Ar., *shafā'a*): "What is the meaning of shafā'a? It is that, as a Muslim person, you will reach the afterlife even if you commit a big rebellion (Sw., *maasi makubwa*). That does not exist for us. This is indeed a fundamental issue."

Sunni Islamic traditions hold that the prophet Muhammad has the power to intercede on behalf of the ummah on Judgment Day. According to Christian Lang, some classical Muslim scholars, like al-Ghazālī, claim that this salvific power to absolve Muslims of their sins so that they may reach paradise and avoid hell extends "to all the truthful (*ṣiddiqūn*), learned (*'ulāmā'*) and pious (*ṣaliḥūn*), [al-Ghazālī, 1:12]."[82] Although piecemeal, this perspective on the issue of intercession again suggests that those seeking salvation must exhibit an uncompromising moral rectitude.

Also, on the matter of the afterlife, he explains the controversial Ibadhi position on the ru'ya that upset Mariam in the opening anecdote of this chapter. "They [other Muslims] say that God can be seen, and we say that God cannot be seen."[83] On the issue of predestination (*al-qaḍā' wa l-qadar*), or whether a person's fate is predetermined by God, Ayman declared, "That is up to God. He knows what is about to happen, but he lets you choose the dangerous path."[84]

He ended our discussion over Ibadhi doctrine by insisting that these points of contention were important in the first centuries of Islam but today hold little import in Muslims' everyday interactions. He also emphasized that these matters were secondary to the fundamentals of the faith:[85] "So, these are the issues of creed, politics, and fight. There are not many; they are very few. Whether [they be] issues of creed or politics, before the start of our madrasas, people were unaware, so after the existence of the madrasas, people understood, and we have institutions and madrasas at the secondary level. Those who graduate are like teachers. They are like imams of the mosques. They educate them in worship."[86]

The Ibadhi leadership that oversees Istiqaama in Oman and Tanzania identified a need to develop schools that would educate their communities on these differences and unify the Ibadhi transregional community around a shared set of Islamic discourses and practices. This was an attempt to raise awareness in Ibadhi youth about their ancestral religious identity and equip them to explain and defend the madhab in the face of outside criticisms. However, as Mariam's emotional reaction to her detractors also shows, the thirst for knowledge among Ibadhi youth is not just a matter of learning how to hold one's own in intra-Muslim theological or legal debates.

In addition, Ibadhi youth find their faith in the positions of their madhab tested when those positions appear to contradict majority views about what it takes to achieve absolution (e.g., by interfacing with Allah on Judgment Day). The Istiqaama madrasas thus serve as both the first line of defense against claims of Ibadhi unorthodoxy or ritual innovation from outsider critics and a space in which Ibadhi ideas about salvation and ritual practice are acceptable, if not the norm.[87] As Ayman pointed out, the graduates of these schools, namely the K–12 Istiqaama Institute in Zanzibar, are the drivers of this educational movement. Many of these youth receive appointments to teach or serve as imams at schools and mosques registered with Istiqaama across the country—narrowing the distance between rural and urban Ibadhi life and Ibadhi communities on the islands and the mainland. This growing transregional cohesiveness of Ibadhi Islam across East Africa and under Istiqaama stands in contrast to the prerevolutionary and sultanate-era reality, where Unguja Island in Zanzibar was the main center of Islamic learning in the region.

## Intra-Muslim Religious and Racial Identity

Regardless of their madhab affiliation, Muslim leaders in Zanzibar often characterize the revolution of 1964 as a watershed moment that precipitated the decline of Islamic education in East Africa and the estrangement of the island's many Muslim communities from each other. However, as Bang notes, such decline narratives were already palpable in learned circles on the islands following the deaths of the scions of the Hadrami Shafi'i and Alawi Sufi traditions, the sheikhs and intellectual companions Ahmad bin Sumayt and Ba Kathir.[88] Prior to the revolution, my interlocutor Ibrahim insisted, Islamic institutions were strong and Ibadhis and Shafi'is would often study and worship, blurring the lines between the two madhabs. In his view, it is only in these two groups' relations to Zanzibar's various Shi'a communities that sectarian differences become discernible.

> There was no sense of identity that these people are Ibadhis, and these others are Shafi'is. Except for the Shi'a, only them, because they have their distinctive mosques. They build housing complexes (*majumba*) which have an area for the mosque and place for their other things, [this space was] only for them. As for the Ibadhi and the Shafi'i mosques, the mosques of those guys are not different [they are open]. They have the shape of a mosque, but for the Shi'a their mosques are in a section inside the *big* housing complexes. In our mosques there is a *qibla*,[89] [but in their mosques] it is only visible to their people, like the Mabohora, there are Isma'ilis, they have all been in Zanzibar for a long time. And they were not fighting, nor did they argue with each other, each one doing what he wants. You do not see differences between the Ibadhis and the Shafi'is. You don't see differences. Except for the Shi'as like the Bohoras because they are from the beginning people of a certain tribe, meaning they are Indians, we say *wahindi*. So, the Shi'a historically were Indians only and the Bohoras were Indians only and the Isma'ilis were only Indians.[90]

Ibrahim's familiarity with the doctrinal diversity within the Shi'a community in Stone Town is a reflection both of his exceptional knowledge of Muslim traditions and a long history of living next door, or around the corner, from Twelver Shi'a, Bohora Isma'ilis, and Nizari Isma'ilis. More than their theological differences and distinctive leaderships, this Sunni perspective suggests that what most distinguishes Shi'a communities in Zanzibar is the scale of their communal properties, their exclusivism and concealment from outsiders, and their undifferentiated racial identity as "Indians." The 1860s saw the fragmentation into three main Muslim identities (Isma'ili, Twelver Shi'a, and Sunni) of the Khoja caste of South Asian to which many "Indian" Muslims in Zanzibar belong. Scholar of religion Iqbal Akhtar explains that "it was through the prism of caste that race entered Khoja collective consciousness in the context of imperial Zanzibar, drawing on Indic attitudes toward particular phenotypes."[91] The colonial government in Zanzibar later reified these preexisting racial attitudes, distinguishing between and imposing a clear hierarchy among Arabs, Indians, Comorians, and Africans. Like the conflation of Ibadhi and Omani identities, there developed a conflation between Shi'a Islam (in all its manifestations) and Indian or South Asian identity.

The "Indian" community complexes mentioned are similar to the caste hall (*mahanjhanavadi*) described by Akhtar, which "shared a profession (merchantry), and had caste-specific religious traditions that were observed in a communal manner in the caste hall."[92] Muslim minorities have faced persecution (Ibadhis included), and a means of maintaining the strict caste and racial hierarchies Akhtar mentions. Modern Ibadhis and Shi'a Muslims struggle with a similar problem of preserving and maintaining the social status and traditions of their communities through seclusion and being more inclusive to better integrate and avoid suspicion from the broader, predominantly African, Zanzibari society. This question is more pressing for the South Asian Shi'a communities in both Zanzibar and Oman who have not had the same degree of rapprochement and intermarriage with the mainstream Shafi'i as have the Ibadhis.[93]

Speaking from an Ibadhi point of view, Ayman also felt that such differences between the madhabs should not affect the day-to-day interactions between Muslims of different schools. He said,

> You know there is no question . . . there is no one who raises the questions of madhabs, people are used to it, for centuries, Zanzibar is famous for it. It is a country in which people live mixed. It is not a surprising thing. It is not a thing that confuses people. Our neighbors live together, there are Christians, they live together, Shi'as, we live with them, Indian Bohoras, we live with them. Thus, in society, we are used to the mix. In Stone Town there are Indian Muslims and non-Muslims, but they come to the farm, eat at home, and if he wants charity, they give him. So, in all, Muslims can live together with other communities without any fight (Ar., *ṣirā'*) occurring. If such a thing happens, it is because people from outside intended it. [They create] strings of stratification. Whereas here on Unguja [island], people live together. And this is reflected in the beginning of the history of Zanzibar. So, there is no instance of arguing over the madhabs, except, when something specific happens to a person . . . say if a person's livelihood is under attack. [Then] our rule is to talk it out until we rejoice (*mpaka tushangulie*). Sure, we have our [own] books but we also consider the issues raised by other madhabs.[94]

The idea of a quintessential Zanzibari cosmopolitanism that defines and derives its definition from its religious and cultural pluralism is recurrent in East African and Indian Ocean Studies, and it has all the trappings of the "nostalgia for a more tolerant past" once defined by the accomplishments of an enlightened class of scholarly, merchant, and landowning elites.[95] In Zanzibar, these elite were particularly characterized by the cosmopolitan Yemeni and Omani Arabs who were the primary purveyors of Islamic textual knowledge on the islands in the prerevolutionary period. In Ayman's view, this cosmopolitan legacy endures in a local Islamic logic and ethic of hospitality that encourages interfaith dialogue and community-based conflict resolution. The only threat to the religious pluralism on the island is radical interference by outsiders.

Indeed, this perception is consistent with much of the scholarship written by the Omani diaspora about the Zanzibar Revolution, which some prefer to characterize as an invasion (Ar., *ghazū*), or coup (Ar., *inqilāb*), orchestrated by African outsiders from the mainland intent on disrupting the peaceful coexistence that marked island life for centuries. Moreover, many Muslims in Zanzibar who are uncomfortable with the growing influence and religious conservativism of radical reformist groups such as the Ansar Sunna[96] or Uamsho[97] often cast these movements and their leaderships as recently arrived outsiders (Sw., *wageni*). They fear that these groups—some of whom maintain ties to authorities and institutions in centers of Islamic learning, Egypt, Sudan, Saudi Arabia, among others—threaten to disrupt the culture of religious tolerance and peaceful coexistence between the various Muslim and non-Muslim groups on the island.

Zayd was keen to emphasize the efforts of the Ahl al-Bayt community in promoting unity among the various religious groups in Zanzibar.[98] Public celebrations of various Muslim holidays, like the celebration of the Prophet Muhammad's birthday (*mawlid*) or Hussein Day, drew over three hundred guests "from different communities" on November 6, 2018, during the holy month of Muharram. The group's Facebook page, like Zayd's offices, displays invitations and photos of the events on the Kiponda school grounds. In the photos the foundation's leadership stand side-by-side with their counterparts from other Muslim communities in Stone Town. The main guest of the 2020 Mawlid celebration was the Mufti of Zanzibar, Sheikh Saleh al-Kaabi. Zayd explained that "the Ahlul Bayt Foundation's (ABF) activities are there to *unite* the Muslim *ummah*, to unite the people of Zanzibar. Because most people are Muslim here, almost 98% people are Muslim. So, one of the objectives of the . . . Foundation is to maintain *unity* in the island. So, when we call any program, we call the peoples, *all* the people whether they are Sunni or Ibadhi, we call [out] to everybody. We call every person."[99]

The work of the foundation that Zayd describes is a kind of daʿwa, or Islamic outreach. Daʿwa often involves discursive practices, such as public celebration of saints' birthdays, as a call to Muslims to deepen their faith and an invitation to religious outsiders to learn about and interact with Islamic traditions in the low-pressure environment of the festival. Shared local traditions of drumming or praise poetry may imbue these festivals, thus affirming the possibility of difference within unity that Ayman suggested is the core of Zanzibar's unique cosmopolitanism. Through these daʿwa initiatives put on by local charities and NGOs, Muslim minorities also find new public spaces to engage in rapprochement with other Muslim groups in Zanzibar without compromising the privacy they enjoy in their daily practice.

## Ibadhi Religious (In)Tolerance under Sultanate Rule

Scholars and residents of Zanzibar alike often remark that though Ibadhi sultans ruled Zanzibar from the 1830s to the 1960s, this did not lead to mass conversions to the Ibadhi madhab. They agree that most Omanis who settled in East Africa focused their attention on political rule (Sw., *utawala*) and trade and relegated religious practice to the private sphere.[100] Historian Randall L. Pouwels characterizes the rule of Sayyid Said and his descendants as (save Barghash in a few instances) "noteworthy for their religious liberalism" and disinterest in imposing an Ibadhi worldview of the island's diverse religious population.[101] The reformist Sultan Barghash (d. 1888), who died just two years before Zanzibar succumbed to British protectorate rule, recurs in writings on sultanate-era Zanzibar as a patron of the literary arts and scholarship. Perhaps his biggest achievement was the introduction of a printing press that enabled the unprecedented dissemination of works by Muslim scholars, especially Ibadhi notables from Zanzibar, Oman, and Algeria who wrote extensively on Ibadhi law and against European occupation of Muslim lands.

Though Omani elites in Zanzibar did not appear to promote their madhab, they did express discomfort in the conversion of Ibadhis to other schools of thought. Indeed, an oft-cited example of the limits of Sultan Barghash's tolerance was his imprisonment of scholars who did not do his bidding, especially those prominent Ibadhi figures who converted to Shafiʿi Islam. For example, Pouwels describes Barghash's imprisonment of Ali bin Abdullah al-Mazrui of Mombasa, who fled the port city of Mombasa (Kenya) with his father in 1837 after its seizure by Sayyid Said. The Mazrui clan of Oman, who ruled much of the East African coast prior to the ascension of the Busaidi dynasty in the region, initially resisted Busaidi rule of Mombasa. However, Ali al-Mazrui eventually returned to Mombasa and served as a qadi under the rule of Sultan Majid bin Sa'id (r. 1856–1870). Originally Ibadhi, Ali came to vehemently defend and teach Shafi'i works in his own writings and study groups he established in Mombasa and Pemba, which inspired other Ibadhis to change their religious orientation to Shafi'i Islam. Because of his defiance, Ali remained in prison until Barghash's death.[102]

I would argue that this shift from an Ibadhi to a Shafi'i orientation during the sultanate period happened on a larger scale in Mombasa and other areas of Mazrui influence than it did in Zanzibar and among the more influential Omani tribal groupings there. This perhaps explains why Zanzibar became the center of Ibadhi reform in East Africa through the Istiqaama schools first established there in the mid-1990s. According to Ibrahim, the Omani diaspora's lack of interest in spreading the Ibadhi madhab created opportunities for other Muslim groups—mainly the Yemenis of Hadramawt or Comorians of Yemeni descent—to assume the responsibility of forming study circles and teaching Islam locally. Indeed, scholars have written extensively on the role of the Hadrami diaspora and the 'Alawiyya and other Sufi orders in the spread of Islam on the coast and into the interior regions of the mainland and the adoption of Shafi'ism as the dominant madhab in East Africa.[103]

## Religious Tolerance in Contemporary Ibadhi Discourse

The term tasāmuḥ is a cornerstone of late-twentieth-century Ibadhi thought as it developed under the leadership of the Ibadhi scholars and institutions cultivated in the modern Omani state founded by Sultan Qaboos. Like his predecessors in Oman and Zanzibar, Qaboos, who we might characterize as a benevolent authoritarian who managed to unify and rule over a previously sharply divided Omani population for a period of fifty years, was also Ibadhi. Nevertheless, he took an inclusive position on religious diversity and had the government treasury fund non-Ibadhi houses of worship and religious institutions. He further gifted the Jāmi'ī Zinjibār (see Introduction) to the government and people of Zanzibar. Oman's Ibadhi heritage is thus detectable only in subtle ways, for example, in the appointment of an Ibadhi cleric, Al-Khalili, as the country's Grand Mufti, and in the publications of the country's Ministry of Endowments and Religious Affairs (MARA or MERA), which invests heavily in the preservation and print of Ibadhi religious and legal tracts.

The question of religious conversion arises, almost without fail, in all my presentations on Ibadhi education and the schools and charities, like those run by Istiqaama that receive support from Gulf-based donors in Zanzibar and Tanzania. The assumption often being that the African communities benefiting from and contributing to such religious institutions are not already Muslim or that they practice a different kind of Islam not quite commensurate with the strict observances of their counterparts in the Arabic-speaking world. What I found in my time spent researching Ibadhi institutions in Zanzibar and Tanzania is that there is a strong correlation between the imagined history of Ibadhi tolerance in the region and the community's aversion to conversion in its common characterization as the act of leaving one religious tradition to adopt another. Representing Istiqaama, Ayman said, "For us, even if he [another Muslim] stays in his, we do not force him (*hatumlazimishi*). So, our approach was not to enter society directly. [Rather] we [focused] on preserving our people."[104]

He went on to explain that people are also free to read the books on Ibadhism available at the mosques and reiterated that the differences between Ibadhis and other schools are too few to "bring about any sensitivity (Sw., *hasasiyya*) in society." The first objective of the Istiqaama Muslim Society in Tanzania and Zanzibar was to "preserve" Ibadhi and Omani traditions and train a cadre of young teachers and imams to transmit these traditions and engage in daʿwa to other communities by establishing schools around the country. Through these efforts, the Istiqaama community can revive local Ibadhi consciousness and attract others *through* mosque outreach in the form of print, sermons, radio shows, social media, and various charitable initiatives described in the chapters that follow.

During our conversation in Kiponda, Zayd insisted that the aim of the Ahl al-Bayt Shiʿa school was to educate and serve as a resource for those seeking knowledge about Islam and that the religious orientation of students was a secondary concern. He insisted that "we teach the people, and they decide. We cannot *force* them ... You cannot force anybody to change their religion. No. They *learn* and *understand* if they have any type of doubt they ask. Then they themselves they change."[105]

It often struck me how my conversations with Muslim authorities in Zanzibar about conversion would often result in a defensive reaction aimed at dispelling any idea I might have that the mosques and schools under their care sought to "force," "coerce," or "compel" (Sw., *kulazimisha*) others to adopt their own beliefs. Others would recite the first part of verse 256 of "The Cow"

(Al-Baqarah) chapter of the Qur'an, which states *la ikrāha fi al-dīn* or "There is no compulsion in religion"[106] as a demonstration of the religious pluralism inherent in local Islamic teachings. I came to view these responses as my interlocutors' preemptive denunciation of any insinuation of religion-based violence in their communities or of an attempt to brainwash students and mosque-goers to adopt a particular interpretation of Islam.

Such responses are not surprising in a postcolonial and post-September 11th world, in which coastal Muslim groups in East Africa find themselves under the rule of Christian majority political leadership and under constant surveillance and harassment by secular government authorities. Moreover, in Tanzania, the government has a history of using Islamophobic rhetoric and threats of jihadist violence by groups like Al-Shabaab as a strategy for maintaining its grip on island politics. Moreover, the finances, sermons, and school curricula of transnational charitable societies and NGOs with ties to the Middle East in Africa are the target of scrutiny by local and foreign intelligence agencies concerned with the spread of extremist ideologies. Compounding the general sense of marginalization shared with other Muslim groups, relatively well-financed ethnic and religious minority institutions in East Africa, such as Ibadhis and the various Shi'a groups, may face suspicion as exclusivist cultural "outsiders" with covert loyalties to religious authorities and governments in their ancestral homelands.

## The Ibadhi Madhab as One Path among Many

To demonstrate the point of the Ibadhi being one path among many, Ibrahim shared an anecdote involving Mufti al-Khalili and his delegation when they came to Tanzania in the 1980s. The mufti and his delegation insisted that Ibadhis resume the obligatory Friday prayer, a practice long neglected by many who remained under the impression that the performance of the congregational prayers was impermissible in the absence of a just Ibadhi imam (Sw., *mwimamu mwadilifu*). As if addressing one of his students at Madrasat al-Noor, Ibrahim gently explained:

> I would like you to know simply that these madhabs are a way to reach God [repeated]. Even when the Mufti of Oman came to Zanzibar, I remember in the Friday Mosque, he gave a lecture in the Friday Mosque, the Friday Mosque is Shafi'i. [You see] at that time, there were no big [Ibadhi] mosques. So, they used the Friday Mosque for the Mufti of Oman. And

there was no problem because people [sometimes] did that. And after the discussion he was asked a question by one of the Ibadhis: "Is it ok for me to follow a person who prays in the Shafi'i way, who recites the *qunūt*?[107] Am I able to follow him?" So, the Mufti gave an example. He said: "all coconuts grow on the same coconut tree." [Meaning] On a coconut tree, there are many coconuts. As for the climbers [of the tree], one uses a rope, other climbs without a rope but they all have the same goal: to reach the top.[108]

The popular name for the sea-facing Friday Mosque where this public teaching moment occurred is the Forodhani Mosque located behind the Old Customs house at the Zanzibar harbor. The invitation for Al-Khalili to address a mixed congregation of Muslims from the pulpit of a legendary Sunni mosque affirmed the fluidity with which religious authority and knowledge flows between the different Muslim schools on the island. However, what this visit and public address by a top Omani state official also symbolizes is a turning point in diplomatic relations between Zanzibar and Oman since an extended period of estrangement following the Zanzibar Revolution.

The anecdote shared by Ibrahim suggests that the mufti appealed to his mixed Muslim audience in Zanzibar by addressing them in their shared native tongue of Swahili and using a metaphor and idiom appropriate for an island shaded by coconut trees that were once also a symbol of local prosperity. The Ibadhi man at the mosque who publicly addressed the mufti about the permissiveness of following the leadership of other Muslim groups further indicates that there were divisions in the Ibadhi community on the question of ritual authority, an issue that I will explore in the next chapter and links the rise of the Istiqaama society to the Mufti's visit. By ending the interview with this anecdote, Ibrahim drove home the Islamic idea of the oneness of God affirmed by Ayman and Zayd, and the notion that in its variant ritual and doctrinal expressions there is just one path among many to reach this realization.

## Conclusion

Drawing primarily from the experience of three representatives from different Muslim communities in Zanzibar, and colonial and postcolonial scholarship about Ibadhis, this chapter has explored the social construction of modern Ibadhi identities in Tanzania. My intention was not to recount historical events and phenomena, as I feel the facts (often a matter of debate) are less significant than from whom or what in the past Ibadhis drew authority in the present. So, while there have been many instances of dynastic succession within the imamate and sultanate that challenge the idea of Ibadhi inclusivity in leadership, it remains important for an Ibadhi in Zanzibar today to demonstrate the non-Arab and, particularly, the claimed *African* heritage of one the earliest imams Abu 'Ubayda. In the examples provided above, I have explained how Ibadhis and their neighbors in Zanzibar understand *identity* and intra-Muslim relations in the late twentieth and twenty-first centuries. This period beginning in the late 1980s is significant because it represented a growth of neoliberal market conditions and forced the hand of former socialist states to loosen their control over local economies, enabling the privatization of education. This in turn inspired the creation of new minority-driven FBOS and NGOs, like Istiqaama and Ahlul Bayt.

My interviews in Zanzibar showed that leaders of Muslim organizations, mosques, and schools in Tanzania tend to downplay differences like the technicalities of ritual practice between the madhabs as matters of secondary importance to religion. Instead, they emphasize what they perceive as their shared roots and the unity of Muslims around religious principles and practices, like the five pillars of Islam. My interlocutors insisted, particularly, on religious pluralism and a culture of intra-Muslim hospitality as defining features of life in Zanzibar—long celebrated as a crossroads of African, Indian Ocean, European societies and a haven of nonsectarian rule. The Mawlid and Hussein Day celebrations described by Zayd are telling examples of how Muslim leaders in Zanzibar today imagine this hospitality and the practice of reaching out (performing da'wa) within and beyond their own madhab. For Ibadhis in Zanzibar, the queues for this friendly engagement with Sunni and Shi'a Muslims comes primarily from Oman and the personality of the Grand Mufti. Since his first public appearance at a major mosque in Zanzibar in the 1980s, the mufti has been a frequent visitor to the islands and advocate of the work of Istiqaama, the central concern of the following chapter.

The opening encounter between Mariam, her sisters, and their detractors at the neighborhood mosque in Abu Dhabi reveals the stakes of knowledge transmission within modern Ibadhi communities in East Africa and the Gulf that frequently find themselves the target of critique. The incident also reveals the persistence of centuries-old debates on theology and religious practice continue to affect ordinary Muslims' sense of who is an insider and who is an outsider of the global Muslim ummah. As Hoffman suggests, knowing the contours of these "obscure and subsidiary issues" and the position of one's madhab on them, is a matter of great urgency for Ibadhis and (I would argue) some Shi'a communities, like the Isma'ilis, who historically showed little interest or found it imprudent to educate the larger Muslim public on their beliefs due to their precarious status as numerical, ethnic, and ideological minorities.[109]

## Notes

1. Mariam (young Ibadhi woman and interlocutor), interview with author, Arusha, Tanzania, March 29, 2016.

2. This is in reference to the grand mufti of the Sultanate of Oman, Sheikh Aḥmad bin Ḥamad al-Khalili, who is the country's supreme interpreter of Islamic law. The mufti is also the world's most high-profile Ibadhi scholar.

3. The Shahādah states that "there is no God but Allah, and Muhammad is the messenger of Allah."

4. Mariam, interview with author, March 29, 2016.

5. Ibid.

6. Ibid.

7. Dale F. Eickelman, "Mass Higher Education and the Religious Imagination in Contemporary Arab Societies," *American Ethnologist* 19, no. 4 (1992): 648.

8. Eickelman, "Mass Higher Education," 648.

9. Shaykh Ahmad b. Hamad al-Khalili, *The Overwhelming Truth: A Discussion of Some Key Concepts in Islamic Theology* (Ruwi, Sultanate of Oman: Ministry of Awqaf and Religious Affairs, 2002).

10. For an interesting discussion on sectarianism in Islam and how sectarian identities tend to wax and wane, see: Adam R. Gaiser, *Sectarianism in Islam: The Umma Divided* (Cambridge: Cambridge University Press, 2023).

11. Abdul Hamid M. el Zein, *The Sacred Meadows: A Structural Analysis of Religious Symbolism in an East African Town* (Evanston, IL: Northwestern University Press, 1974), xix.

12. Important critiques and questions have been raised in recent decades about how well Islam fits in the category of religion that scholars have convincingly showed was the brainchild of the European Enlightenment and its proponents among Protestant missionaries and European colonial governments. While I recognize these problematic origins of the term *religion*, I use it here as a general way of referring to a community of monotheistic believers who follow the prophecy of Muhammad ibn Abdullah (570–632). For critical perspectives on religion as a Western construct and the colonial origins of the term *world religions*, please read David Chidester, *Savage Systems: Colonialism and Comparative Religion in Southern Africa* (Charlottesville: University of Virginia Press, 1996); Daniel Dubuisson and William Sayers, trans., *The Western Construction of Religion: Myths, Knowledge, and*

*Ideology* (Baltimore: Johns Hopkins University Press, 2003); Tomoko Masuzawa, *The Invention of World Religions, or, How European Universalism Was Preserved in the Language of Pluralism* (Chicago: The University of Chicago Press, 2005). See also Shahab Ahmed's discussion regarding the problems of directly translating the Arabic term "dīn" with the English term and concept "religion": Ahmed, *What Is Islam?*, 194–95.

13. Stuart Hall. "Introduction: Who Needs 'Identity'?" In *Questions of Cultural Identity*, 1–17 (Los Angeles: Sage, 2011), 2–4.

14. For a discussion on the relationship between discourse and force in the study of religion, see Bruce Lincoln, *Discourse and the Construction of Society: Comparative Studies of Myth, Ritual, and Classification* (New York: Oxford University Press, 1989).

15. Lincoln, *Discourse*, 3 and 9.

16. Janet McIntosh. *The Edge of Islam: Power, Personhood, and Ethnoreligious Boundaries on the Kenya Coast*. Duke University Press, 2009.

17. Ahmed Al-Ismaili, "Ethnic, Linguistic, and Religious Pluralism in Oman: The Link with Political Stability," *Al-Muntaqa* 1, no. 3 (December 2018): 58–73.

18. Hussein Ghubbash and Sue Lees, *Oman—The Islamic Democratic Tradition* (London: Taylor and Francis Group, 2006), 33.

19. Shahab Ahmed, *What Is Islam? The Importance of Being Islamic* (Princeton and Oxford: Princeton University Press, 2016), 93.

20. However, as Iqbal Akhtar points out, members of the South Asian Khōjā community in Dar es Salaam refer to themselves as *"Asian* as opposed to *Indian,"* due to the politicization of the term *Indian* in recent times. See Iqbal Akhtar, "Negotiating the Racial Boundaries of Khōjā Caste Membership in Late Nineteenth-Century Colonial Zanzibar (1878–1899)," *Journal of Africana Religions* 2, no. 3 (2014): 298.

21. Hussein Day, also known as Ashura, is a significant day for Shia Muslims that marks the martyrdom of Imam Hussein, the grandson of the Prophet Muhammad, at the Battle of Karbala in 680 AD.

22. His emphasis.

23. Zayd's characterization of Ismailis is a misnomer on two levels. First, the usual term that Muslims and non-Muslims use to distinguish Ismaili Muslims from Ithna 'Ashara, or Twelver Shi'a, is *sevener*, not *sixer*. This, they say, is because Ismailis hold that, following the death of the sixth Shi'a imam, Jafar al-Sadiq, the seventh imam, his successor, went into occultation and planned to return to guide the community when it was safe to reveal his identity. For the Ithna 'Ashara, it is the twelfth imam who went into hiding. Nevertheless, the term *sevener* is considered inaccurate and even offensive. Moreover, most Ismailis today claim that the Aga Khan is the direct descendant of an unbroken chain of imams going back to the seventh.

24. Adam R. Gaiser, "Khārijīs," in: *Encyclopaedia of Islam, THREE*, Edited by Kate Fleet, Gudrun Krämer, Denis Matringe, John Nawas, and Devin J. Stewart

(Leiden: Brill, 2020), accessed March 15, 2024. https://referenceworks.brillonline.com/entries/encyclopaedia-of-islam-3/*-COM_35487.

25. Ibadhis later preserved this phrase and recited it three times when electing an imam to lead their community (Wilkinson, *The Imamate Tradition*, 149). The phrase also appeared on early Ibadhi coins found in the 1970s in the interior of Oman, where the imamate was based, which suggests an attempt by Ibadhis to distinguish themselves as a morally superior Islamic sect in the manner of the Kharijites, though they continued to emphasize their pacifism and religious tolerance (Gaiser, "Khārijīs," 185).

26. For more on early Ibadhi and Kharijite history, see Adam Gaiser's rich discussion on Ibadhi understandings of martyrdom and asceticism; Adam R. Gaiser, *Shurāt Legends, Ibāḍī Identities: Martyrdom, Asceticism, and the Making of an Early Islamic Community* (Columbia: University of South Carolina Press, 2016).

27. Adam R. Gaiser, "Khārijīs."

28. John C. Wilkinson, *The Imamate Tradition of Oman* (Cambridge: Cambridge University Press, 1987), 150.

29. Gaiser points out, however, that bias against Kharijites in Islamic sources makes it difficult to conjure an accurate representation of their notions of leadership. See Gaiser, "Khārijīs."

30. Valerie J. Hoffman, "Ibadism: History, Doctrines, and Recent Scholarship," *Religion Compass* 9, no. 9 (2015): 173.

31. B. Wheeler and V. Hoffman, "Oman: Country Overview," in *Worldmark Encyclopedia of Religious Practices*, 2nd ed. (Farmington Hills, MI: Gale, 2015), 172–78, accessed March 15, 2024, https://search.credoreference.com/articles/Qm9vaoFydGljbGU6NDQ3OTIyOQ==?aid=107358.

32. For more on this comparison between the Ibadhi conceptualization of shura and modern democratic institutions, see Ghubbash and Lees, *Oman*.

33. Hoffman, "Ibadism: History, Doctrines, and Recent Scholarship," 1–2; John C. Wilkinson, "On Being Ibāḍī," *Muslim World* 105 (2015): 105.

34. Ersilia Francesca, "Ibāḍī Law and Jurisprudence," *Muslim World* 105 (April 2015): 209.

35. Sunni Muslims later changed this position and "accepted any ruler who could unite the majority of Muslims" (Hoffman, "Ibadism," 1).

36. Ayman, interview with author, February 24, 2016.

37. The Rustamid Dynasty eventually succumbed to the Fatimid expansion across North Africa in 909, but its legacy endures in the longstanding Ibadhi communities of Tunisia, Libya, and Algeria.

38. Libyan Ibadhi scholar ʿAlī Yaḥyā Muʿammar provides an extensive biography of Abu Ubayda based on al-Shammākhī (d. 1522) in the biographical dictionary of Maghribi scholars in the *Siyar*. See Hoffman, "Oman," 175.

39. Adam R. Gaiser, "Imāmate in Khārijism and Ibādism" (Encyclopaedia of Islam, THREE, 2017).

40. Wilkinson, *The Imamate Tradition*, 150.
41. Wilkinson, *The Imamate Tradition*, 150–152.
42. Henri Lauzière, *The Making of Salafism: Islamic Reform in the Twentieth Century* (New York: Columbia University Press, 1983), 5.
43. Gaiser, "Khārijīs"; Wilkinson, *The Imamate Tradition*.
44. Mubarak bin 'Abd Allah al-Rashidi uses the term *zanj* (the origin of the word *Zanzibar* or *zinjibar*, meaning "the land of the blacks") in reference to Abu Ubayda in the first chapter of his dissertation on the life and works of the Ibadhi imam. In describing the personality of Abu Ubayda, he refers to the Persian scholar Abu al-Faraj al-Isfahani and the Arabic prose writer Al-Jahiz, among others. See Al-Rāshidī, Mubārak bin 'Abd Allāh, "Al-Imām Abū 'Ubayda Bin Abī Karīma al-Tamīmī Wa Fiquḥu," (PhD diss., Zaytuna University, 1996), 25.
45. There is no clear origin of this term, though Marina Tolmacheva has argued that in the context of the caliphate, it generally referred to enslaved people of African descent or those who came from a dependent and lower socioeconomic class. "In West Africa, too, the word denotes a category of serf population, whereas in the East African context, to the contrary, the reference is generally to free inhabitants of the area. Here they are implicitly recognized as the majority, if not the sole population group." See Marina Tolmacheva, "Toward a Definition of the Term Zanj," *Azania: Archaeological Research in Africa* 21, no. 1 (1986): 105.
46. Edward E. Curtis IV, "African-American Islamization Reconsidered: Black History Narratives and Muslim Identity," *Journal of the American Academy of Religion* 73, no. 3 (2005): 659.
47. Chanfi Ahmed, "Networks of Islamic NGOs in Sub-Saharan Africa: Bilal Muslim Mission, African Muslim Agency (Direct Aid), and Al-Haramayn," *Journal of Eastern African Studies* 3, no. 3 (2009): 426.
48. Curtis, "African-American Islamization," 663–64. In his discussion on African American Muslim appropriations of Islam in the remapping of Islamization, Curtis mentions a Liberian missionary named Edward Wilmot Blyden, who "was the first prominent African American to advocate Islam as an efficacious religious tradition for black people."
49. Ahmed, 426.
50. Often perceived as "other" in the regions they travel and reside in, Ibadhis sometimes find themselves the target of critique by local political leaders. For example, Ibadhis living in relative seclusion in the Nafusa Mountains in Libya face ongoing surveillance and threats of violence by the government. In the regions of the Persian Gulf and Arabian Peninsula, polemical Emirati and Saudi clerics criticize Ibadhi ritual practices or theological beliefs as unlawful innovations (*bid'a*).
51. Ayman (Istiqaama leader), interview with author, Stone Town, Zanzibar, February 24, 2016.
52. Valerie Hoffman, "The Articulation of Ibadi Identity in Modern Oman and Zanzibar," *Muslim World*, 2004; Enki Baptiste, "Des vallées du pays Ibadite aux

littoraux du sultanat: une histoire patrimoniale des manuscrits Ibadites Omanais," *Arabian Humanities*, 2022; Adam R. Gaiser, *Sectarianism in Islam: The Umma Divided* (Cambridge: Cambridge University Press, 2023).

53. The Arabic acronym for the Islamic State of Iraq and the Levant (*Al-Dawla al-Islamiyya fī al-ʿIraq wa al-Sham*).

54. My emphasis.

55. Ayman, interview with author, February 24, 2016.

56. Emily Goshey, "Eternal Punishment in Modern Ibāḍī Discourse: A Moral Argument." In *Local and Global Ibadi Identities*, Eds. Yohei Kondo and Angeliki Ziaka, 13: 327–45. Studies on Ibadism and Oman (Hildesheim: Georg Olms Verlag, 2019).

57. Goshey, "Eternal," 337.

58. Will McCants, "Oman, the Land of No Jihad," *Jihadica*, July 18, 2008, http://www.jihadica.com/oman-the-land-of-no-jihad/.

59. McCants, "Oman."

60. Ingrams also spent significant time in southern Arabia, an experience he recorded at length in H. Ingrams, "Arabia and the Isles," in *Arabia and the Isles* (London: Taylor & Francis Group, 1998).

61. My emphasis.

62. W. H. Ingrams, *Zanzibar: Its History and Its People* (London: Stacey International, 1931), 191.

63. Ingrams precedes these lines with a reference to Burton, who, in his view, portrayed Ibadhis as exclusivist and "fiercely intolerant." See Ingrams, *Zanzibar*, 190–91.

64. My emphasis.

65. B. G. Martin, "Notes on Some Members of the Learned Classes of Zanzibar and East Africa in the Nineteenth Century," *African Historical Studies* 4, no. 3 (1971): 526.

66. Ibid.

67. Anne K. Bang, "Teachers, Scholars and Educationists: The Impact of Hadrami-ʿAlawī Teachers and Teachings on Islamic Education in Zanzibar ca. 1870–1930," *Asian Journal of Social Science* 35, no. 4/5 (2007): 458; Anne K. Bang and Knut S. Vikør, "A Tale of Three Shambas Shāfiʿī-Ibāḍī Legal Cooperation in the Zanzibar Protectorate: Part I," *Sudanic Africa* 10 (1999): 1–26.

68. My emphasis. John Middleton, *The World of the Swahili: An African Mercantile Civilization* (New Haven, CT: Yale University Press, 1992), 161.

69. Here Middleton also claims that an "Ibadi can only be born not converted," though this is not something I ever heard in my fieldwork; Middleton, *The World of the Swahili*, 161.

70. Ibrahim (Sunni teacher and imam), interview with author, Stone Town, Zanzibar, March 15, 2016.

71. Ibid.

72. My emphasis.

73. Ayman, interview with author, February 24, 2016.

74. Ersilia Francesca, "Ibadi School of Law," *Oxford Encyclopedia of the Islamic World: Digital Collection,* 2022.

75. Ingrams, *Zanzibar,* 189.

76. Richard Martin, "Createdness of the Qur'an," in *Encyclopaedia of Islam, THREE,* 2015.

77. Ayman, interview with author, February 24, 2016.

78. Shaykh Ahmad b. Hamad al-Khalili, *The Overwhelming Truth: A Discussion of Some Key Concepts in Islamic Theology* (Ruwi, Sultanate of Oman: Ministry of Awqaf and Religious Affairs, 2002), 91–2.

79. Khalili, *The Overwhelming Truth,* 93.

80. Wilkinson, "On Being Ibāḍī," 152.

81. Najam Haidar makes a convincing case that the study of everyday practices of Shi'a Muslims in Iraq in the eighth century is a more effective way (than abstract theological debates) to show how communal boundaries and memberships were formed. See these arguments in Najam Haidar, "Prayer, Mosque, and Pilgrimage: Mapping Shīʿī Sectarian Identity in 2nd/8th Century Kūfa," *Islamic Law and Society* 16, no. 2 (2009): 154.

82. Christian Lange, "Eschatology," in: *Encyclopaedia of Islam, THREE,* Eds. Kate Fleet, Gudrun Krämer, Denis Matringe, John Nawas, and Devin J. Stewart, (Leiden: Brill, 2020), accessed March 15, 2024, https://referenceworks.brillonline.com/entries/encyclopaedia-of-islam-3/*-COM_26227.

83. See also Ingrams, *Zanzibar,* 189.

84. Ayman, interview with author, February 24, 2016.

85. While this is not the place to list points of divergence between Ibadhi political, legal, and theological positions with those of other Muslims, such concerns are nicely outlined in the first chapter of Valerie J. Hoffman, *The Essentials of Ibadi Islam* (Syracuse, NY: Syracuse University Press, 2012).

86. Ayman, interview with author, February 24, 2016.

87. As will be discussed in chapters 2 and 3, the Istiqaama K–12 school in Tungu, Zanzibar, follows the curriculum for religion set by the Tanzanian government, which adopts Sunni perspective. However, many of the teachers and students at the school are Ibadhi and the curriculum is offset by religious studies textbooks imported from Oman. So, it is normal for students to encounter both Ibadhi and Sunni perspectives on campus.

88. Anne K. Bang, *Sufis and Scholars of the Sea: Family Networks in East Africa, 1860–1925,* Indian Ocean Series (London: Routledge Curzo, 2003), 99.

89. The *kibla* (or *qibla*) usually refers to the invisible line pointing in the direction of Mecca, the same direction that Muslims face when they pray. In Zanzibar, the term *kibla* also refers to the prayer niche or door-like outline inscribed on the interior wall of a mosque, which indicates this direction of prayer. Historically,

Ibadhi *kiblas* were visible only from the inside of the mosque, whereas Sunni *kiblas* had a deep recess that would protrude to the extent that it would be visible from the outside.

90. Ibrahim, interview with author, March 15, 2016.
91. Iqbal Akhtar, "Negotiating," 299.
92. Ibid.
93. Hoffman has credited Mufti al-Khalili with bringing modern Ibadhism closer to Shafi'ī Islam. See Hoffman, "Oman," 175.
94. Ayman, interview with author, February 24, 2016.
95. For an in-depth critique and discussion of the use of approaches to cosmopolitanism in Middle East studies, see Will Hanely, "Grieving Cosmopolitanism in Middle East Studies," *History Compass* 6, no. 5 (2008): 1,346–67.
96. "The followers of the Sunnah" are one of the "fastest growing Salafi organizations in Tanzania." They are known for their puritanical interpretation of early Islamic traditions and teachings and their critique of what they perceive as un-Islamic practices—such as drumming at funerals or visiting the shrines of Sufi saints—as ritual innovations (*bid'a*). All major cities have at least one branch of the group popularly known as "Ansar Sunna," though their formal names may differ from location to location. Many of the leaders of the Ansar Sunna received their education in Salafi-learning circles in the Middle East and North Africa around the same time Tanzania began shifting away from socialism toward a more open economic policy in the early 1980s. Like Istiqaama, their mosques and schools receive significant foreign funding from those world regions. See Søren Gilsaa, "Salafism(s) in Tanzania: Theological Roots and Political Subtext of the Ansār Sunna," *Islamic Africa* 6, no. 1–2 (2015): 30–59.
97. This Islamist organization derives its name from the word for *awakening* or *revival* in Swahili. Its full translated name is the Association for Islamic Mobilisation and Propagation. In the past, they have promoted Zanzibar's autonomy from mainland Tanzania, causing friction with both governments under the influence of the dominant Party of the Revolution. In 2021, two leaders of Uamsho were freed after eight years in prison, after "terrorism-related charges against them dropped." See Ali Sultan, "Leaders of Islamist Group in Tanzania Freed, Charges Dropped," *Associated Press*, June 16, 2021.
98. The slogan of ABF reads, "To promote unity, social, cultural, economic and educational development."
99. Zayd, interview with author, March 16, 2016.
100. Randall Pouwels also encountered this narrative among "field informants," who insisted that the Omani ruling elite were invited guests in indigenous coastal communities and thus "not allowed to interfere in local affairs." They could govern, but they could not proselytize. He concludes, "At Zanzibar, too, because of the great variety of sects and religions, tolerance was required of the Omanis." See

Randall L. Pouwels, *Horn and Crescent: Cultural Change and Traditional Islam on the East African Coast, 800–1900*, African Studies Series (Cambridge: Cambridge University Press, 1987), 116.

101. Ibid., 126.

102. Ibid., 117–18.

103. See especially August H. Nimtz Jr., *Islam and Politics in East Africa: The Sufi Order in Tanzania* (Minneapolis: University of Minnesota Press, 1980).

104. Ayman, interview with author, February 24, 2016.

105. Zayd, interview with author, March 16, 2016.

106. The remainder of the verse reads, "true guidance has become distinct from error, so whoever rejects false gods and believes in God has grasped the firmest hand-hold, one that will never break." See: Abdel Haleem, M. A. *The Qur'an: A New Translation* (Oxford: Oxford University Press, 2016), 29.

107. An article published by the Arab news outlet *Al-Bawaba*, which covered the 2005 imprisonment of Islamists who attempted to overthrow the sultan of Oman, claimed that Ibadhis refrain from reciting the *qunūt* (a prayer of supplication offered while standing during prayer) because, historically, "this is where enemies were cursed during prayers." While I had not before heard this reasoning, it is consistent with popular and nationalist narratives about Ibadhi tolerance and moderation in Oman. See "Ibadi-Islam's Distinct Sect," *Al-Bawaba*, May 3, 2005, accessed March 15, 2015, https://www.albawaba.com/news/ibadi-islams-distinct-sect.

108. Ibrahim, interview with author, March 15, 2016.

109. Valerie Hoffman, "Articulation," 201.

# 2

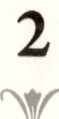

# Building a Righteous Muslim Society

The main Ibadhi congregational mosque in Dar es Salaam towers above a bustling street tightly packed with Indian-owned shops and apartments and a Shiʿa congregational mosque enclosed by a wall adorned with latticed-screen (*jali*) windows. Just as the banners that read "Ya Fatima" (Oh Fatima!)[1] are a clear indication of the latter mosque's Shiʿa identity, the identity of the Ibadhi mosque is indicated by its namesake: Jabir bin Zayd. The director of the mosque, Maher, is a Zanzibar native who was among the first generation of youths from East Africa to be sent to Oman for religious education with the support of Mufti Al-Khalili. He met me for an interview before the noon prayer in his shared office on the roof of the mosque, which overlooks the city center. Here he explained that Istiqaama emerged through two "doorways" (Sw., *milango*) in Tanzania. The first was the unification of the Omani diaspora, which had been scattered all over (Sw., *wametawanyika kote*) following the revolution in Zanzibar. Instead of coming together in a moment of crisis, "everyone was looking out for themselves,"[2] making it impossible to establish a sense of community. Even if religious leaders in Oman had wanted to bring aide to Tanzania in the 1960s and 1970s, they wouldn't have known where to start or who to connect with. Maher continued: "In the beginning the goal was to gather them across Tanzania as a whole, not just Zanzibar; that is how the community of Istiqaama was established. Branches were [then] selected in each of the regions where Ibadhis and Omanis were present."[3]

Once the branches were established in the 1990s, another "door" opened for educational initiatives focused on youth development through religious and secular education. As Zanzibar had always been the regional center of Ibadhi

**Figure 2.1**: Jabir bin Zayd Ibadhi Mosque, Dar es Salaam, 2019. Photo by author.

learning and scholarship, the first schools developed on the islands. Over time, however, young men of Omani-Ibadhi heritage were recruited from branches on mainland Tanzania and other regions in East and Central Africa to attend the new Istiqaama Institute in Zanzibar. This chapter argues that beginning with the religious diplomacy and reformist messages of Al-Khalili and his Ibadhi delegation from Oman in the 1980s, Istiqaama developed as a transnational faith-based organization (FBO) that maintains obvious financial and authoritative ties to religious actors in Oman's government but tries to downplay these in an effort to demonstrate the inclusive and apolitical image of the organization in Tanzania.

## Biography of a Modern Ibadhi Reformer from Zanzibar

Ahmad bin Hamad al-Khalili was born into a conservative Ibadhi family in the village of Mfenesini (literally, "where the jackfruits grow") in Zanzibar on

July 27, 1942.[4] Along with thousands of others, he fled the chaos and violence of the Zanzibar Revolution for Oman in 1964. In returning to the islands of his birth as both a celebrated Ibadhi authority and a member of the Omani government two decades later, the mufti and his delegation delivered a series of lectures at congregational mosques across Tanzania focused on Muslim unity and collaboration in education and development. At the same time, he gathered leaders of the Omani diaspora with the goal of educating the community on Ibadhi thought and practice and encouraging its rapprochement with the country's Shafiʿi Sunni majority. The mufti's delegation stressed that Ibadhism was in danger of effacement by fundamentalist groups like the Wahhabi movement, which originated in Saudi Arabia, and that it was time to educate their youth about the madhab so they could pass this knowledge on to future generations. This transmission of knowledge was critical not only for the long-term survival of the Omani-Ibadhi diaspora in Tanzania but also for Ibadhi identity, which was increasingly less understood by religious outsiders. The delegation from Oman began its open lectures in Sunni congregational mosques while also addressing Ibadhis in more intimate settings, such as in the historic Omani family mosques in Stone Town. They reproached their Omani-Ibadhi kin for their mutual estrangement following the revolution, which, as Maher related it, brought on an "every man" and "every family" for himself/themselves mentality. This estrangement presented an obstacle to community development as foreign donors from Oman, for example, were wary of sending aide to Tanzania as there was no centralized Ibadhi leadership or organization that could speak to the needs of the entire community and ensure the trusted transfer of funds and implementation of building projects and charitable initiatives.[5]

Talks between the Omani delegation and local Ibadhi leaders in Tanzania eventually led to the decision to establish an Ibadhi religious and charitable society called Istiqaama, which would unify the diaspora around their common origins in Oman, their belief in Islam, and their adherence to the teachings of the Ibadhi madhab. Beyond its commitments to reviving Ibadhism in the diaspora, the founders stressed the importance of outreach to the broader Muslim community. They worked to revive and demarcate Ibadhi space by labeling old and new mosques after the madhab's founding figures, hanging up portraits of Al-Khalili in their homes and offices and creating a transregional network of private schools all under the name Istiqaama. From its foundation Istiqaama was a transnational initiative with a translocal reach, connecting Omani and Ibadhi communities of coastal and northwestern Tanzania and into central Africa. So far was the organization's reach, that once the Istiqaama

Institute was established in Zanzibar (see chap. 3), Ibadhis in Burundi, Democratic Republic of Congo, and Rwanda gradually began to send their youths to Tanzania to study at the Istiqaama Institute. The rise of Istiqaama, then, must be contextualized in terms of the 1980s and 1990s, when Tanzania, and much of Africa, was undergoing a transition from socialist to democratic governance, multiparty elections, and neoliberal reforms centered on structural adjustment policies and the privatization of the economy in a way that enabled the proliferation of FBOs and NGOs across the country. Moreover, during this period, the country's borders opened to trade and foreign investment, welcoming diplomats and businessmen from Oman, among other places. Al-Khalili's delegation was an example of Tanzania's openness to reviving its cultural ties with Oman and interest in pathways toward mutual economic growth.

Istiqaama is an example of what geographer Mona Atia has called "pious neoliberalism," or a meeting point of neoliberalism and Islamism where "subjects engage in a moral economy that is inextricably linked with the market, self-government, and faith."[6] Moreover, it is a way of doing good works (*khayr*), which brings one closer to God, while also attempting to engage in socioeconomic development that will improve effectiveness and efficiency of governing structures.[7] As Atia cautions, this is not necessarily a top-down process, as much as governments and government authorities may try to monitor, control, and co-opt, for diplomatic or civil purposes, the activities of religious groups within their purview. Nor do all neoliberal faith-based organizations around the world look the same or relate to governance in the same kinds of ways.[8] International diaspora organizations like Istiqaama offer a unique vantage point from which to examine how the same organization may take on varied leadership and economic structures or be more or less explicit about their religious identities, depending on how near or far they are to what they consider their ancestral homeland. At the same time, religious organizations like Istiqaama have the potential to create transregional and transnational solidarities around diaspora identity by engaging in religious diplomacy that conveys a particular interpretation or vision of Islam. This is seen nowhere more clearly than in what I call the "Friday prayer movement," the main case study in this chapter, which was initiated under the leadership of Al-Khalili as a means of bringing Ibadhis into proximity with Shafi'i Sunni Islam in Tanzania through public sermons at old and new mosques across the country.

The Friday prayer movement was essential to Al-Khalili's religious diplomacy in Tanzania as it drew on the rhetoric of religious tolerance and Muslim unity, which are central to the sultanate's self-image, while at the same time resonating with local discourses about peace and security in postrevolutionary Zanzibar. The Omani mufti's personal connections to Zanzibar and his knowledge of Swahili and familiarity with Muslim cultures and practices in East Africa enabled him to reach and connect with a wide public. Ibadhi calls for religious reform in Zanzibar have intersected with Omani public diplomacy in the formation of the Istiqaama Muslim Society of Tanzania.

## A Lost Son Returns: Al-Khalili and Omani Public Diplomacy in Tanzania

Omani writer Nasser Abdulla Al-Riyami's biography of Al-Khalili begins with two hagiographic anecdotes about his early childhood in rural Zanzibar that portray him as the lost son of exceptional piety and discernment who would become the key figure driving the religious reforms of the modern Omani state under Sultan Qaboos. In the first of the two incidents, the four-year-old Al-Khalili purportedly reproached his mother for attending a co-ed, though gender-segregated, celebration of Mawlid without the permission of his father. When his mother explained that she could not seek permission as his father was out of town, the young Al-Khalili made a fuss until she took him home in defeat.[9] In the second account, we learn that Al-Khalili was precocious and could recite the Qur'an by the age of six. The boy prodigy also studied closely with, and attended the public lectures of, the Algerian Ibadhi Sheikh Abu Ishaq Atfayyish during his first and second visits to Unguja island. By the age of seven, he had begun to serve as the mosque's muezzin, where his father served as imam, and by age nine, he had become a hafiz, having memorized the entire Qur'an. Al-Khalili learned under the tutelage of several other scholars in Zanzibar and studied the Qur'an, hadith, Arabic grammar, law, and inheritance, among other subjects. He read the Ibadhi legal primer *Talqīn al-ṣubiyyān mā yalzamu al-insān* (Educating the Youth on What Is Imperative of the Human) and the two-volume legal poem *Jawhar al-Nidhām* (Jewel of the Legal System) both by Nūr al-Dīn ʿAbd Allāh bin Humayyid al-Sālimī (1869–1914). When the Zanzibar Muslim Academy opened in Stone Town in the early 1950s, Al-Khalili was unable to attend because he lived far away. Moreover, he was responsible for tending to the family business whenever his father was out of town.[10] Disturbed by the lack of parity in rural and urban education, Al-Riyami claims that Al-Khalili once addressed the issue in a speech delivered to members of the Arab Association in Zanzibar. The eloquent young orator stressed the importance of making Islamic education available to children in the rural areas who for various reasons could not attend the elite institutions of the town.[11] These stories establish the impeachable and righteous character of Al-Khalili, an image consistent with the reverential manner with which Ibadhis in Tanzania regard him.

At the time of the Zanzibar Revolution, Al-Khalili's father spent time in jail along with "many tens of thousands of Arabs," most likely under suspicion that they would try to undercut the revolution and reinstate the sultanate.[12] After his father's release, the Khalili family joined the waves of Arabs fleeing the island by boarding a Pakistani ship for the weeks-long journey to Muscat, Oman. From Muscat, they left for the mufti's home region of Bahla, located in Oman's interior region (Al-Dakhaliyya). As Al-Riyami tells it, there the young Khalili began to seek out local scholars and study groups, and it was not long before he gained notoriety for his extensive knowledge of Islamic studies. He accepted a position teaching the Qur'an and religion to local children and held study groups at the Bahla Mosque. As the word about his intellectual abilities spread, Al-Khalili received and accepted an offer to teach advanced Islamic sciences at a college in Al-Khoor Mosque in Muscat. In 1975, following the death in a car accident of the mufti who preceded him, Al-Khalili was appointed the grand mufti of Oman by Sultan Qaboos, who had only just risen to power following a British-backed coup that overthrew his father five years earlier. Starting in 1986, Al-Khalili served as undersecretary of the Ministry of Justice, Awqaf and Islamic Affairs until a severe illness required him to take a sabbatical from this post to seek treatment abroad. Al-Riyami writes that after Al-Khalili's recovery, the sultan made him a minister of the same office, now called the Ministry of Endowments and Religious Affairs (MERA).[13] The biography ends here and, surprisingly for an author focused on the legacies of Zanzibar elites and exiles who went on to build Oman, does not mention the mufti's role in the creation of Istiqaama or the significance of this transnational Ibadhi movement in shaping the future of Oman-Tanzania relations. His narrative, like that of many Omani exiles whose focus is on the history of Zanzibari elites the first two decades after the revolution, is a nostalgic one, concerned with celebrating and archiving an idealized past without examining present struggles and achievements. When the Ibadhi imamate dissolved in Oman in the late 1950s and Sultan Qaboos rose to power in Oman in 1970, he worked quickly to legitimize himself as the sole ruler capable of creating a sense of shared identity or an "imagined community."[14]

The new leader's legitimacy-building project relied largely on the promotion of shared national myths about Omani identity and "on [establishing] standardized collective references."[15] Chief among these references is the idea of a distinctively Omani nationalist articulation of Islam, which draws heavily from the Ibadhi ideals of justice and equality, and a history of downplaying and concealing one's religious identity. Strong links continue to exist between the history of Ibadhi Islam and state power in Oman. Yet Sultan Qaboos was reticent about his own Ibadhi heritage, and state representatives in Oman, in general, tend to downplay the political significance of Ibadhi Islam as part of its policy to promote religious unity. They elevate the ideal of religious unity by promoting what Political Scientist Marc Valeri called "a consensual and 'generic' Islam that is peculiar to Oman and that neglects both controversial past influences and foreign ones, such as the Saudi Wahhabi influence."[16] The idea of a generic and unified Islam necessarily undermines sectarian identities and debate in the interest of maintaining political neutrality and regional stability. The irony of Oman's philosophy of Muslim unity is that its justification derives in large part from a sectarian identity (i.e., Ibadhi Islam). While state actors emphasize the need for tolerance in public pronouncements on religion, the Omani government also works hard to undermine any religious voices that threaten to challenge the existing political order or that highlight sectarian differences.

Eickelman shows that the Omani state's preoccupation with religious tolerance and accommodation is, in many ways, a response to the consciousness of religion and sectarianism that emerged in post-1970 Oman. Driving this consciousness is a better-educated younger generation that has come into greater contact with alternative interpretations of Islam and the role of religion in the modern world.[17] Ibadhis in Oman have taken advantage of the increased literacy, new community and institutional arrangements, and new media at their disposal to project a controlled image of Ibadhi Islam.[18] What defines this new Ibadhi consciousness is its unique relationship to the state in Oman. This relationship relies on Ibadhi religious and political ideals, such as moderation and mediation, as a basis from which to disseminate a hypercontrolled discourse on tolerance.

The sultanate also closely monitors religious organizations and congregations through MERA. "All religious organizations must register with the government. Groups seeking registration must request meeting and worship space from one of the sponsor organizations recognized by MERA. Muslim groups must register, but the government—as benefactor of the country's mosques—serves as their sponsor."[19] Oman recognizes several Christian churches and Hindu and Sikh temples and appoints an official sponsor to oversee each one. "The sponsors are responsible for recording the group's doctrinal adherence, the names of its leaders, and the number of active members, and for submitting this information to the ministry."[20] MERA has branches in the major governorates across the country and is the umbrella organization housing both the mufti's office, the Institute of Shariah Sciences, and all other religiously related institutions, including the departments of zakat, waqf, hajj affairs, and preaching.[21] The sultanate's structured religious bureaucracy is identifiable in schools and houses of worship that follow very clear curricular and building guidelines.

The building of Friday mosques in cities across the sultanate is another visible manifestation of the state's "generic Islam" and a good example of the inextricable link between religious and state authority in Oman. The construction of mosques requires the approval of the local and national governments and is well monitored with strict guidelines for their location and function.[22] The government appoints all imams in the sultanate, and the state issues a uniform Friday sermon delivered weekly in every mosque there. The International Religious Freedom Report states that "all individuals who deliver sermons in recognized religious groups must register with MERA. Unlicensed lay members are prohibited from preaching sermons in mosques, and licensed imams must follow government-approved sermons. Lay members of non-Muslim groups may lead prayers if they are specified as leaders in their group's registration application."[23]

According to this report issued by the US government, its Omani counterpart accepts proposals for each week's sermon, and MERA checks these for stylistic errors, accuracy of information, and the quality of their content before the selection.[24] The government then publicizes the name of the author for each week's selected sermon, adding a degree of competition and prestige to the practice of sermon writing. The state's appointment of mosque religious leadership and its monopoly over the Friday sermon is part of a comprehensive strategy under MERA to incorporate Islam and the country's religious leadership into the state, thus enabling a more effective transmission of the national message on Muslim unity.[25] Valeri suggests that this "bureaucratization of men of religion" is the reason "why relations with Ibadhi communities of Tanzania, Algeria, Tunisia, and Libya remain weak after 1970. By confining religious personalities within the national framework, the regime has not only controlled their voice and influence more easily but also involved them personally in the promotion of a national identity."[26] Providing government subsidies for transnational religious charities such as Istiqaama and working with these groups to shape national discourses on Islam and Ibadhi Islam, the Omani state is beginning to revive its ties to Ibadhi networks in East and North Africa.

In early sermons and lectures addressing the Ibadhi community, the authorities from Oman and their supporters in Tanzania focused on self-knowledge as a first step in removing a veil of ignorance about Ibadhism. Ayman from chapter 1 explained:

> Our goal is first to bring in those Ibadhis who realized that they did not really know themselves and those who had not yet reached this realization [of lack of self-knowledge], i.e., those who were uneducated. You could say that before the 1980s, there was no [madhab] education at all [*haipo kabisa*]. Even the youth were not educated, [a person] would just exist, almost ashamed to discover a path to learn more. So, the first step was to introduce the Friday prayers. We started in Stone Town near [the business called] Stone Traders. The first day in that location was April 4, 1986.... So first it was prayer then they began to inform the community [about the madhab] and people began to recognize each other. The jumuiya did not start right away; it happened by way of the madrasa, madrasas of Istiqaama... over there in Mkunazini. To this day, the Shaksi madrasa continues to teach children, and we ourselves studied there, so it became our first identity until we realized it is up to us to bring understanding. Before getting outsiders to understand. So, people from other madhabs [come] without being called, see the mark of the Ibadhi works.[27]

Ayman implies that the collective "forgetting" or willful dissociation from their madhab was due to a lack of guidance and consensus among Ibadhis about where religious authority lay. According to this line of reasoning, the revival of Ibadhi group consciousness[28] first required that individual members of the community face the shame of recognizing their lack of self-awareness. This self-realization demanded the humility that comes with submitting oneself to the care of another deemed more learned and authoritative, who would serve as a guide on the path to righteousness in a manner like the relationship between the Sufi master and disciple. To submit to a more knowledgeable authority was as much the prerogative of "uneducated" elders as it was for the youth. Still, the situation for youth was more urgent due to their affinity toward new religious movements with more articulate religious ideologies that were adept in recruiting followers through new media and educational programs that combined religious knowledge with modern technologies.

Ibadhis who I spoke with or whose works I read during my research on mainland Tanzania and the islands would often describe their communities as having been in a state of spiritual slumber or, like Ayman put it, of existing without purpose or meaning. For example, in *Qamusi-Ssalaa* (2010) a Swahili language primer designed to teach school-age children about Ibadhism and prayer, a Pemban scholar, Sheikh Khalfan Tiwani, explained that there are two reasons that other Muslim groups misunderstand and sometimes shun Ibadhis. First is because of the propagation of what he calls sectarian hate, which he attributes to the failure of non-Ibadhis to read and engage with scholarship written by Ibadhis themselves, so he provides references for those seeking to understand the tradition on its own terms. The second reason is that Ibadhis themselves have been asleep and are in part to blame for the ignorance of others about the madhab because they do not attempt to explain it beyond their immediate families or communities, if they even do that. He cited the dearth of books about Ibadhism written in Swahili as evidence of this spiritual lethargy and claimed that therefore young people go in search of other paths to gain clarity about their faith. They then return to their Ibadhi parents and critique the way they pray and behave. He credited Al-Khalili with "activating" Ibadhism "after a long time of bitter sleep" and praised the work of his relative Sheikh Mohammad Suleiman Tiwani, an acolyte of the mufti, for using his talents and education to awaken Ibadhis in Pemba.[29]

Related to the recurrent trope of the "sleeping" madhab or Muslim is shame that comes with not knowing one's own history or the reasons for one's beliefs. From Ayman and Sheikh Khalfan's point of view, shame that derives from a lack of self-knowledge has the potential to destroy communal and familial bonds, making one vulnerable not only to moral corruption but also to other religious groups and ideologies that are intolerant to other ways of life. They describe a deeply ontological struggle to uncover a sense of both spiritual "consciousness and intersubjectivity."[30] Summing up major philosophical positions on how shame affects our sense of self, philosopher Luna Dolezal explains that "without shame, we would not have the capacity for reflective self-awareness nor eventually become relational political subjects."[31] She suggests, in her rereading of John Paul Sartre's work on the topic, that there is a strong connection between "shame, the body and vulnerability" and that this interconnection reflects a basic human need for belonging.[32]

When viewed through a similar lens, Ayman's experience of shame can be seen as a productive force that prompts spiritual reform. Rather than serving as an obstacle that prevents someone from advancing on the path to spiritual reform, shame enables the self-awareness essential for the first step to joining a righteous society. Ayman's words are also a commentary on the suppression of religious education and associational life in Zanzibar following the revolution and a reference to the secularization of Tanzanian society under socialist governance in the 1960s and 1970s. While Istiqaama's leaders shy away from involvement in public politics, their critique is not so different from that of earlier Muslim reformists, such as the forerunners "of contemporary Sunni Islamist thought,"[33] like the Egyptian scholar Sayyid Qutb (1906–1966). Qutb blamed the spiritual depravity of humanity on the cultural and political hegemony of an "unbelieving" Western civilization. In adopting Western and Eastern systems of governance such as a secular legislative authority, democracy, and socialism, Muslim leaders were themselves ignorant (*jahili*) of the authority of Allah and were not able to serve as righteous guides for the umma. The only way to restore the earth to righteous leadership, in his view, was to create a vanguard of reformers who would at once maintain distance from and closeness to the ignorance (*jahiliyya*) surrounding them and follow the example of the Prophet Muhammad and the Salaf (pious ancestors) in leading their communities to spiritual enlightenment.[34] The challenges faced by Ibadhi youth in integrating into the capitalistic aspects and secularizing projects of modern nation states, as well as navigating calls for global Islamic revival, emphasize the importance of a framework to make sense of their multiple identities and experiences of modernity. This tension between conforming to the expectations of the modern nation-state and adhering to conservative Islamic teachings reflects a broader struggle within Tanzania's Ibadhi-Omani community to build and sustain its aspirational righteous community in the diaspora.

The Islamic revival of the 1980s presented a challenge to local Muslim practices that Islamist reformers criticized as deviating from the teachings of the Qur'an and Sunna and the example of the Salaf from the first century of Islam. Muslim youths were facing the challenge of how to integrate into postcolonial and quasisocialist local environments that were hostile to political Islam while also responding to the call for them to don the mantle of religion and propagate the faith. During this dual pressure to conform to the exigencies of the modern nation-state and Islamic reform, Ibadhi youth also felt pressure to articulate their place in this global Islamic revival while not having the religious framework to help them make sense of this double consciousness[35] and the ways in which their diasporic identities intersected with their Islamic ones.[36]

Like the earlier movement described by Amal Ghazal, the postrevolution Ibadhi revival began in the mosque. Yet now it was not only the mosque study circles where issues of moral reform and Muslim unity were highlighted; the Friday prayer and sermon were also involved. The prayers were a call to action for young people, inspiring them to assume their new role as the vanguard of the imagined righteous community that would later refer to itself in Swahili as the Istiqaama Muslim Community. The creation of the organization allowed Ibadhis the opportunity to redefine their collective identity in the unstable postrevolutionary present as an inclusive and tolerant madhab that other Muslims would want to follow. This reorientation toward inclusivity in a community that (in Zanzibar especially) had historically kept to its own networks of Arab family mosques, depended greatly on the charismatic authority of the foreign delegates and the religious literature and spiritual resources they brought with them.

### The Ibadhi Friday Prayer Movement

The Ibadhi Friday prayer movement began in what is today Stone Town's largest Ibadhi mosque located near and across the street from the landmark Ismaili-owned Stone Town Traders stationery shop. The location of the mosque is on Gizenga Street, part of the old city's upscale Shanghani neighborhood and the main tourist thoroughfare and center for souvenir shopping. Indeed, the somewhat awkward encounter between brightly—and sometimes, scantily—clad tourists and the outpour of crisply dressed Muslim male worshippers following the Friday afternoon prayer is a commentary on both the tolerance and the unease with which Stone Town residents have learned to maintain the town's religious integrity amid the material signs of a Westernized modernity.

When Sultan Qaboos assumed power in Oman in the 1970s, state-funded Friday mosques proliferated, as did efforts to standardize the Friday sermon in government mosques. According to Al-Siyabi, the Friday sermon in the first Istiqaama mosques came from MERA.

> Oman sends them podium books especially preaching books that are prepared by the Ministry.[37] They preached from them, and [practice of] the khutba [sermon] was new to the people, as the khutbas were delivered in the Friday mosques that are connected to the other ancient madhabs. And among the teachers were Egyptians and Sudanese, coming to pray in the

Ibadhi mosque, and we sent to them [text of] the khutbas constantly. There were so many people praying to the point that they filled the mosque, and the Ministry of Endowments set out to expand the Muharrami mosque so that now it consists of two floors. Then the Istiqaama Mosque broke away from it, so the Istiqaama Mosque used to be the Al-Muharrami mosque, and it was appropriate for the Omani man from the tribe of al-Muharrami in Oman.[38]

The imagery of Muslims crowding into the mosques eager to hear the sermons given by Omani visitors or provided by the Omani government suggests both a renegotiation of authority in Zanzibar in the 1980s, when the movement began, and an openness and curiosity for the new expressions of Islamic knowledge coming from Oman. I prefer the term "(re)negotiation" of authority over "crisis" or "fragmentation" of authority because it is less suggestive of intra-Muslim antagonism and also better explains how a reform movement led by Ibadhis and religious authorities from Oman could gain such momentum in primarily non-Ibadhi spaces. Moreover, the presence of Omani religious authorities at the podiums of a Sunni congregational mosque on Friday gave those Ibadhis who had previously opposed the practice on the grounds of Omani "tradition" a reason to enter the space, observe the practice, and join the dialogue over Muslim unity that was key to the reforms. Beyond the rapprochement with Sunni Islam, however, the revivalists sought to bridge a generational gap within the Omani diaspora that threatened the longevity of the madhab, which was already obscure even to most Ibadhis in Tanzania. According to sectary general of Oman's Mufti's Office, Sheikh Ahmad Ibn Al-Siyabi,

> The idea of holding a Friday prayer in Zanzibar motivated the Ibadhi youth to oppose the sheikhs and elders. I was among the strong supporters of the prayer. When I traveled to Zanzibar, I would give lectures in several of the mosques. I seized the opportunity to persuade them, and to encourage them to perform the Friday prayers. There were heated conversations with the opposition, who argued that the ancestors did not perform [the Friday prayers] in their time, and the rule in Zanzibar was an Omani Arab Islamic [state].
>
> There were many protests. So, I quoted the Qur'an and Sunna to them, and [gave examples of] the precedent of the pious ancestors in the performance [of the Friday prayers]. I made clear to them the intellectual arguments that the Friday prayers are among the things that will protect the madhab because there were some youths who had been lured into sectarian destruction.[39]

The prayer movement both destabilized and challenged existing structures of Ibadhi authority based primarily on one's seniority rather than learnedness. Moreover, it reflected larger debates about correct Islamic practice that formed part of the Islamic revival and that migrated with students who traveled to and from Tanzania and the Arabic-speaking countries, such as Saudi Arabia, Sudan, and Egypt. In these major urban centers of Islamic learning and Salafism, the students were in proximity to some of the most famous preachers (Ar., du'āt, sing m. dā'ī, sing. fem. dā'īyya) and mosque lecturers (Ar., khuṭabā') and had the opportunity to participate in public debates about the virtues of different schools of thought. Moreover, they inhabited a pious "sensorium" of new Islamic media, sounds, and conservative dress that heightened their sense of piety and primed them to protest the low quality of religious and secular education in their home countries and the moral corruption and/or lack of representation of Muslims in government.[40] Siyabi comments on the talismanic quality of prayer, something that is well documented in studies on Sufism but that is rarely discussed in the case of minority Muslim politics. When the question is raised, say in the case of Muslim minorities in Europe, prayer as protection is usually seen as antiassimilationist rather than as a means of downplaying the sectarian identity of an individual or group, or as an attempt to assimilate into the Sunni Muslim mainstream. For the Omani diaspora in Tanzania, mimicking the prayer practices of other Muslims was not only critical to narrowing the distance between the madhabs but was also essential for the transformation and expansion of Ibadhi space across the country.

Mainstream Shi'a were less likely to attend congregational prayers owing to the frequent absence of a Shi'a imam who is both a political and spiritual leader. In Ibadhi-dominated territories, a similar opinion prevailed. At various periods in Omani history when there was a power vacuum in Nizwa, the historic seat of the imamate, the local community would refrain from prayer. Valerie Hoffman explains that the prayers could "be done only in the traditional capital cities like Nizwa in the presence of a just imam."[41] In the diaspora, Omani clans such as the Kharusi of Zanzibar remained staunchly supportive of the imam and ambivalent about the leadership of the sultans at Muscat and Zanzibar. A widespread belief circulated within the Swahili-speaking Ibadhi community in sultanate-era Zanzibar that in the absence of a just imam (Sw., *imamu mwadilifu*) and leader of the Islamic polity, the performance of the Friday prayers was impermissible. This belief held sway in Zanzibar and Ibadhi circles on the mainland until at least the 1980s, when the mufti's delegation from Oman began to tour the region promoting the practice of Friday prayers as necessary for the revival and survival of the Ibadhi madhab on Zanzibar. This set the example for the community elsewhere in the country.

Historically Ibadhis did not perform the Friday prayer owing to a belief that because the island's rulers were sultans and not elected imams, it was impermissible to congregate in prayer. The stance of Ibadhis particularly in Zanzibar, who refused to recognize the sultans as legitimate religious authorities, reflected a deep-rooted allegiance to the Ibadhi imam in Nizwa and historical ties with Omani families such as the Kharusi clan. Through this historical context, we see the complexity of religious authority and political leadership within the Ibadhi community, and the ongoing negotiation of practices and beliefs in the face of changing social and political circumstances.

Moreover, factions within the Omani-Ibadhi diaspora in Zanzibar, especially, the resistance to congregational prayers is what had long distinguished them from other Muslims and ethnic groups in the highly cosmopolitan and religiously plural coastal context of Zanzibar. The Ibadhi practice of abstaining from performing the Friday prayer historically served as a key distinguishing factor in Sunni and Ibadhi practice in Tanzania. According to Hoffman: "Traditionally Ibadi scholars were divided over the permissibility of performing the Friday congregational noon prayer under the reign of any but a just imam, but it is now normative for all Muslim townsmen to attend."[42] The Friday prayers were historically incumbent on all adult males who had reached the age of puberty, unless they were sick or traveling. Additionally, scholar of Islamic law Marion Katz remarks: "Women, slaves, villages, and nomads are all regarded in Islamic law as responsible religious actors, but all of them are [at least according to some schools] permanently exempted from Friday prayers."[43] For Shafi'is, the Friday prayer could only be held in settlements "whose populations afforded a quorum of at least forty resident male worshipers, without which the prayer was invalid."[44] The practice requires the presence of an imam who stands in front of the rows of congregants, "synchronizes the prayer," and guides the recitation of the Qur'an. The imam plays a fundamental mediatory and sacramental role in the weekly communal ritual.[45]

The Ibadhi practice of abstaining from Friday prayers was a defining feature of the Omani diaspora's identity which the older generation was desperate to preserve. This practice and the new Ibadhi spaces it created led to contestations within the diaspora as they demanded a rethinking of the meaning of righteous behavior among Ibadhis in Tanzania.[46] As historian Linda Gale

Jones notes, the Friday *khutba* and communal prayers have been critical in bridging the generational gap between seasoned religious authorities and youth in local and global protest movements and calls for religious reform.[47] During the so-called Arab Spring, for example, communal space of the mosque and the premodern practice of the sermon gave moral weight to protest and the struggle against injustice in a way that mass "modern media and social networks," as effective as they are in sustaining and spreading awareness about the movement, could not do.[48]

The congregational prayer also offered Ibadhi Muslims a space in which to identify each other, reaffirm their commitment to the religion of their ancestors and to reimagine the meaning of madhab in the present. Maher explained: "So it started with prayer then [through it] we began to inform the community [about Ibadhism] and people began to recognize each other."[49] As the movement gained momentum, space in Stone Town became an issue and the Ibadhi leadership gathered to discuss how to modify existing mosques to accommodate the influx of worshippers. He continued,

> Those restorations happened because the number of people grew. The number of people praying filled [the mosque]. That was the reason for the additions. And, when we wanted to pray on Friday we sat in a meeting, which mosque do we want [to pray in]? Should we add [a section] to the Binti Juma Mosque, or that of Shangani which has more room in the front [for expansion]? On one [of the mosques], the back wall had to be demolished because it was not permissible to take down the front. We looked and we found that if we were to add a section in front and above, it would create a lot of [extra] space.[50]

Maher alludes to the politics and trials that residents of Stone Town face in their attempts to build, expand, and improve historic buildings such as Ibadhi mosques, many of which were built at the height of sultanate rule on the islands in the mid- to late 1880s.

Several studies in Islamic art, architecture, and ritual practice have sought to destabilize normative understandings of what constitutes Muslim space.[51] Historian Barbara Metcalf poses and responds to this question with the suggestion that we ought to reimagine Muslim space as more than just the visual markers of mosque domes, arabesque designs, and minarets, some of which are emblematic of Middle Eastern architectural traditions. Instead, we should turn our attention toward the sacred words, typically in Arabic, that make a space Islamic. Unlike mosque architecture, which looks dramatically different in style and material from Mali to Iran to Zanzibar, congregants of the space in all these places share a vocabulary of Islam drawn from the Qur'an, the Hadith, popular supplications, and the practice of everyday life in admonitions such as *Bismillah* (in the name of God) or *InshaAllah* (God willing). These sacred words also adorn the interior and exterior of mosques and other Islamic spaces, globally, and punctuate ritual practices like the five daily prayers and the Friday sermon. Drawing on the work of Clifford Geertz, Metcalf reflected: "And beyond the words, one encounters shared practice. The linkage between sacred word and practice is clear."[52] Sacred words in Arabic and ritual practice are often the ways in which non-Muslims identify Muslims and the ways in which Muslims identify differences among themselves—however big or small. In the case of the Omani-Ibadhi diaspora in Tanzania, the introduction of the Friday prayers and the attendance of adult men at the weekly sermon not only ignited a sense of group feeling with a broader Muslim community but also led to the reorganization, creation, and spread of Ibadhi space across the country. It announced the presence of Istiqaama in local communities as founding ceremonies of new mosques or the restoration of old ones usually entailed the visit of delegations from Oman, the naming of mosques after prominent living and historic Ibadhi scholars, and the labeling of the mosques as belonging to Istiqaama. The mosque came to serve as a way of marking diaspora identity as Ibadhi while also signaling the minority group belonging in the broader ummah.

## Religious Education in a State of Revolution

Among the effects of the Zanzibar Revolution was the tightening of government control over associational life on the islands and ethnic and religious-based organizations. This was in part due to the fear that unmonitored religious, social, and political activities could foster disunity among the islands' residents and solicit help from foreign governments and organizations to overthrow the revolutionary government. For many people from the Zanzibar archipelago, the revolution is not only a marker of time but is an ongoing event and state of being. It is a recurring theme inscribed on the slogan of the undefeated party of the revolution and reenacted through red fireworks reminiscent of spilled blood and celebratory gunfire every January 12 and in the layers of faded and new party campaign posters and green-and-yellow flags on city walls and government office buildings. When we spoke on the baraza outside his home one evening in Ziwani, Pemba, Mzee Bakari, an elderly representative of Istiqaama, explained that the constant awareness and fear of revolution among island residents is a deterrent of religious fanaticism and intra-Muslim conflict. "In this country we have a revolution (Sw., *tunayo mapinduzi*), it is not permitted to organize anything, they have made it militant (*walifanya ni militant*). You understand? So, everyone is careful of that. They *only* teach . . . without entering political language that labels Ibadhis as this, and the Ansar Sunna as that. So now, we do not fight (*hatugombani*) we go together to the funerals, to the weddings not to . . . they have their beliefs, and we have ours."[53]

The Zanzibar government's constant invocation of the revolution, whether through symbolism or militarization, is an effective and at times brutal means of social control. Mzee Bakari distinguishes "teaching" about religion and religious identity as a benign act that contrasts with the more divisive practice of "labeling," whereby group identities reflect attitudes toward outsiders. Such attitudes might map onto politicized traits often used by insiders and outsiders to characterize modern Islamic movements as "tolerant," "moderate," "extremist," or "fanatical." He describes the situation in Zanzibar as one of self-censorship, where every group knows the power of language to foment division and justify violence, especially when deployed to politicize religious, racial, and class identities. In a state of revolution where language can be a dangerous signifier of identity, Mzee Bakari suggests that public religious ceremonies such as weddings and funerals were a way of maintaining Ibadhi religious distinctiveness while also practicing hospitality toward non-Ibadhi neighbors.

## The Istiqaama Muslim Community of Tanzania

The constitution of the Istiqaama Muslim Community of Tanzania states that a "member of the Association shall be any Moslem who belongs to the Ibadhi sect."[54] Members attend Friday prayers at Ibadhi mosques and group meetings and activities organized by Istiqaama. They must not affiliate with "opposing organizations" but should engage in da'wa with the aim of unifying "all the Moslems of the Ibadhi sect in the Republic, both mainland and the Isles."[55] As a group, their mission is "promoting understanding and cooperation between Moslems of the Ibadhi sect and all other sects of Islam, and to endeavor to find ways of resolving differences that exist between them in theory and in practice."[56] The main vehicles for carrying out this mission are the various schools and institutes for Islamic and Arabic studies under the purview of Istiqaama, some of which offer vocational training and advanced studies "with religious and environmental perspectives among others."[57] They also provide social services, assisting in disaster relief (e.g., fire and floods) and the care of orphaned children.

The organization is bureaucratic, with its international headquarters and leadership based in Oman and branches in East Africa, each of which adopts similar leadership and hierarchies, including a president or chairperson, vice president, secretary, treasurer, etc. However, there was no corporate office for Istiqaama in Muscat at the time of my research and, unlike in Tanzania—where Istiqaama buildings often bear the community's name—the group's presence in Oman seemed to be much more understated. The relative invisibility of the organization relates to the role of religion in public life and the government's policies regarding religious pluralism and tolerance, which strictly regulate the activities of religious organizations. The pervasive discourse on religious tolerance generated by the state differs from that of other Muslim majority countries in that it depends largely on the underlying perception that Ibadhism, the religious heritage of Oman, is an inherently moderate and tolerant expression of Islam.

According to its constitution, Istiqaama derives its funds from tithes (*zakāt*) and voluntary charitable donations (*ṣadaqa*). The association's governing committee sets the amount of membership dues. They may also receive funds from other associational groups and Islamic organizations and any "lawful economic activities"[58] conducted by members of the community to raise funds for its various projects. On both the mainland and Zanzibar, my Ibadhi interlocutors responded with only vague answers to questions about sources of funding and the shilling or dollar amounts donated for their various community initiatives and building projects. I learned that the various branches of Istiqaama across the country provide the government with year-end reports of donations received and funds spent and that they are subject to auditing by the state, though none of these records is publicly available. In other instances, I heard that they did not want to share information about funding for major projects such as multimillion-shilling mosque building projects because they were afraid the government would tax them heavily. As a result, only a qualitative assessment of Istiqaama's sources of funding, costs, and investments was possible.

According to Ayman, the bulk of donations received by the organization come from wealthy actors (Sw., *watu wazito*) in Tanzania and Oman. He explained that there are at least three meetings per year. Two meetings occur after the big and little Eid holidays and the third is an official (Sw., *rasmi*) meeting where the Istiqaama leadership gives a report on the work of the society and people make donations. Ayman explained,

> Some people [come to] give their thoughts and others give complaints. At those meetings it is just regular people [not the wealthy] who contribute what they can, or they offer to volunteer. They are not people who take initiative themselves; [rather] they wait for the jumuiya to help them. These are the challenges [we face], these are not people of initiative, [meaning] the members of the jumuiya carry the burden, we spoon-feed everything; this type of assistance is a problem for us.... The jumuiya performs extra work for the sake of serving people. They know what exactly is there for them. However, little by little people are changing.[59]

The periodic open meetings held by Istiqaama are an opportunity for people in the community to raise questions or complaints about the operations of the organization or ask for assistance in personal matters. Yet Ayman's concerns about the dependency of those seeking aid suggests that the organization aspires to create institutions that will not only cater to the immediate needs of those who participate in them but will also empower them to eventually support themselves. At first blush, Ayman's complaints sound very similar to neoliberal logics that view poverty as an impediment to development and that require an ethics of self-help to overcome it. While such logics certainly do inform many of Istiqaama's works in Tanzania, such as the for-profit health care centers they have opened to generate revenue for other projects, socioeconomic development is not the only, or even the primary, focus of their outreach.

Anthropologist of religion Amirah Mittermaier shows how this religiously oriented view of giving serves as a critique of conventional understandings of charity: "Rather, it is dutiful and directed at God. Placing God in the foreground, and the suffering Other in the background, disrupts both the liberal conceit of compassion *and* the neoliberal imperative of self-help."[60] Islamic communities, like Istiqaama, often conflate good works or "charity" with daʿwa and Islamic ethics in which charitable giving brings one closer to God and prepares the givers for the afterlife. The leaders of Istiqaama hope that by providing various kinds of aid and making space for prayer and discussions, they will create moral subjects who will become not just professionals or entrepreneurs but also members in a righteous society.

As is the case with most other NGOs and FBOs in Tanzania, Istiqaama is run by elites and was created to primarily serve the interests of the Omani-Ibadhi diaspora, which tends to be concentrated in major urban centers where the branches are located, though many members trace their roots to rural farms and towns. Legal Studies scholar Issa Shivji has observed that while NGOs do exhibit concern for improving the conditions of "working people" or nonelites in Tanzania, most were not designed to include the masses in their memberships or organizational decision-making, even though they may, as in the case of Istiqaama, host *barazas* or meetings where the grievances or requests of nonmembers may be voiced. The relationship remains one of "benefactors and beneficiaries"[61] rather than a radical collaboration between a relatively well-funded transnational charitable organization with a distinctive religious and ethnic identity and the non-Arab majority that it serves. Membership in Istiqaama, like NGOs, is limited to a minority of people, and this creates a problem of transparency and accountability beyond the exclusive community[62] that is constructed from Omani-Ibadhi ideas of diaspora, kinship, and ancestry and is beholden to international donors who identify largely, though not exclusively, with the same community.

Just as framing Istiqaama's giving practices in the language of charity makes the organization more readable to non-Muslim authorities and international collaborators so does the language of "volunteerism," (Sw., *kujitolea*) which members in Oman and Tanzania use to describe their work. By calling themselves volunteers, they simultaneously distance themselves from association with sectarian or political interests while also framing their work as altruistic and meant to serve both humanity and the ummah.[63] Historian Felicitas Becker notes that Muslim organizations often face more difficulties in striking collaborations with Western donors in Tanzania "whose conceptions of civil society and volunteering do not accurately reflect the institutional practices of Muslims."[64] Moreover, Becker explains, Muslim organizations in Tanzania often prefer to work independently from the government, which they mistrust[65] for reasons stemming from the marginalization of coastal Muslim communities under European colonial rule and the persistence of state Islamophobia during the socialist era and following the Zanzibar Revolution. Even in Zanzibar, where the islands' government has a Muslim majority, Islamophobic rhetoric tends to amplify around election periods, when the ruling party invokes the threat of international terrorism as a scare tactic. Opposition candidates who may seem to have a large following within the Arab diaspora or who may advocate for loosening restrictions on land acquisition and business permits for investors from the Gulf are often presented as supporting neo-Arab colonialism in Tanzania. While Muslim organizations like

Istiqaama that are financially independent from the government are in danger of being accused of such designs, they may also be viewed as more legitimate *religiously* as they do not serve as puppets to the regime.⁶⁶

Indeed, there is a general sense that Islamic morality was corrupted, and learning lost in Tanzania, generally, and Zanzibar, in particular, following independence with the revolution and the rise of a socialist regime that sought to minimize and control the impact of religion in public life. That this project of social control was successful is evident in the absence of extensive archival information about Islam and Muslim organizations in state institutions or newspapers in the 1960s and 1970s. In a rhetorical turn, Istiqaama members often associate this decline in religious scholarship and institutions with state xenophobia toward Arabs and Islamophobia, which they argue deprived the country of righteous leadership and moderate expressions of Islam, like Ibadhism.

## Istiqaama and State Islamic Authorities in Tanzania

Despite the appearance of unity in Istiqaama projects, notable divisions within the organization and between its branches occurred over time. For example, while it began as one organization based in Dar es Salaam and registered under BAKWATA, the Zanzibar leadership of Istiqaama eventually decided to register independently with the Grand Mufti's Office (GMO) or in Swahili, Ofisi ya Mufti Mkuu wa Zanzibar, which has branches on both Unguja and Pemba islands. The GMO is a government department established in 2001, with its budget controlled by the state. The divisions within Istiqaama are a touchy subject. In Pemba, Mzee Bakari explained to me that in the past an argument over leadership had occurred between the big men of Istiqaama and the community became divided because of human selfishness. Therefore, each group developed its own mission statement, but relations remained amicable. He continued, "There is no hate, we work together as one people (*watu moja*)."⁶⁷ The objective of all Istiqaamas is to serve society through ground-up organizing centered on distribution and missionizing. "They are for society ... here in Pemba you know there is a lot of poverty from a long time ago, people don't have money for the food that is available, there is no money. It overwhelmed me. So, Istiqaama does not have money [of their own] but they ask for funding. They brought food, rice, clothes, and whatnot, you see. They go to Chake Chake [first], not here, and they take food to Zanzibar... to help. Then if they have books like Qur'ans, they bring and distribute them in all the mosques."[68]

Mzee Bakari explained that most of the aide comes from local and international religious institutions and individuals, but occasionally they receive funding from the government in Zanzibar. He claimed that direct funding from foreign governments occurs by way of the Zanzibar government, which suggests that much of the funds and materials donated from the Gulf come through informal networks, for example as cash donations from family members or visitors from Oman.

The distribution of copies of the Qur'an alongside nonperishable food and clothes is an indication of how Istiqaama's giving practices connect to a larger religious mission to spread awareness about Islam. The symbolism of offering copies of the Qur'an along with base-level nutrition suggests a clear statement about a perceived necessity for both material and spiritual nourishment among the beneficiaries of this aid. There is little publicly accessible information about the number and sources of donations the headquarters of Istiqaama receives in Oman and how much goes toward projects in the country or abroad in countries of influence, like Tanzania. However, the projects range from establishing regular programmatic schools (*madāris nidhāmiyya*); building schools for Islamic and Arabic education; digging wells; establishing public libraries, computer labs, sewing centers, and large and small mosques; buying land to generate income for local branches of Istiqaama; and purchasing four-wheel drive vehicles "in order to carry out da'wa in remote areas."[69] The da'wa vehicles are an indication of Istiqaama's self-identification as a harbinger of righteous reform to communities both near and far and of the intimate connection between charitable giving and bringing oneself and others closer to God.

African students who study Islam and Arabic (among other subjects) in Istiqaama madrasas and schools can receive scholarships to study abroad in Oman at the College of Sharia Sciences in Muscat. There they deepen their intellectual and personal engagement with the faith, become part of an international network of Ibadhi-oriented religious youth, and are prepped to serve as teachers of Arabic and religion on graduation. Since the founding of Istiqaama in the 1990s, many of the youth from Tanzania who studied abroad in Oman have returned to their home countries to become du'āt and serve as teachers, imams, administrators, and leaders for Istiqaama in their communities. In the language of Sayyid Qutb, this vanguard are the ideal figures to spread Istiqaama's vision of righteousness.

## State Authorities and Muslim Associational Life in Tanzania

The socialist dream of Ujamaa in Tanzania required the nationalization of the means of production across the country, a move that proved disastrous for the Indian business community and Arab landowning elites on the mainland, especially in Zanzibar.[70] Moreover, the Christian-dominated Tanganyika African National Union (TANU) leadership reneged on their promises to address colonial-era inequities in Muslim and Christian access to education. TANU added salt to this wound by banning the country's first major pan-Islamic, East African Muslim Welfare Society (EAMWS), established by the global Ismaili Muslim leader, the Aga Khan, in 1945.[71] In place of the EAMWS, in 1968 the TANU government founded the state-sponsored Baraza Kuu la Waisilamu of Tanzania (BAKWATA) or, the National Muslim Council of Tanzania.[72]

BAKWATA and its counterpart on the islands, the Grand Mufti's Office in Zanzibar, serve as the premier Muslim religious authorities in Tanzania. All religious organizations in Tanzania, including Istiqaama, must receive approval from BAKWATA to operate, but the state institution does not typically provide financial support to its affiliated private religious organizations, and it is widely perceived as representing the interests of the country's majority Sunni Muslim population. In the eyes of Ayman, this lack of support has led some private organizations, like Istiqaama, to rely on their own resources for development and maintenance. "Now we drive ourselves forward. This means that if you think of doing something, you get it done. For example, when you see our mosques here, do not think that we depended on BAKWATA... they did not contribute a single shilling. They failed to contribute to the development of the decrepit mosques until they began to crumble, [even then] they did not contribute."[73] This self-reliance demonstrates a sense of agency and determination within the community to drive themselves forward, even in the face of limited support from state-sponsored institutions. This dynamic reflects a broader trend of grassroots initiatives and self-sufficiency within religious communities in Tanzania.

When Ibadhis in rural areas need assistance for the maintenance of the mosque or religious programming, they send a delegation to the larger mosque communities in Mwanza, Shinyanga, and Meatu to request assistance. According to Mzee Bakari, many who contribute to the mosques are Ibadhis and members of Istiqaama. Were they to approach BAKWATA for help, say in hiring a Qur'an teacher, they would have to follow government guidelines for the religious curriculum and accept whoever the organization assigns to teach at the mosque. Going through Istiqaama, on the other hand, is preferable because while they must report their activities to the government, they also have a degree of autonomy in the training and selection of the teachers for Ibadhi mosques and schools around the country.[74]

In Tanzania, the state does not exercise the same degree of control over religious organizations as it does in Oman, in large part because groups like Istiqaama are financially independent of the state and the government has limited resources to standardize and monitor the production and dissemination of religious knowledge across the country. Still, Muslim groups frequently voice concerns about what they perceive as the disproportionate amount of government surveillance at mosques, schools, and charities bearing an Islamic identification. On Zanzibar, the main Muslim authority with which all organizations must register is the GMO. On the mainland, "The two most important Muslim apex bodies are the National Muslim Council of Tanzania (established in 1968), known as BAKWATA, and the Supreme Council of Islamic Organizations and Institutions in Tanzania (established in 1992), known as Baraza Kuu."[75] The GMO and BAKWATA are "umbrella bodies" for Islamic institutions on the islands and mainland and the latter runs a number of educational, healthcare, and entrepreneurship programs throughout the country while also writing and recommending "policy priorities and guidelines to the *ulama*."[76] It is exceedingly difficult for Muslim groups to operate independently of the two government religious authorities.[77]

The head office of BAKWATA is in the Kinondoni district of Dar es Salaam, and other main branches exist in the nation's administrative capital in central Tanzania, Dodoma. BAKWATA has about twenty-four of its own schools and supervises hundreds of mosques across the nation, all considered Sunni institutions and all run through a complex hierarchy of district and regional sheikhs appointed by BAKWATA in cooperation with the local communities. According to a senior official at BAKWATA, Yasser, religious organizations in Tanzania must receive the endorsement of his office before they can register with the government, and the office bases its endorsement on approval of the contents of each group's constitution. "The only thing we manage now is whether they go against the principles stated in their constitution. When a religious organization wants to register with the government, they must first present their constitution to BAKWATA. We read [the constitution] carefully, and if it is OK, we sign and endorse it."[78]

On presenting their group constitution and receiving the council's endorsement, religious organizations like Istiqaama are then eligible to register under the Tanzanian government's Societies Act, originally established under the British colonial regime in 1954 through the Ministry of Home Affairs and still in use today.[79] According to the act "a 'society' includes any club, company, partnership or association of ten or more persons whatever its nature or object," with several exemptions, including political parties and sports associations. (See points g–h of chap. 337.2.) Once officially recognized by the state, the society or organization in question must proceed to register its trustees under the Trusteeship Act, governed by the Registration Insolvency and Trusteeship Act (RITA).[80] The registering of trustees, Yasser from BAKWATA explained, "makes clear who is responsible for the governance of the organization and who owns it. The minimum time to complete the registration process is one year."[81] Istiqaama registered as an organization under the Societies Act in 1995.

The Societies Act suggests that there is strict government oversight in the activities of all religious NGOs on the mainland. In theory, the president of Tanzania can declare an organization unlawful in the "public interest," just as the registrar can cancel a group's registration should they prove to have any external political affiliation or demonstrate "any purpose prejudicial or incompatible with the maintenance of peace, order and good government."[82] Under the act, the government can also perform an audit of any organization at any time (sect. 22) and has the power to "enter and search meeting places or business places" (sect. 31) and make arrests according to its own discretion (sect. 32). The Tanzanian government does occasionally demonstrate its power of search and seizure, entering Muslim communities and spaces of worship to assess the content of public lectures and, in more extreme cases, arrest Muslim religious leaders perceived to have ties to foreign terror networks and fundamentalist groups. Popular Islamic newspapers such as the weekly *An-Nuur* routinely condemn the government's indiscriminate arrest of both ordinary citizens and high-profile preachers without due process and call for the institutionalization of special courts on the mainland that could protect the interests of Tanzanian Muslims.[83]

Additionally, many Tanzanians feel as though the government officials representing Muslim interests on the mainland (BAKWATA) and the islands (the GMO) function primarily as handmaidens to the state and do not adequately represent their aggrieved Muslim constituency. For this and other reasons, nonstate actors such as Istiqaama are becoming increasingly more attractive sources of education and social services because they are economically independent of the state, though they may be subject to annual audits and government surveillance (see chap. 6).

Anas, a representative of the GMO in his late thirties whom I met at its main branch in Chake Chake, Pemba provided some historical context. He stated that before the office of the mufti, all the roles were the work of the office of the chief kadhi or judge. Anas is originally from the Mkoani district of southern Pemba, and after completing his primary and secondary education in government schools, he began an independent search for religious knowledge (Sw., *taaluma*), attending the study groups offered by various sheikhs on the island. He later went to Dar es Salaam and had the opportunity to travel to the region of Hadramaut in Yemen for his higher education. There, Anas enrolled first at Ribat University in Tarim city for one year before entering a program in Islamic and Arabic Studies at Al-Ahqaff University. He traveled to Yemen independently and paid for his own studies, emphasizing that "the government did not pay even a shilling for me."[84] He explained that this was before the war in Yemen, which has since ravaged the entire country and left tens of thousands dead (2014–present), displaced, or at risk of hunger. Hadramaut was then very safe and the only conflict that emerged was a result of "tribal politics," which rarely erupted into anything of great concern.

When Anas returned to Zanzibar, he served as a teacher in a primary school on Unguja island before accepting a position in 2010 in the Office of Islamic Research at the mufti's office. He explained that he assisted in issuing fatwas and used comparative fiqh, drawing on legal methods and interpretations from the different Sunni and Ibadhi madhāhib represented in Zanzibar. When a person approaches the mufti's office for an opinion on a given issue, he explained, they assess whether the person has the learning to receive different interpretations and then they provide fewer or many explanations according to their ability. While most employees of the GMO, including Anas, identify as Shafiʿi Sunni, Anas insisted that "the mufti's office is for all Muslims that are in Zanzibar. There are Ibadhis, there are Sunnis, there are Shiʿa, and others whatever they may be."[85] He continued, "They come to the office for everything that pertains to the office of the mufti. If you go to the mufti's office, he does not choose between the Ibadhis and the Sunnis or the Ansari Sunna or anyone else."[86]

Like BAKWATA, the GMO in Zanzibar oversees all registered Islamic organizations in the archipelago. According to Anas, his office can call out any Muslim individual or organization on matters pertaining to Islamic law. However, the mufti or his representatives are frequently guests or collaborators in the celebrations and charity events hosted by the various Muslim groups on the islands. The support Muslim organizations like Istiqaama receive from the GMO is largely symbolic and does not provide funds for building private mosques and Islamic schools. However, Islamic groups must apply for and receive permission from the mufti to carry out such building projects. According to Anas, Istiqaama and other Islamic organizations in Pemba typically host an annual public prayer at a community mosque in Chake Chake to welcome the start of Ramadan. They also use this time to discuss their work and plans and suggest collaborations with the GMO.

## Conclusion

While Al-Khalili is frequently credited with founding the International Istiqaama Charitable Society based in Muscat, the majority of the organization's branches are in Tanzania, where they play an important role in shaping Ibadhi and Islamic identity across the country through the many schools, mosques, radio stations, and charities under Istiqaama's leadership. These branches are successful because they depend on long-established Omani-Ibadhi kinship networks that occur throughout the country and strong family ties to Oman, which enable the informal transfer of funds and resources, such as textbooks, dates, clothing, and religious knowledge between the two countries. Istiqaama presents itself as an apolitical and nondiscriminatory organization guided by Ibadhi principles of tolerance and moderation in religious affairs. It demonstrates inclusivity by welcoming male and female Ibadhis and non-Ibadhis into its mosques and schools, though the organization's leadership is male and of Omani ancestry. This suggests that though there is a push to bring Ibadhi Islam closer to more popular Islamic practices and communities in Tanzania, the Istiqaama community also clearly demarcates insiders and outsiders through its exclusivist membership policy.

Moreover, because of the organization's deference to the religious authority of Oman, and as will be shown in the next chapter, Islamic learning in Istiqaama schools is heavily imbued with Omani cultural practices, as seen in the content of school textbooks, the dress of many of the students and teachers at the schools, and the popularity of scholarship programs that allow graduating students from the Istiqaama Institute in Zanzibar to pursue advanced training in Islamic law and Arabic in Muscat. These opportunities for study abroad enable students to expand their social networks and deepen their faith while also creating an educational pipeline that enables graduates of religious colleges in Oman to return to teach religion and Arabic at Istiqaama schools in Tanzania.

## Notes

1. Fatima bint Muhammad (d. 632) was the daughter of the Prophet Muhammad who married his cousin 'Ali bin Abi Talibin. The twelve imams revered by most of the world's Shi'a population are descendants of Fatima and 'Ali and thus members of the "House of the Prophet" (Ahl al-Bayt).
2. Maher (representative of Jabir bin Zayd Mosque), interview with author, Kitumbini, Dar es Salaam, May 15, 2019.
3. Ibid.
4. In the English translation of Al-Riyami's book, he dedicates pages 388–395 to the mufti's biography. See Nasser Abdulla Al Riyami, *Zanzibar. Personalities & Events (1828–1972)* (Muscat, Oman: Beirut Bookshop, 2012).
5. Ibid.
6. Mona Atia, *Building a House in Heaven: Pious Neoliberalism and Islamic Charity in Egypt* (Minneapolis: University of Minnesota Press, 2013), xviii.
7. Ibid.
8. Ibid., xix.
9. Al Riyami, "Personalities," 388–90.
10. Ibid., 390–91.
11. Ibid., 392.
12. Ibid., 393. This number varies from hundreds to tens of thousands, depending on who is narrating the events of the revolution.
13. Ibid., 394–95.
14. Benedict Andersen, *Imagined Communities: Reflections on the Origin and Spread of Nationalism* (London: Verso, 1983).
15. Marc Valeri, "Ibadism and Omani Nation-Building Since 1970," in *On Ibadism*, eds. Abdulrahman al Salimi and Heinz Gaube, Studies on Ibadism and Oman (Hildesheim, Zurich, New York: S, 2014), 166.
16. Ibid., 167.
17. Dale Eickelman, "The Modern Face of Ibadism in Oman," in *Studies on Ibadism in Oman*, ed. Angeliki Ziaka (Hildesheim, Zurich, New York: Georg Olms, 2014), 154–55.
18. Ibid., 153–54.
19. *Oman 2016 International Religious Freedom Report*, 2.
20. Ibid.

21. "Organization Chart" (Ministry of Endowment and Religious Affairs, Sultanate of Oman), accessed March 16, 2017, www.MERA.om/MERA/organization-chart/.

22. According to the *Oman 2016 International Religious Freedom Report*: "The law states the government must approve construction and/or leasing of buildings by religious groups. In addition, mosques must be built at least one kilometer (0.6 miles) apart from each other" (3).

23. Ibid.

24. Drawn from notes recorded in a conversation with a longtime American resident of the Gulf and active participant in interfaith initiatives between Muslims and Christians in Oman (December 2016).

25. MERA and the mufti's office are patrons of Islamic and Ibadhi studies and produce several publications on these topics, many of which can be found in Istiqaama libraries across Tanzania. One notable publication of MERA's is the multilingual and "quarterly Islamic intellectual magazine" called *Tafahum* (previously Tasāmuh). Contributors come from all over the world, and their work focuses on, among other issues, "Strengthening an Islam that is based on understanding, [and the] right to difference and diversity of views." As an international scholarly publication committed to the elaboration of the ideals of pluralism and religious accommodation in Islamic thought, *Tafahum* gives scientific weight to the project of Muslim unity and interfaith cooperation. Moreover, the journal carries with it a reformist mission aimed at reinstating intellectual rigor in Islamic thought and practice and making Islamic ideals compatible with the exigencies of the modern world. Characteristic of other calls for reform in Islamic thought, this process involves an intensive "weeding-out" process that identifies areas of degeneration or neglect within the tradition and calls for a revival or reinterpretation of texts and practices in such a way that will serve to substantiate the national vision of Islamic unity. The underlying paradox of reformist discourses that aim to create a uniform narrative of religious tolerance is that they sometimes require, at least initially, a high degree of intolerance of differences of opinion to achieve such harmony.

26. Valeri, "Ibadism and Omani Nation-Building," 167.

27. Ayman, interview with author, February 24, 2016.

28. Émile Durkheim (1858–1917) and Karen E. Fields (translator), *The Elementary Forms of Religious Life* (New York: Free, 1995).

29. Sh. Khalfan Tiwani, *Qamusi-Ssalaa*, first edition (N/A: Publication rights are reserved for the author., 2008), 82–91.

30. Luna Dolezal, "Shame, Vulnerability and Belonging: Reconsidering Sartre's Account of Shame," *Human Studies* 40, no. 3 (2017): 421. See also J. P. Sartre and H. E. Barnes (trans.), *Being and Nothingness: An Essay on Phenomenological Ontology* (London: Routledge, 2003).

31. Dolezal, "Shame," 422.

32. Ibid., 421.

33. Roxanne L. Euben and Muhammad Qasim Zaman, "Sayyid Qutb 1906–1966," in *Princeton Readings in Islamist Thought: Texts and Contexts from al-Banna to Bin Laden* (Princeton and Oxford: Princeton University Press, 2009), 129.

34. Ibid., 139.

35. W. E. B. DuBois, *The Souls of Black Folk* (New York: Vintage, 1990).

36. Kimberlé Crenshaw, "Mapping the Margins: Intersectionality, Identity Politics, and Violence against Women of Color," *Stanford Law Review* 43, no. 6 (1991): 1241–99.

37. MERA.

38. Sayfī, Muḥammad ibn 'Abdullah ibn Sa'īd ibn Nāṣṣor al-. *Al-Namīr, Hikāyāt Wa Riwāyāt: Al-Ibāḍiyya Fī Zinjibār Wa Mā Jāwarahā Min Duwal Sharq Ifrīqiyyā* (Nizwa: Al-Ghantaq) 2013, 357. v. 6:357.

39. Quoted in Muhammad bin 'Abd allah bin Sa'īd al-Sayfī, *Al-Ibāḍiyya Fī Zinjibār Wa Mā Jāwarhā Min Duwwal Sharq Ifrīqiyya*, first, vol. 6 (Mascat, Oman: unknown, 2013), 356.

40. Charles Hirschkind, *The Ethical Soundscape: Cassette Sermons and Islamic Counterpublics* (New York: Columbia University Press, 2006).

41. Hoffman, *Oman*, 175.

42. Ibid., 176.

43. Marion Holmes Katz, *Prayer in Islamic Thought and Practice* (Cambridge and New York: Cambridge University Press, 2013), 131.

44. Ibid.

45. Ibid., 139.

46. Anthropologist Patrick Desplat has observed how sites such as shrines and mosques have always been the objects of contestation throughout Islamic history, but these arguments often have less to do with the nature of the space itself than with the practices that define them (See: Patrick A. Desplat. *Prayer in the City: The Making of Muslim Sacred Places and Urban Life*, edited by Patrick A. Desplat, and Dorothea E. Schulz, (Bielefield: transcript, 2012), 11). For related work see Jonathan Berkey, "Tradition, Innovation, and the Social Construction of Knowledge in the Medieval Islamic Near East," *Past and Present*, no. 146 (1995): 38–65; Felicitas Becker, "Islamic Reform and Historical Change in the Care of the Dead: Conflicts over Funerary Practice among Tanzanian Muslims," *Africa: Journal of the International African Institute* 79, no. 3 (2009): 416–34.

47. As Jones points out, the mosque sermon has been a popular topic of anthropologists interested in how this premodern practice "foments normative or revivalist Islam in contemporary Muslim societies and thus how this institution has been transformed under modernity." Linda Gale Jones, *The Power of Oratory in the Medieval Muslim World* (Cambridge: Cambridge Studies in Islamic Civilization, 2012), 3. See Richard T. Antoun, *Muslim Preachers in the Modern World: A Jordanian*

*Case Study in Comparative Perspective* (Princeton University Press, 2014); Patrick D. Gaffney, *The Prophet's Pulpit: Islamic Preaching in Contemporary Egypt* (Berkeley: University of California Press, 2019).

48. Jones, *The Power of Oratory*, 2.
49. Maher, interview with author, May 15, 2019.
50. Ibid.
51. See especially Barbara Metcalf, *Making Muslim Space in North America and Europe* (Berkeley: University of California Press, 1996); Patrick Desplat and Dorothea Elisabeth Schulz, *Prayer in the City: The Making of Muslim Sacred Places and Urban Life* (Germany: Biefeld University Press, 2012); Michelle Apotsos, *The Masjid in Contemporary Africa* (Cambridge: Cambridge University Press, 2021).
52. Metcalf, *Making Muslim Space*, 5.
53. Mzee Bakari, interview with author, February 2, 2016.
54. "Katiba" (Dar es Salaam: Jumuiya ya Kiislamu ya Istiqaama Tanzania, n.d.), http://istiqaamatz.org/tz/images/documents/katibaenglish.pdf.
55. Ibid.
56. Ibid.
57. Ibid.
58. Ibid., 13.
59. Ayman, interview with author, February 24, 2016.
60. Amira Mittermaier, *Giving to God: Islamic Charity in Revolutionary Times* (Oakland: University of California Press, 2019), 4.
61. Issa Shivji, "Reflections on NGOs in Tanzania: What We Are, What We Are Not, and What We Ought to Be," *Taylor & Francis, Ltd. on Behalf of Oxfam GB* 14, no. 5 (2004): 689.
62. Ibid.
63. Felicitas Becker, "Obscuring and Revealing: Muslim Engagement with Volunteering and the Aid Sector in Tanzania," *African Studies Review* 58, no. 2 (2015): 111–33.
64. Ibid., 111.
65. Ibid.
66. Ibid., 124.
67. Mzee Bakari (Ibadhi elder and Istiqaama representative), interview with author, Ziwani, Pemba, February 2, 2016.
68. Ibid.
69. Istiqaama Arabic Webpage, "Alistiqaama.Org," accessed June 15, 2016, http://alistiqama.org.
70. For more about the effects of nationalization policies on Indian and Arab communities in urban Tanzania between 1958 and 1975, see James R. Brennan, "Blood Enemies: Exploitation and Urban Citizenship in the Nationalist Political Thought of Tanzania, 1958–75," *The Journal of African History* 47, no. 3 (2006): 389–413.

71. Bruce E. Heilman and Paul J. Kaiser, "Religion, Identity and Politics in Tanzania," *Third World Quarterly* 23, no. 4 (2002): 701.
72. Ibid.
73. Ayman, interview with author, February 24, 2016.
74. Mzee Bakari, interview with author, February 2, 2016.
75. Robert Leurs, Peter Tumaini-Mungu, and Abu Mvungi, "Mapping the Development of Faith-Based Organizations in Tanzania," UK Aid (International Development Department, University of Birmingham, January 2011), 31.
76. Ibid.
77. Ibid., 54.
78. Yasser (senior BAKWATA official), interview by author, Kinondoni, Dar es Salaam, June 21, 2017.
79. According to a working paper published by a development branch of the Ministry for Foreign Affairs of Finland (KEPA), the NGO Act of 2002 under the Ministry of Community Development, Gender and Children aimed to streamline the requirements for NGOs by adding the requirement that all NGOs apply for a certificate of compliance from the government. However, this did not change the basic guidelines of the original societies' act through which religious organizations and others register as NGOs in Tanzania. See Evod Mamanda, "NGO Work in Tanzania: Highlights of Relevant Facts, Policies and Laws," KEPA's Working Papers (Helsinki, Finland: Service Center for Development Cooperation (KEPA), 2012), 3, accessed March 15, 2024, https://fingo.fi/wp-content/uploads/2020/10/ngo-work-in-tanzania-2012-update.pdf.
80. Yasser, interview with author, June 21, 2017.
81. Ibid.
82. The United Republic of Tanzania, "The Societies Act 337" (Registration Insolvency and Trusteeship Agency, June 1, 1954), 8.1a, accessed March 28, 2024, http://www.rita.go.tz/eng/laws/History%20Laws/Societies%20Ordinance, 1954%20(cap.%20337).pdf.
83. See for example Mwandishi Wetu (unnamed author), "Tanganyika Si Guantanamo Ya Kutesa Masheikh (Tanzania Is Not a Guantanamo Where Shaykhs Can Be Tortured)," *An-Nuur*, September 11, 2015, headline and 2–3.
84. Anas (the Grand Mufti's Office), interview with author, Chake Chake, Pemba, February 4, 2016.
85. Ibid.
86. Ibid.

# 3

## Ibadhi Schools and Their Transnational Networks

Hidden behind lengthy walls about thirty miles east of Stone Town lies a prestigious, private K–12 institute (ma'had) that specializes in Arabic and Islamic studies. Two large, guarded gates shield the Muslim boarding school students from the hustle generated by passenger buses (*daladalas*), trucks, and tourist vans that travel to and from the town and villages of the island's famously laid-back east coast. A basic sign that reads The Istiqaama Institute of Zanzibar[1] in Swahili and Arabic alerts the visitor of the school's location. The sign is an indication of the bilingualism of the campus and the mixed heritages of many of its students, teachers, and administrators. Students come from all over East Africa, among them are Ibadhi-Omanis whose families are members of local branches of Istiqaama in the region. The recruitment and admissions process at the school is rigorous and includes a written questionnaire that serves as an entrance examination. Only high-scoring students receive acceptance. The ma'had is an example of efforts to revive Islamic and Arabic language education in Zanzibar following extended efforts by the British colonial administration to eliminate Arabic and qur'anic study from the national curriculum and the postcolonial government's seemingly antireligious and anti-Arab policies following the revolution and fall of the sultanate in 1964.

Specifically, this chapter explores the collaborations in education that occur across national borders in Ibadhi education.[2] Specifically it focuses on the importation of religion and Arabic language textbooks from Oman to the Istiqaama schools in Zanzibar. These textbooks, although printed exclusively for Istiqaama by the Ministry of Education in Oman, primarily reflect an Omani nationalist and Gulf-based environment that is unfamiliar to many non-Omani students at the schools. I ask first, how does the Omani nationalist tone of the donated Istiqaama textbook series used in the schools impact the teaching of Arabic language and religion to a primarily non-Arabic speaking student body? Second, how do the predominantly Swahili-speaking Zanzibar students, teachers, and administrators at Istiqaama view the influence of Omani culture and language in their learning materials and school environment?

Given the sometimes distrustful relations between Zanzibar and Oman since the revolution and ongoing public debates about the potential for renewed Arab economic and political influence on the islands, examples of Omani soft power like this are likely to draw attention. However, through my conversations with teachers, an administrator, and former students associated with Istiqaama, I have discovered that the imported textbooks and other educational materials are primarily valued as useful tools for learning Arabic and enhancing students' knowledge of Islam. Furthermore, the work of this chapter builds on previous examinations of transregional circulation of Islamic texts, ideas, and traditions of learning and reform during the era of British colonial rule in the Western Indian Ocean from the late nineteenth century to the first half of the twentieth. These previous studies primarily draw on Sufi texts, Islamic newspapers such as the bilingual (Swahili and Arabic) *al-Islah* (*Reform*) based in Mombasa, and *al-Falaq* (*Dawn*) based in Zanzibar.[3]

Additionally, earlier studies emphasize the importance of portraying an Arabic cultural and religious identity in discussions of reform, an identity that was locally constructed through Swahili discourses of Arab gentility (ustaarabu), gentlemanliness (uungwana), respectability (heshima), and social practices, such as patrilineal descent and marriages between social equals.[4] This chapter expands on these discussions by shifting the focus beyond the colonial period and archival sources and instead examining the context of postcolonial Zanzibar, where being perceived as Arab, particularly Omani, can be socially advantageous but also controversial. I argue that although the learning materials, attire, and academic training at Istiqaama reflect symbols of Omani culture and nationalism, local actors in Zanzibar are eager to assert a unique Swahili Muslim identity.

## Islamic Education in Zanzibar

Schools such as those funded by Istiqaama that maintain ties to the Middle East or the "Arab" regions (Sw. *sehemu za kiArabuni*) appeal to students and parents as they boast newer buildings and facilities, can recruit foreign-trained teachers, maintain low acceptance rates, and benefit from transnational religious and economic networks that enable greater social mobility. Sociologist Simon Turner noted that the liberalization and privatization of schooling in Zanzibar coincided with a global Islamic revival. "Since the 1980s wealthy individuals from the Gulf States have funded mosques, *madrasas* [Islamic schools], health clinics, secondary schools, teachers' training colleges and universities in Zanzibar, and young Zanzibar men have been given scholarships to study in Medina, Khartoum and elsewhere."[5] The rise of private Islamic institutions of education during this period further enabled the dissemination of religious literature in the form of textbooks and pamphlets from abroad in addition to "CDs and DVDs [and now social media] in Arabic, English and Swahili" both in and beyond formal schools' structures.[6] State actors in Zanzibar frequently denounce new religious activists who studied in North Africa and the Arab Gulf and promote foreign religious literature as the work of "fundamentalists," "radicals," or "Arabcentric." This in turn has led some Muslims to lose trust in state institutions,[7] even those tasked with representing Muslim interests in Tanzania and Zanzibar, such as BAKWATA and the Zanzibar Mufti's office.

A similar education movement began in Zanzibar in the Istiqaama School established in the old Ibadhi mosque of the Al-Lemki family of Oman. When he returned from Oman, Maher, from chapter 2, began teaching at the school and in the Istiqaama mosque in Baghani. As enrollments increased and more funds became available, the Istiqaama community built a new campus that comprised a K–12 school and institute for advanced Arabic and Islamic Studies in the lush island village of Tungu, which is about a thirty-minute drive east of Stone Town. In the school's early years, students from the mainland would first go to Pemba to study at Istiqaama in Chake Chake. Maher explained that students in Zanzibar typically were at a higher level (Sw. *kiwango cha juu*) in their Arabic and religious studies than students from the mainland (bara), who had to pass through Pemba to learn the basics first. After studying in Pemba for two or three years, some of the students would go to Unguja to study in the institute at Tungu, where the staff there would place them in the appropriate class level. On graduation, high-performing students would receive opportunities to study at the College for Shariʻa Studies in Muscat. Other students from Pemba would get opportunities to study at another Ibadhi institute in Algeria called Maʻhad al-Hayah (see chapter 4).

In addition Istiqaama hosts several free religious studies and Arabic lessons for adults in local mosques. Students at the K-12 ma'had in Zanzibar do pay tuition. According to Ayman, from chapter 1,

> We are looking for funding, one that supports food and another that supports teachers' salaries, another supports the building of things. So, there are small projects. Then there is the third element, a school where everyone studies. An integrated school that supports (*skuli ya integration inasupporti*) all studies. Meaning there is a school, the syllabus of the ministry of education in Zanzibar, then there are a few periods when the costs are high ... but together with that, the jumuiya contributes ... it is 8% that they give ... 50% without minding whether he is Ibadhi or not Ibadhi. So many who study are not Ibadhi. Many who study in all these organizations are not Ibadhis. The Ibadhis are a small percentage[8]

He claimed that there was no way to know precise numbers of Ibadhis as "it is not permitted by the government to do our census."[9] He estimated that there could be up to twenty-four thousand students studying in Istiqaama schools and only a quarter of them Ibadhi. Moreover, most of the students who attend the schools are from families who are members of Istiqaama and therefore participate in the organization's elections or serve on its councils and committees. However, lack of membership does not preclude local students and their families from receiving charity (sadaqa) in the form of scholarships for students to attend Istiqaama schools or the care of orphans. When we met for the second time in 2016, Ayman told me that the Unguja branch of Istiqaama paid the school fees for 161 orphaned and impoverished students.[10]

## The Istiqaama Institute in Zanzibar

The school uniforms at Istiqaama are noticeably Islamic. Female teachers and older girls wear long black robes (Sw. *buibui* or Ar. *abaya*). The male teachers also dress conservatively in kanzus and embroidered prayer caps distinctive of the different Ibadhi communities of Oman and Algeria. The teachers often joke among themselves that their journey back and forth between the separated girls' and boys' sections of campus is like running between the two hills of *al-Ṣafa* and *al-Marwah*, a ritual that Hajj pilgrims perform annually when visiting the sacred enclosure in Mecca. This ritual commemorates the

Islamic matriarch Hajar's desperate run in search of water when abandoned in the desert with her young son, Isma'il. Students at the Istiqaama Institute learn to pray at the small campus mosque and can conduct research at two school libraries that contain volumes of legal and theological texts written by modern and classical Ibadhi authorities. The library has a collection of student theses that serve as the basis of a growing archive of local Ibadhi and Islamic knowledge. Many of the books in the library are publications of the Ministry of Endowments and Religious Affairs in Muscat and are donated to the library by Omani investors and visitors to the school. The library books offer advanced students opportunities to deepen their knowledge of Islam and Arabic after they have completed a series of introductory courses in grammar, Islamic education, and reading comprehension. These subjects are taught through a series of imported textbooks from Oman donated to the schools for use in the religion and Arabic language classes.

According to Salim, a former Sunni Muslim chemistry teacher at Istiqaama, students from families that cannot afford to pay the monthly fee of approximately TZS65,000(US$30) receive scholarships from the Istiqaama school board in Zanzibar. Salim explained that the scholarship opportunities provided through Istiqaama enable greater economic and racial diversity at the school because most students receiving financial aid are from non-Arab Swahili backgrounds. On an island where the estimated average annual income is around US$250, most parents on Zanzibar would find the cost of attendance at the Istiqaama Institute prohibitively expensive.[11] Students who excel at the Istiqaama Institute may receive scholarships to study at the College of Shari'a Sciences in Muscat after they graduate, where they deepen their knowledge of Islamic law and Arabic. Istiqaama recruits many of its teachers and school administrators from the college. Religious studies are not a compulsory subject in public schools in Zanzibar and Tanzania, but community members may teach them on an ad hoc basis. In most private Islamic K–12 schools in Zanzibar, religion is compulsory, but the secular courses taught at these institutions, such as math and science, follow the curriculum set by the Tanzanian government. Students at the Istiqaama ma'had also take the national O-level and A-level exams, which determine entrance into high school and university. The religious studies curriculum at the school is presented as nonsectarian, and Ibadhism is only visible in times of prayer, in the Omani kanzus worn by some students and teachers on Fridays, and in the numerous volumes of scholarship written by Ibadhi scholars in the girls' and boys' libraries. Ibadhism also appears in subtle ways in the Istiqaama religion textbooks that are imported from the Ministry of Education in Oman.

## Omani Textbooks in Zanzibari Schools

The first textbook, *Tarbiyya*, is from a series entitled Islamic Education (or *al-Tarbiyya al-Islamiyya*). It is a primary school–level guide to Islamic ritual practice and norms and is similar in content to a series by the same title used in the national religious studies curriculum in Oman. (See Limbert 2007) This textbook is printed by the Ministry of Education in Oman and bears the printed Istiqaama Tanzania name and logo. The series, first published in 1998, has six sections: Qur'ān, prophetic hadith, *'aqīda*, acts of worship, biography of the prophet (*sīra*), and ethics and good manners (*akhlāq*). Anthropologist Mandana Limbert's study of equivalent textbooks in Oman explores the ways in which the books used by elementary school students serve "in the production of good citizens" and instill a sense of "personal piety and seriousness of purpose" from an early age.[12] According to Limbert, the Ibadhi orientation of the textbook writers and the primarily Omani audience is detectable only in several references to prominent Ibadhi figures, in stories about succession disputes and tribal politics in early Islamic Arabia, and in pictorial representations of distinctively Ibadhi prayer practices.

The Sultanate of Oman is never mentioned explicitly in the *Tarbiyya*, but images depicting "typical" Omani landscapes and dress and features of a stereotypical middle-class lifestyle of modern toilets, homes, and public buses serve as representations of what the ideal modern state should look like. These "wish-images," Limbert explains, are as much a part of Oman's particular modernist vision and state-building narratives as they are of preexisting notions of behavioral propriety and civil obedience. As ideals, however, they are often in tension with the realities of daily life.[13] The *Tarbiyya* used by Istiqaama describes ritual practices with emphasis on neighborliness and cleanliness and includes scenes of Omani domestic life and physical environment (e.g., desert landscape, Omani houses, craggy mountain ranges, and water canals).

As the literal meaning of its title suggests, the *Tarbiyya* (Sw., *malezi*) focuses on topics related to the "upbringing" or "guidance" of Muslim youth and its audience is children in primary school or the early stages of development. It seeks to impart "social skills" related to Islamic ideals and norms concerning physical appearance, family, neighborliness, and gender roles. In the series images demonstrating how a child should pray are of men and boys, while those depicting household chores such as cooking and cleaning are of young girls wearing *hijab* and colorful housedresses. Ibadhi women in Zanzibar and Tanzania typically perform their daily prayers at home; however, mosque attendance among women is growing in regions with newer mosques that have designated women's prayer halls. The textbook ideal that suggests the duties of the Omani Muslim woman lie primarily in the domestic sphere is at odds with Istiqaama's or, for that matter, Oman's many initiatives to promote education for its female students, for example, at the Istiqaama ma'had in Zanzibar.

The religious studies textbooks printed by the Omani government make no explicit reference to Ibadhi Islam, although Ibadhi-centered narratives and demonstrations of prayer are discernible.[14] In fact, if one were to remove the Istiqaama Tanzania logo from the book's cover, little would distinguish the series from those described by Limbert as the basis of Oman's religious studies curriculum. The presence of the logo suggests some degree of Omani governmental investment in, or at least awareness of, its role in the Istiqaama's educational efforts in Zanzibar and Tanzania. Oman's role in educational development in East Africa appears, on the surface, to be unidirectional and absent of collaborative pedagogy, or dialogue, between the writers of the donated textbooks and their recipients. The textbook audience at Istiqaama is a Swahili-speaking and non-Arab, coastal, East African Muslim community who do express discomfort with the wholesale adoption of Arabic and Islamic studies textbooks that appear to privilege Arab Muslim and Arab nationalist discourses. Coinciding with this discomfort is an attitude of indifference that suggests the textbooks serve only a practical objective—to teach Swahili-speaking students from Zanzibar the basic principles of Islam and Arabic language—while the rest of the content is superfluous and does little to change students' perceptions of their physical or social selves. The willingness to accept the gift of unmodified textbooks from Oman points to two things: First, that material constraints and lack of expertise in the relevant subjects do not allow the East African branches of Istiqaama to produce their own textbooks or contribute to the modification of the books to reflect the local environments in which they learn. Second, the religious authority of Oman within Ibadhi circles in Zanzibar is clear because of the Ibadhi community's strong kinship ties to the ancestral homeland. This authority is also linked to charismatic figures such as Mufti al-Khalili, who is often credited with the vision to establish the transnational Istiqaama Charitable Society.[15]

## Student and Teacher Perspectives on Imported Learning Materials

Students learning Arabic and Islamic studies at neighborhood Ibadhi mosques in Stone Town also use the Istiqaama textbooks donated from Oman. One student, Jalali, attended the evening classes during his school days and, at the time of our interview, was pursuing a degree at a local college in Zanzibar Town. Jalali's mother is Zanzibari of Indian and Sunni heritage and his father is a member of a well-known Omani family in Zanzibar Town. Jalali and several other Ibadhi students attended evening classes funded by Istiqaama at an Ibadhi mosque from the ages of eight to fifteen while also attending school full-time at the Cutchi Indian Sunni madrasa (Islamic school) in the Mkunazini neighborhood. The madrassa is large and has a distinctive facade of white walls with leaf-green trim. It sits in a prominent location across from the island's main branch of the CRDB bank. The Sunni madrasa is a private school, but like the K–12 school located within the Istiqaama campus, it follows the Tanzanian national curriculum in which religion appears as only one subject out of many and English is the primary language of instruction. Jalali explained that the religious education offered in the school is from a completely "Sunni perspective." Moreover, students who are not Sunni are obliged to conform to mainstream Islamic ritual practices while in school, and they learn about Islam from exclusively Sunni sources.[16] In the evening, however, Ibadhi students enter a new epistemological sphere at an Istiqaama school that privileges Ibadhi norms and practices. This phenomenon of crosscultural appropriation and subject formation is strikingly like Jalali's description of a school life that compelled him to be Sunni by day in the Cutchi school and Ibadhi by night in the Istiqaama one.

Former students and teachers in the Istiqaama schools explain that the Swahili language permeates all aspects of Arabic language pedagogy and mediates between the ideal of Omani-Arab nationalism portrayed in the imported Istiqaama textbooks and the cosmopolitan context of the Istiqaama classroom. Like the *Tarbiyya*, the Istiqaama *Iqrā'* textbook series designed for Arabic language pedagogy is also replete with reading passages and pictures drawn from an Omani context and projects an identifiably more nationalist tone. When asked about his experience studying religion and Arabic from the Istiqaama textbooks printed in Oman, Jalali explained that while he was generally comfortable with the Omani examples and pictures, the centrality of the Arabic language to the Istiqaama curriculum was an adjustment.

Well to me it [the textbook's depictions of life in Oman] was normal. You know, my family, from when I grew up ... so many of them were Arab so ... going into these classes it was easy for me to adapt. Although it was difficult to learn [the material] because of the language ... because I did not know Arabic very well ... I grew up talking Hindi a lot more than Arabic. So, I did not understand Arabic. You know, I understood a little bit, but it was not my language, so it was difficult for me to adapt for some time. Then days passed and it became normal, so it was like an everyday situation ... but at first it was difficult, but it became normal.[17]

Jalali's experience of growing up in a multicultural but patrilineal Muslim society of Zanzibar, in which children of Arab heritage typically assume the religion and tribal identity of their fathers, was good preparation for the digestion of the Omani customs presented in the textbook. However, like most Omani-Zanzibari children of his and his parents' generation (born in the fifties and sixties), knowledge of the Arabic language and Arabic script consisted of that learned in Qur'an classes or a few key religious phrases and greetings while Swahili (and in Jalali's case, Hindi) served as the dominant mode of communication. This is in contrast to a long history of local Swahili writings using Arabic script—a cultural and intellectual practice that British colonial officers and missionaries disrupted and transformed by enforcing the romanization of Swahili as part of a broader civilizing mission to make the language and its speakers "legible" to Europeans.[18] Other narratives suggest that the loss of Arabic-language abilities on the island is a partial result of the anti-Arab and Zanzibari nationalist policies adopted by the government in the years following the revolution.[19]

The experience of several formative years spent in a bilingual, dual confessional, and multicultural Zanzibari educational milieu is likely to produce occasional moments of confusion. In this postcolonial context, where independence and revolution came from both European and Arab imperial powers, such conflict persists in the Muslim student's attempt to navigate between a local Swahili African culture heavily influenced by Arabic and Islam and the idealized Arab Islam presented in the textbooks. Like any subject, learning Arabic is something that takes time, sustained exposure, and discipline until it becomes an everyday situation, a habit, or something normal. Inculcating a sense of normalcy in Arabic is among the distinguishing factors of the Istiqaama school curriculum in relation to that of other similarly faith-based educational institutions in Tanzania's primarily Swahili- or English-speaking educational context. The cultivation of Arabic language skills within the

Istiqaama association also bestows the minority Muslim group with a degree of religious authority in a religious playing field in which knowledge of Arabic often means greater access to higher truths and symbolic capital.[20] This capital affects not only campus life but also one's ability to accumulate material wealth on graduation as it enables access to trade networks in Arabic-speaking countries such as the United Arab Emirates or Dubai.[21] Yet, the emphasis placed on Arabic as a prestige language is not without its critiques; some religious elders, such as Sheikh and Ramadan lecturer Abdilahi Nassir of Mombasa, caution against mistaking "appearance for substance."[22] Functionality in the language of Islam is different from having knowledge of Islam.[23]

Given the competition that Istiqaama faces from other Gulf-funded institutions and actors in Zanzibar and Tanzania, it is no wonder that Arabic is at the core of the group's current educational initiatives. Despite the high premium placed on knowledge of Arabic in the region, Zanzibar's Istiqaama teachers (several of whom attended college in Oman or studied at the ma'had) frequently employ Swahili in their classrooms to facilitate the process of foreign-language acquisition. Jalali expressed his admiration at the intelligence and skill of his teachers at Istiqaama who, he explained, attended college in Oman. They were non-Arabs—he referred to them as "Swahilis" and then clarified that they were "Africans." Jalali said, "It was not like they [the teachers] were talking Arab, Arab, Arab, no no no. He would read a passage or a story and then translate it into Swahili, and that helped me a lot to understand the words and how Arab is used."[24] This dual-language pedagogical approach adopted by the Istiqaama teaching staff demonstrates a sensitivity to and awareness of the various learning needs of their primarily Swahili-speaking student body.

The fifth lesson in the fourth part of the *Iqrā'* textbook focuses on the "Omani armed forces" and their role in the Omani Nahḍa, which began in the 1970s under Sultan Qaboos. The lesson includes patriotic pictures of the armed forces, including a plane from the Omani air force and a military march in front of a building bearing the Omani crest, two crossed ceremonial swords, and a ceremonial dagger (*khanjar*) (Ministry 1997: 44). The passage reads: "[The Nahḍa] realized major successes in the way of building powers aimed at the spread of peace and tranquility in the souls of the citizens in [every] corner of the Sultanate and the protection of the dear homeland [*al-waṭan al-'azīz*]."[25] The passage also discusses the various branches of the Omani military (the army, the air force, the navy, and the sultan's guard) and their phases of development, along with the various academies established by the sultan for the training of those aspiring to join the forces. The appearance of military propaganda in a primary school textbook apparently intended for students in Omani government schools and madrasa systems at home and abroad is an indication of the vast reach of the country's vision for modernization and the intersection of different sites of development—military, education, language, and religion. Moreover, the textbook links Oman's achievements in modern development (*al-tanmiyya al-ḥadītha*) to the intellectual acumen and military might of the former sultan.

Textbooks published by governments for use in their public schools, in Oman as elsewhere, frequently contain nationalist rhetoric.[26] It is also not uncommon for students studying abroad to return home influenced by the rhetoric and the images espoused in their host country's curriculum and public discourses, such as occurred with many of the leaders of modern Saudi-inspired Wahhabi or Egyptian- and Sudanese-inspired Salafi movements across coastal East Africa. What is less clear is how the content of such textbooks influences student perceptions of their own national history and culture vis-à-vis that imported from abroad and how local students process, filter, and interpret the content of these books. To what degree do students and teachers in Zanzibar actively engage the textual and pictorial narratives displayed in the textbooks and to what degree is the foreign textbook just a means to a very practical end—acquiring the ritual and linguistic knowledge required for being a "good" Muslim? Jalali described his own experience with the *Tarbiyya* and *Iqrā'* textbooks as one of passive engagement with the "foreign" nationalist message imbuing the textbooks.

> We didn't go beyond what we were reading, or we were discussing. It is kinda like, you read the passage and then you answer the questions, you understand what was taught—that's it. Because if you go beyond, it is different from our traditions, you know? They are Omanis and we are Zanzibari. And we are taught things very differently, you know. Our traditions, our customs, it is very different, so it is something like that. But the main thing, the main thing was to understand Arabic. It doesn't matter what we were talking about... [or] whether they were talking about the [Omani] air force, or the port, or something like that. The main thing is just to understand Arabic. That is, it. How to pronounce the words, how to do the *tadrībāt*, you know, how to answer the questions. How to do the *i'rāb*. That's it, nothing more.[27]

From this perspective the Omani textbooks were, in a very practical sense, drills (*tadrībāt*) for improving one's knowledge base and not a replacement or competitor for Zanzibari students' hearts and minds. Jalali makes clear that the two cultural contexts are distinct—despite the familiarity of Zanzibari Arabs with Omani customs and traditions. It also appears that the Istiqaama teachers, though they previously lived and studied in Oman, were very conscious of not engaging in any dialogue with students that might touch on issues of political sensitivity in Zanzibar, such as the virtues of the sultan and his armed forces. Still, it was striking the degree to which even years later a student from the ma'had could remember very acutely the themes of the passages and the images of the textbooks, suggesting a degree of passive learning that transcended the acquisition of merely technical knowledge. However, this can also be understood as a form of resistance to the imposition of foreign cultural values, like political philosopher Frantz Fanon's call for decolonization through the rejection of colonial culture and a recognition of the pitfalls of nationalist power structures.[28] The Istiqaama students may maintain a sense of their own distinct cultural identity and traditions, even as they are exposed to external influences. This tension between foreign influences and local cultural identity is a key aspect of the struggle for Zanzibari self-determination and autonomy vis-à-vis Oman.

This lack of motivation and engagement with the Omani curriculum in Zanzibar could stem from a variety of factors. Firstly, the absence of a national exam on the material may make it seem less important or relevant to students who are not required to demonstrate their knowledge in a formal setting.[29] Additionally, the fact that the textbooks used in Zanzibar are essentially the same as those used in Oman, suggests a lack of consideration for the cultural and social context in which they are being used.

Furthermore, the religious knowledge students receive in school is only one small component of the religious socialization they encounter elsewhere through the various print and electronic media, Friday sermons, and daily conversations with friends, families, and teachers outside the official classroom.[30] The broader religious environment may shape their beliefs and practices more significantly than the formal education they receive. Jalali explained that during his time in the dual-learning environment of the Cutchi madrasa and Ibadhi classes, he and his fellow Ibadhi students would often engage in debates with their Sunni classmates over the merits of the different schools of thought in Islam.[31]

The experience of Jalali in engaging with Sunni classmates highlights the complexity of religious identity in Zanzibar. Students like him may feel compelled to defend their beliefs in the face of criticism, indicating the importance of personal conviction and understanding in navigating diverse religious perspectives. Ultimately, the disconnect between the formal curriculum and the lived experiences of students in Zanzibar indicates the limits of formal education in shaping religious identities.

## Arabic as a Prestige Language

Accompanying the heavily Gulf-influenced social environment at the Istiqaama Institute is familiarity with the Arabic language that students come to embody beginning in nursery school. Nuhu—a dark-complexioned Zanzibari university student who recently graduated from Istiqaama in Tungu—explained that for many students at Istiqaama who studied in a madrasa prior to enrolling in the school, learning religion and the Arabic language from Omani textbooks is not at all strange. "For me, it was simple because since a long time ago I had started to study Arabic . . . For me, I saw that it was only normal, it was good, because I already understood something that was written, and it was easy to understand." Similarly, students who come to campus quickly learn that knowledge of Arabic is essential to their success in and outside of the classroom. "It is the rule for *everyone* to speak Arabic, and *they know it*."[32] The physical and social environment of the school appears as a lusher version of the idyllic Omani village scenes represented in the textbooks from which the students learn Arabic grammar, reading comprehension, and the behaviors befitting a good Arabic-speaking Muslim.

Like the students, few of the teachers who come from Omani families at the Istiqaama schools are native speakers of Arabic. Moreover, Arabic is only their second or third language after, in most cases, Swahili. Even the Algerian teachers who have a more natural command of Arabic from the Arab nationalist context, in which they originated, are ethnically Amazigh and speak a mix of Arabic and Berber dialects among themselves. Former students and current teachers at the Istiqaama schools have noted that the cultural and linguistic diversity present among the teaching staff and student body impacts the translation and interpretation of the curated image of Islam and Muslims that is presented in Omani educational materials. Nuhu explained that some teachers would draw on examples from the cultural context with which they themselves were most familiar (e.g., Algeria) when teaching religion or Arabic reading comprehension. "Others stick to this [Zanzibar's] environment, they teach about this or that stream, meaning, they use [examples] of different kinds."[33] This observation underscores the teachers' awareness of the diverse learning needs of their students and highlights the fact that the Omani textbooks are just one set of tools among many in their pedagogical toolbox. It is utilized alongside other approaches, reflecting the adaptability and responsiveness of teachers at the ma'had to effectively communicate knowledge of Arabic and religion at Istiqaama.

Bi Aida, a longtime teacher and administrator at Istiqaama, explained that as a private institution of learning, the school affords teachers relative freedom to select classroom materials and experiment with a variety of pedagogical methods.

> As for teaching, the teacher is not required to focus on just one book. We are a private school [*skuli binafsi*], but we received permission from the Ministry of Education [Wizara ya Elimu] that we can import skills—other skills—that we think can help advance the education of our students. So, the Omani and Arabic books are used because there are some things that must be taken from there. They [the Omanis] do well in Arabic, so we want to do as well as them. So, we use their books as supplementary books so that our students can be at that same average as the students that do well over there in Oman.[34]

From this perspective, it is only natural that Zanzibari students would learn from textbooks printed in a country where Arabic is the official language, if not always the primary mode of communication. The question is not necessarily one of Omani or Arab supremacy but one of utility: How can we use the various materials at our disposal to enhance the pedagogy of our teachers and address the learning needs of our students? The association Bi Aida makes between knowledge of Arabic and being from Oman invokes a deeply ingrained assumption in Zanzibar that the Gulf countries are home to the "pure" Arabic language and culture to which young Muslims must aspire. A successful Istiqaama student is the one who achieves the same level of Arabic as their Omani counterparts who attend the national school system in Arabic. This does not consider that many students of East African heritage or the Zinjibari diaspora in Oman are themselves struggling to navigate between their Arab and African linguistic and cultural heritage. For example, some students may grapple with the expectation of being fluent in the standardized Swahili taught in schools, though their home dialects may differ drastically from the Tanzanian standard that uses a roman orthography and flattens some of the guttural sounds characteristic of Arabic and Islamic vocabulary.[35]

At the Istiqaama Institute in Tungu, math and science teachers tend not to use Arabic. Salim, who left the maʿhad to teach chemistry in a government school, explains: "However there are some books written in Arabic for science, but we do not use those. For example, I, myself, cannot use Arabic books to teach. I can read Qur'an [that is all]."[36] While there are some science textbooks in Arabic available in the school library, English and Swahili is the preferred method of communication for these subjects. Salim's experience is an example of the distinction made between English as a language of industry and Arabic as the language of Islam and Arab culture that also serves the socioeconomic purpose of maintaining business and kinship ties with the Gulf. Salim further gestures to a desire to immerse students in what many view as the primary language of Islam; this is also a primary reason for which Zanzibari parents may send their children to study at the maʿhad. According to Salim, because of Istiqaama's success in graduating students with high marks on national exams—Ibadhi and non-Ibadhi, Arab and non-Arab—parents and teachers alike aspire to send their children to the Istiqaama-supported schools to learn Arabic and the behaviors and cultural practices befitting a virtuous Muslim. "I am sorry, but to me, Arabic is the best language. However, I do not speak it. But it is my first language. Because ... even the poems, when they sing songs, they are very nice even [more so] than English songs or Swahili. Sometimes Swahili [becomes] nice because of some Arabic words. So, I want my children to know this. To me [myself] now it is not important but for my children it is important. And I prefer them to know English, and when they are there, they will speak both languages."[37]

These comments are reminiscent of a perception held by visitors, archaeologists, linguists, historians, and ethnographers to the East African coast that the main aspects distinguishing Swahili as a prestige language, in comparison to the indigenous African languages and cultural traditions of the mainland and interior, are its Arab and Persian influences. These perceptions map onto a longstanding practice among coastal residents of "emphasizing their descent from immigrants from Shiraz in Persia and from Arabia who had come centuries earlier to the African coast to trade and who stated to settle, build coral towns, live a sophisticated urban life, and rule."[38] Despite these claims, however, historical linguists such as Derek Nurse and Thomas Spear have made convincing arguments against the centrality of Arabic to Swahili language and culture, emphasizing the language's Bantu grammar structure and sound system. While Swahili remained an important language of trade, oral and written culture, and social life, the establishment of the Omani sultanate in

Zanzibar during the first half of the nineteenth century saw greater emphasis placed on the role of Arabs and Arabic in trade and economic life on the coast. It was during this period that merchants and scholars from noble lineages (*ashrāf/shurafā'*, sing. *sharīf*) in Hadramaut became "prominent community leaders" and harbingers of Islamic reform in Zanzibar, in line with trends that were already underway in Arabic-speaking lands.[39] Even after the process of emancipating enslaved persons began in 1897, knowledge of Arabic and one's ability to demonstrate Arabness through lineage, dress, and manners became the measure of the civility and gentility on the islands.[40]

Over a century later, Salim, who himself claims distant Omani heritage but is Sunni, articulates the importance of early Islamic education and Arabic in ensuring the social standing and respectability of his children. Just as Swahili is sometimes viewed as the language that distinguishes Muslim coastal residents from their non-Muslim counterparts, he views Arabic as a prestige language that yields more symbolic capital than his native Swahili. His insecurity is shared by many of the island's educated Muslims: that failure to learn or lack of opportunity to study Arabic in depth deprives them of a certain symbolic capital and religious authority that would enable greater integration into Arab economic and social circles in Zanzibar and the Gulf. Parents may transfer this anxiety to their children, who have the burden of mastering Arabic for its religious value and English for the opportunities it affords Zanzibaris in achieving success in education, the local tourism industry, and international business, among other sectors. Parents in Zanzibar choose to send their children to private religious schools, like Istiqaama, to increase their earning potential but also to improve their social standing in a local context where virtuous Muslim behavior is still strongly linked to regular attendance at prayers, knowledge of Arabic, modest dress, and knowledge of Arab culture.

## Conclusion

This chapter has examined the place of Ibadhi private schools in postrevolutionary Zanzibar through the lens of educational materials imported from Oman for use in religion and Arabic-language classrooms. The schools discussed here are housed under the Istiqaama Muslim Society of Tanzania and Zanzibar, which emerged as a collaborative effort between Ibadhi leaders in Oman and members of the East African diaspora in the 1980s and 1990s. The chapter has further shown that while Istiqaama supports the use of educational materials designed for an Omani national audience, Zanzibaris affiliated with Istiqaama make clear that they view donations from Oman as mere tools for social and economic advancement. Zanzibari relations with their former rulers remain contentious in public debates; however, state institutions such as the mufti's office approve of educational collaborations between both states. The Istiqaama schools reveal that Tanzania-Oman relations since the revolution are driven by economic development, knowledge exchange, and religious activism. Indeed, Istiqaama is a primary example of how religious institutions are today influencing power relations between the formerly colonized states and their colonizers and between institutions of the global south. These relations extend beyond the Indian Ocean to North Africa, where Istiqaama sends students to and recruit teachers from Algeria. These crosscontinental ties are in part a reflection of the pan-African solidarity that has endured between Algeria and Tanzania since at least the 1950s when both countries were engaged in a struggle for independence against European colonial rule.

Stuart Hall's theory of representation illuminates the educational environment at Istiqaama, in analyzing how cultural and religious identities are constructed and perceived in the transnational Islamic school setting. According to Hall, representations are not direct reflections of reality, but rather constructions that are shaped by social, historical, and cultural contexts. They are produced through cultural codes and norms that are influenced by power dynamics and ideologies, which may include religious to nationalist discourses.[41] The materials donated to Istiqaama from Oman reflect a particular representation of Arab culture and religious identity, which may not fully resonate with the experiences and identities of Zanzibar students. By incorporating local Zanzibari culture and language in the learning environment, teachers at ma'had Istiqaama are engaging in a process of re-presentation. This can disrupt the dominant representations found in the donated materials and provide a more nuanced and inclusive understanding of culture and identity for the students.

Though associated with a religious and ethnic minority in contemporary Zanzibar, the Istiqaama Institute in Unguja has managed to position itself as one of the most sought-after K–12 Muslim schools in Tanzania. The school's success is due, in part, to its modern educational resources and rigorous learning environment but also to its direct ties to Omani-Arab society and culture, which once served as a standard for respectable Muslim behavior in Zanzibar. In this way, Istiqaama differs from other Gulf-supported Muslim private schools whose founders are not so directly entangled in Zanzibar's complex histories of imperialism, Arab landownership, class-based and racial discrimination, and revolution. More than any other cultural project spearheaded by the Omani government or private actors in Zanzibar today, the faith-based Istiqaama organization and educational networks it has established across Tanzania have been critical to reimagining the Ibadhi-Omani diaspora as a locally rooted, inclusive, and bilingual Muslim community.

## Notes

1. In Swahili, "Maahad Istiqaama Zanzibar."
2. An earlier version of the arguments and materials presented in this chapter can be found here: Kimberly T. Wortmann, "Ibadi Muslim Schools in Post-Revolutionary Zanzibar," *Africa: Journal of the International African Institute* 92 (2022): 249–64.
3. See for example: Anne K. Bang. *Sufis and Scholars of the Sea: Family Networks in East Africa, 1860-1925*. Indian Ocean Series. London: RoutledgeCurzo, 2003; Amal N. Ghazal. *Islamic Reform and Arab Nationalism: Expanding the Crescent from the Mediterranean to the Indian Ocean (1880s-1930s)*. Culture and Civilization in the Middle East. Taylor and Francis, 2010.
4. See for example: McMahon, Elisabeth. *Slavery and Emancipation in Islamic East Africa: From Honor to Respectability*. 1st ed. (New York: Cambridge University Press, 2013).
5. Simon Turner, "'These Young Men Show No Respect for Local Customs'—Globalization and Islamic Revival in Zanzibar," *Journal of Religion in Africa* 39, no. 3 (2009): 238.
6. Ibid.
7. Ibid.
8. Ayman, interview with author, February 24, 2016.
9. Ibid.
10. Ibid.
11. Salim (former Istiqaama teacher), interview with author, Stone Town, Zanzibar, May 31, 2018.
12. Mandana E. Limbert, "Oman: Cultivating Good Citizens and Religious Virtue," in *Teaching Islam: Textbooks and Religion in the Middle East* (Boulder, CO: Lynne Rienner, 2007), 103–4.
13. Ibid., 121.
14. Ibid.
15. Kimberly T. Wortmann, "Omani Religious Networks in Contemporary Tanzania and Beyond" (PhD diss., Harvard University, 2018).
16. Jalali (former Istiqaama student), interview with author, Skype, August 15, 2017.
17. Ibid.

18. Caitlyn Bolton, "Making Africa Legible: Kiswahili Arabic and Orthographic Romanization in Colonial Zanzibar," *The American Journal of Islamic Social Sciences* 33, no. 3 (2016): 61–78.

19. Roman Loimeier, *Between Social Skills and Marketable Skills; The Politics of Islamic Education in 20th Century Zanzibar* (Leiden, Netherlands: Brill, 2009).

20. Pierre Bourdieu, *The Field of Cultural Production: Essays on Art and Literature* (New York: Columbia University Press, 1993).

21. Akbar Keshodkar, "Who Needs China When You Have Dubai? The Role of Networks and the Engagement of Zanzibars in Transnational Indian Ocean Trade," *Urban Anthropology and Studies of Cultural Systems and World Economic Development* 43, no. 1/2/3 (2014): 105–41.

22. Kai Kresse, "The Uses of History : Rhetorics of Muslim Unity and Difference on the Kenyan Swahili Coast," in *Struggling with History: Islam and Cosmopolitanism in the Western Indian Ocean*, eds., Edward Simpson and Kai Kresse (New York: Columbia University Press, 2008), 240.

23. Ibid., 240–41.

24. Jalali, interview with author, August 15, 2017.

25. "Iqrā': Lil Saff Al-Rabi' Al-Ibtidā'ī, al-Taba'a al-'ashira," *Ministry of Education in Oman*, (Istiqaama Muslim Community of Tanzania, 1997), 47.

26. Eleanor Abdella Doumato and Gregory Starrett, *Teaching Islam: Textbooks and Religion in the Middle East* (Boulder, CO: Lynne Rienner, 2007).

27. Jalali, interview with author, August 15, 2017.

28. Frantz Fanon and Philcox Richard. *The Wretched of the Earth*. New York: Grove Press, 2004, 97–144.

29. James A. Toronto and Muhammad S. Eissa, "Egypt: Promoting Tolerance, Defending against Islamism," in *Teaching Islam: Textbooks and Religion in the Middle East* (Boulder, CO: Lynne Rienner, 2007), 47–48.

30. Ibid., 47.

31. Jalali, interview with author, August 15, 2017.

32. Nuhu (former Istiqaama student), interview with author, Zanzibar, May 31, 2018.

33. Ibid.

34. Bi Aida (Ma'had Istiqaama administrator), interview with author, Tungu, Zanzibar, May 29, 2019.

35. Sara Hillewaert, *Morality at the Margins: Youth, Language, and Islam in Coastal Kenya* (New York: Fordham University Press, 2019), 79.

36. Salim, interview with author, May 31, 2018.

37. Ibid.

38. Derek Nurse and Thomas Spear, *The Swahili: Reconstructing History and Language of an African Society, 800–1500* (Philadelphia: University of Pennsylvania, 1985), 4.

39. Ibid.

40. Laura Fair, *Pastimes and Politics: Culture, Community, and Identity in Post-Abolition Urban Zanzibar, 1890–1945* (Athens: Ohio University Press, 2001).

41. Hall, Stuart. "The Work of Representation." In *Representation: Cultural Representations and Signifying Practices*, 13–64 (London: SAGE Publications Ltd, 1997).

# 4

## Ibadhi Students and Teachers between Tanzania and Algeria

One evening during Ramadan, in June 2019, I met with a group of current and former male students at the Ibadhi mosque in Ilala, Dar es Salaam. They had all received scholarships to study at a sister school of Istiqaama's in Algeria. The school, located in the Mzab Valley, is called Ma'had Al-Hayat (est. 1925), which means the Life Institute. From now on, I will refer to this institute simply as Al-Hayat. The students, all Tanzanian nationals with Omani heritage, were recruited to speak with me by Suleiman, a preacher and teacher at the mosque in his early thirties who also runs the Istiqaama Youth Organization. All the young men at the meeting were from Ibadhi families that migrated from Pemba to Dar es Salaam between the 1970s and 1980s, where their Arab ancestors had originally settled.

The Ibadhi mosque in Ilala, a one-story building with a pale-green exterior, may seem modest in size, but it has a corrugated iron roof and protruding prayer niche (*mihrab*). Near the entrance are rows of cubbyholes where worshippers leave their shoes before entering through a large wooden door. During the day, a local resident regularly supervises the drying cloves on a mat outside the mosque, possibly imported from Pemba, where the spice is abundant. Others display used kanzus (traditional robes) and kofias (caps) for sale on a wall that blocks the view to a private residence facing the mosque.

Next to the mosque, there are classrooms and offices, including a library and the office of the youth organization. This complex in Ilala is part of the work and service of the Dar es Salaam branch of Istiqaama. This chapter explores the relationship between Istiqaama and Al-Hayat and what it reveals about the enduring connections among Ibadhis in East and North Africa.

Figure 4.1: Ibadhi Mosque, Ilala, Dar es Salaam, 2019. Photo by author.

The story of this relationship is not only important for showcasing the extent of Tanzanian Ibadhi transnationalism but also for demonstrating that Istiqaama is part of a longer and global reformist tradition focused on Ibadhi understandings of moral rectitude, involving cross-continental migrations and the exchange of ideas and resources, such as those between Istiqaama and Al-Hayat in the postcolonial period. I argue that these collaborations are also a reflection of and a contribution to larger Tanzanian-Algerian educational and diplomatic efforts. Having already discussed the impact of Istiqaama on education reform, this chapter now focuses on the history of Al-Hayat and its role in shaping Ibadhi identity in Algeria and Tanzania.

## Tracing the Histories of Istiqaama and Al-Hayat

Tracing the histories of Al-Hayat and Istiqaama, two institutions situated thousands of miles apart, as well as their efforts towards reform (al-islāh) along Islamic lines, reveals the profound impact of North-West Ibadhi reformist and educational initiatives. These endeavors have their roots in the Middle Ages but gained momentum in the mid- to late-nineteenth through the pan-Islamic and pan-Ibadhi policies implemented by the sultans of Zanzibar, particularly Sultan Barghash, who established an Arabic printing press on the islands.[1]

By studying the post-independence Ibadhi history in Tanzania and Algeria from the work of these two educational institutions, it becomes evident how transnational Ibadhi reform initiatives have continued to progress into the twenty-first century. These programs have adjusted to and accommodated various colonial and/or national circumstances, addressing both the spiritual and pragmatic requirements of students and educators who travel to acquire and share knowledge in both locations.

An examination of the attempts of Al-Hayat and Istiqaama to revive Ibadhi education in both countries demonstrates what historians Amal Ghazal and Augustin Jomier have already shown—that Islamic reformism is not an exclusively Sunni or, by extension, Shiʿi, phenomenon.[2] Indeed, Ibadhi networks and mobilities that focus on "the circulation of pilgrims and merchants between the Maghreb and Egypt (including the Hejaz and Oman)" date back to the early modern period, when connections between the "islands" of the Ibadhi archipelago,[3] enabled by institutions such as the Buffalo Agency in Cairo, which included an Ibadhi trade agency, school, and library.[4] These connections continued into the twentieth century with the financial support of the sultans of Zanzibar and the Ibadhi printing press, which Sultan Barghash established on the islands in the 1880s.

## Situating Al-Hayat within the Mzab Region

The Mzab lies about "600 km south of Algiers," the country's capital, and is the primary home of the country's Amazigh Ibadhi population.[5] While the majority of Algerians are Sunni Muslims who follow the teachings of the Maliki Sunni madhab, the Mzab is an ethnically and linguistically diverse region comprised of five *quṣūr*, or fortified towns and cities.[6] People from the region are a confessional (Ibadhi) and linguistic (Tamazight, a Berber language) minority and refer to themselves using the ethnotype "Mozabite," a term "forged in French from the 1830s, from the Arabic name Bani Mzab (or Mizāb)."[7] According to the Algerian teachers at Istiqaama,[8] being Mozabite in Algeria means being Ibadhi in the way that being Ibadhi in Tanzania implies having Omani ancestry.

The Algerian territory was home to the world's second Ibadhi imamate, which the Persianate Rustamid Dynasty founded in the historic trade city of Tahert in 761. The Ibadhi imamate continued to rule in North Africa until its defeat at the hands of the Fatimids in 909.[9] Following the fall of the imamate, the Ibadhi community migrated farther south toward the Mzab, where they established a unique governing system represented by elected members of the community called *niẓām al-ʿazzāba* in Arabic.

North African Ibadhis first established the 'azzāba in the eleventh-century to address their religious, educational, and social needs while they practiced kitmān (concealment) in the absence of a ruling Ibadhi imam. The 'azzāba is made up of twelve members, each assigned specific roles. Traditionally, an elected member of the 'azzāba is a man who possesses good manners and politeness, is an active seeker of knowledge, and has memorized the Qur'an because such a person is considered "willing to sacrifice for the sake of God and in the service of the Muslims."[10] The 'azzāba members collectively supervise the building and management of mosques as well as community endowments (awqāf, sing. waqf), educational institutions, and local market accounts. They also determine the terms of association (walāya) and dissociation (barā'a) with other non-Ibadhis and work closely with women's organizations.[11]

The wealth generated by Berber-Ibadhi merchants during the trans-Saharan trade, combined with the early success of the lost imamate and the 'azzāba system that developed in its place, have all contributed to the organization, preservation, and elaboration of Ibadhi thought and practice in North Africa. For example, Arabic is the primary language of instruction in government schools at Al-Hayat, in part because the Algerian government has invested in an intensive Arabization campaign that seeks to unify the population around an Arab Islamic identity. French is also taught, as it has remained an important language of business and international relations in Algeria since the colonial period.

## The Birth of Al-Hayat amid Islamic Reform in the Mzab

Two decades after the 1882 annexation of the Mzab, the colonial regime imposed the military draft for World War I on men from the Mzab and others who lived in the north of the country, first in 1912 and again in 1918. Although there were rumors that conscription would be imposed in the south, it never was.[12]

During the war, Ibadhi scholars from the Mzab supported the Ottoman Muslim power over the French and joined the anticolonial movements already underway in Tripolitania (today Libya) and Tunisia. They hoped that by forming solidarity networks with other Ibadhis in North Africa and promoting resistance to colonial rule, they would liberate their own Berber region from French-controlled Algeria.[13] It was against this sociopolitical backdrop that Al-Hayat was established as a study group in the home of Sheikh Ibrahim bin 'Umar Bayyud (1899–1981), a well-known Ibadhi reformist figure. As such, he and his students faced continuous harassment from the regime. After time, the close-knit study circle responded to the pressure by transferring its activities to a local mosque in Guerrara.[14]

## Al-Hayat: An Algerian Ibadhi Educational Movement

Al-Hayat was established as a secret study group during the time when Algeria was under French colonialism. The school's Facebook page states that it was developed "in secret" under the colonial regime, which "sought to erase all the features of Islamic and Arabic character of the Mzab Valley."[15] The group would gather at the residence of Sheikh Bayyud. He hailed from Guerrara, a city in the Ghardaïa province, which is where Al-Hayat is still located today, in the Mzab Valley. Eventually, this group's activism fueled an Islamic reformist renaissance (Ar. *al-nahḍa al-islāḥiyya*) that focused on religion, science, society, and politics, serving as a precursor to a network of local Ibadhi schools and associations, such as Al-Hayat.

Ibadhis today admire Muslim scholars like Bayyud for their dedication to the resistance against colonialism in North Africa and their fight for independence of the Imazighen.[16] However, Jomier wisely advises against taking the Ibadhi origin stories of revival and reform in the region too literally. This is because much of the history of the Mozabite community under colonial rule is written from a nationalist perspective, emphasizing the perceived resistance of local scholars and heroes (such as Attfayish and Bayyud) in the anti-colonial struggle. Such narratives are accompanied in later periods by a narrative of decline, similar to that of the Ibadhi community in Zanzibar following the revolution in 1964, which suggests that subsequent generations of Ibadhis failed to capture the essence of the madhab's teachings. Such declinist perspectives have led to a teleology of the Ibadhi Nahḍa, in Algeria, which prioritizes their networks at the expense of lesser-known exchanges of knowledge between the Ibadhi East and North West.[17]

Nevertheless, the Ibadhis of the Mzab view Sheikh Bayyud as the "the pioneer of the southern renaissance" (*rā'id al-nahḍa fī al-junūb*).[18] They recognize his role as the "leader of Ibadhi reformism in Algeria after Muḥammad bin Yūsuf Aṭfiyyash (1820–1914),"[19] who Ibadhis in the Mzab refer to as the pole of the imams (*quṭb al-a'imma*). Furthermore, Bayyud is celebrated as a leader of the "Ibadhi opposition to French colonialism in the Mzab Valley in Algeria" and someone who "educated a generation of Mzabi scholars who became leading figures in several anti-colonial movements spanning the Maghrib as well as the Mashriq."[20]

Bayyud earned this reputation "by the prolixity of his work," which includes more than one hundred titles, poetry and correspondence excluded, written for the ma'had he established in his home—which attracted Ibadhi students from outside Algeria—and, for this study in particular, for the Ibadhi intellectuals of Zanzibar that he formed a strong connection with in the late nineteenth and early twentieth century.[21] He was in close contact with Ibadhi reformers in Oman such as Nur al-Din al-Salimi and the "Zanzibari sultans who sponsored the publication of his works, honored him with high ranking medals and provided him with financial support."[22] Finally, on October 21, 1937, under the leadership of Sheikh Bayyud, Al-Hayat received official recognition by the French colonial government.[23] Going forward, the association's leadership would focus on "its curriculum, expanding its scope in accepting students from different parts of the country and from friendly countries."[24] Like the Istiqaama Institute in Zanzibar, the Algerian school has expanded to include a combination of secular and religious subjects in its curriculum at the primary and secondary school levels. Additionally, the school campus features a college dedicated to advanced Islamic Studies and Arabic.[25] The academic year at Al-Hayat lasts for nine months, with classes being held for eight hours a day, five days a week. Students are given breaks during religious and official holidays, as well as select local events. They can participate in various school clubs that focus on law, literature, science, and art. They are taught to deliver speeches and engage in debates, and their written work is published in school magazines. The students also organize religious and national concerts.

To gain admission to university, students at Al-Hayat must pass a baccalaureate exam after completing three years of high school. The education system at Al-Hayat consists of three main levels:

1. The intermediate level (*marhala at-ta'līm mutawwasit*) which lasts for four years and enables students to take the Ministry of Education exams to obtain a basic education certificate.
2. Secondary education lasts for three years and qualifies the student to take the Ministry of Education examinations to earn a secondary education certificate (baccalaureate).
3. Education in Islamic law is pursued at the university (*ta'līm shar'ī*).[26]

The stated objective of Al-Hayat is "to promote God-consciousness (*taqwa min Allah*) and good will (*riḍwān*) and to provide the Mzab Valley, Algeria, and the global Islamic community (*ummah*) with an elite (*nukhba*) of men competent in various fields of life."[27] To achieve this objective, Al-Hayat now has transnational networks in place and a relationship with the international Istiqaama community in Oman and Tanzania.

## A Bridge between Al-Hayat and Istiqaama: Mohammed Tiwani and Pemba's Ibadhi Revival

In the office of the Istiqaama Youth Organization in Ilala, mentioned at the beginning of the chapter, there are bookshelves stretching from floor to ceiling. These bookshelves hold volumes of Ibadhi fiqh, which are embossed with gold titles published in Oman. There are also works by East African Ibadhi writers in Swahili, notably these include the apologetic works of Juma Muhamamd Al-Mazrui, an Omani writer and national whose Swahili language corpus includes a book aiming to dispel misconceptions about the Khawarij and their relationship to Ibadhism and another on the Islamic caliphate, the former a publication of the now closed Istiqaama Library in Muscat. On a wall behind a wooden desk, there is a large photo of the grand mufti of Oman, Mufti al-Khalili. Hanging next to it is a picture of Sheikh Muhammad Tiwani, an Ibadhi activist from Pemba who is credited with establishing religious and educational missions between Algeria and Zanzibar.

The relationship between these two men is described in a biography of Sheikh Mohammad, that appears in the Swahili language ritual manual called Qamusi-Ssalaa (the Prayer Dictionary). The manual was written for Ibadhi youth by Sheikh Mohammad's relative in Pemba, Khalfan Tiwani. In the manual, Sheikh Mohammad is referred to as a "Muslim activist" (*mwanaharakati wa kiislamu*) and a disciple of Mufti al-Khalili. It is mentioned, "in adulatory language," that Al-Khalili was impressed by Mohammad's intellect and his tendency to challenge established wisdom. Through Al-Khalili's influence, Mohammad got the opportunity to study in Oman, where he developed a passion for education and spreading knowledge about Ibadhi Islam. He then brought this passion back to his birthplace, the island of Pemba.

According to the notes in his biography, Sheikh Mohammad initiated various educational and social projects aimed at awakening Ibadhis (*aliamsha hisia za watu*) in Pemba and Oman to the need for grassroots reform. In the 1990s, the opportunity to send students from Zanzibar to Algeria emerged

**Figure 4.2**: Istiqaama Youth Office, Ilala, Dar es Salaam, 2019. Wall portraits of Ibadhi Sheikhs Ahmad bin Hamad al-Khalili (Oman) and Mohammad Tiwani (Pemba). Photo by author.

**Figure 4.3**: Al-Khalili Istiqaama Mosque and School, Pemba, Zanzibar, 2015. Photo by author.

from extensive conversations that Sheikh Mohammad had with Algerian Ibadhi scholars whom he had met during his studies in Oman. When he returned home, these connections played a critical role in generating support for student missions in the form of scholarships, learning materials, and instruction from the Algerian Ibadhi community in the Mzab Valley. Tiwani wrote that, through Sheikh Mohammad's international contacts, he was not only able to secure tuition and room and board for Pemban student missions to Algeria but he even raised enough to pay for students' flight tickets and to support underprivileged students.

In the *Qamusi*, Sheikh Khalfan also lists the various initiatives Sheikh Muhammad developed at home in Pemba. These initiatives included securing scholarships for students to study abroad in Oman and Algeria as well as building libraries, a men's and women's college, a Friday Mosque named after Mufti al-Khalili, Qur'an schools, an orphanage, a computer center, and a radio station. Sheikh Muhammad also supported concerts for the holiday (Eid) following Ramadan and was something of a matchmaker for young

Ibadhis, matching couples according to their "tendencies and attitudes"[28] rather than their physical appearances (*sura*). According to the biography, he accomplished all these tasks in a period of just fifteen years, even in the face of heavy opposition from Pemban elders and local authorities. The author emphasizes his relative's resilience in the face of this fierce opposition: "For many, if you mention [those things], they think it just came about [effortlessly]. But it came at a great cost to him. Insults, accusations, breaches of honor, convictions, letters of sedition to international organizations, letters of intimidation and slander, [he was] taken to the police, taken to the courts."[29]

While the author does not call out Sheikh Muhammad Tiwani's detractors by name, it is possible that some of this opposition came from the Ibadhi leadership in Pemba's northern port town of Wete, where there is also a large Omani diaspora. In the early years of the organization, there was only one branch of Istiqaama on the island. Like its counterpart in Chake Chake, the northern branch in Wete has its own leadership and collection of schools, including a boys' school called Istiqaama College. The *Qamusi* explains,

> He selected some of the youth [of Pemba] to go to Oman to continue their education. [Moreover], while he was studying [abroad in Oman] he initiated relationships with the North African [Ibadhi] 'ulamā', especially in Algeria. After conversations over a long period of time, the rain of the opportunity of [his] studies started to pour from Algeria. The flight ticket (*nauli*) was an obstacle (*kikwazo*), so he had to mobilize [people] until they understood [and could help]. At the same time, he was raising money to help those who do not have the means. Now the youth have started to return with degrees in different fields (*nyanja tofauti*), Islamic law, secular law (*kanuni*), diplomacy, history, etc.[30]

The *Qamusi* portrays Sheikh Muhammad not only as a self-sacrificing community leader and charismatic authority who leads a vanguard of youth abroad to train in the secular and religious sciences and then use their acquired skills to build their communities back on Pemba but also as a man who is mindful of the precarious socioeconomic position of his home island.

## How Pemban Migration Contributed to Ibadhi Transnational Education

Although it is the smaller of the two islands in the Zanzibar archipelago, Pemba is arguably richer in natural resources, with "good soil and well-watered valleys."[31] Pemba receives marginal attention in scholarly works on Zanzibar, and its inhabitants often appear as socially regressive, religiously conservative, superstitious, and suspicious of any outsider synonymous with political opposition to the ruling party in Tanzania including the Zanzibar isles, Chama cha Mapinduzi (CCM). The island's residents have experienced severe economic and political marginalization as well as ongoing harassment from the Zanzibar authorities since the 1964 revolution.

In the decade that preceded the revolution, however, residents of Pemba had enjoyed extensive periods of bounty from the fruitful harvest and international sale of cloves.[32] This economic fortune enabled them to maintain relative autonomy from the highly stratified urban society of Unguja, where economic prosperity and respectability connected intimately to affiliation with the Arab ruling class. Then, in the years following the revolution, Pembans of all racial and economic backgrounds found themselves the target of revolutionaries and the central government for not supporting the African nationalist coalition in Zanzibar, the Afro-Shirazi Party (ASP), in the contentious elections of 1961 (preceding the revolution) and not participating in the massacre of their Arab and Indian neighbors as occurred in Unguja.

According to anthropologist Nathalie Arnold Koenings, in 1964 "the Revolutionary Government established an army camp and two new Field for Unit enclaves on Pemba (where there had been none in the past), at the same time significantly increasing police presence."[33] Koenings has examined how the militarization of Pemban society led to a series of humiliating and "infantilizing" detainments and the canings of respected male elders who had previously served as the island's authorities and arbiters. Also, during this period, the government "nationalized and redistributed wealth" on Pemba.[34] This process resulted in the divvying up of agricultural lands among several poor tenants, rendering it less profitable. At the same time, the government imposed a prohibition against imported goods and travel outside Pemba.

Then in 1971, an island-wide famine, locally referred to as *"wakati wa njaa"* or "the time of hunger," hit local communities in Pemba hard. Islanders finally began to see relief from the food scarcity but only after the death of Zanzibar's first president in 1972. Although more food became available during that time, and life on Pemba began to improve "in small ways deep distrust, surveillance, and widespread physical and economic hardship" endured.[35]

As a result, many of the residents who had not had the opportunity to flee the island before—whether for Unguja, the mainland countries of Tanzania and Kenya, or the Gulf—began to do so in large numbers, hoping to secure better futures for themselves and their families. The members of the Omani diaspora and the business community from Pemba who settled in Ilala thus became part of a new wave of Ibadhi migrations from the islands to the mainland. Significantly, their children, who grew up in Dar es Salaam but attended school in Pemba (and, in some cases, Algeria) had become part of a new generation that inherited a strong sense of both Pemban and Tanzanian national identity. In fact, the male students I interviewed in Dar es Salaam were first sent by their parents to the Istiqaama school in Chake Chake, the island's southern capital, and then to Al-Hayat.

Sheikh Muhammad Tiwani was, and continues to be, influential among the large Pemban Ibadhi community that settled in Dar es Salaam in the decades following the Zanzibar Revolution. So, in the 1990s, my interlocutor Suleiman said, the sheikh developed the transnational educational network between Al-Hayat and Istiqaama. At that time, many Ibadhi parents began to send their children to Pemba to study at the nursery and primary school appended to the gleaming Al-Khalili Friday Mosque in Chake Chake.

Now, Pemban students of non-Omani and Sunni origins[36] also attend the mosque school and may receive scholarships to study abroad in Algeria, although such opportunities are not widely advertised in the local media. Regardless of whether students are Ibadhi or Sunni, however, Suleiman said, "You must first go through Pemba, then you can go to Algeria. However, mainlanders don't really like [this arrangement]; they prefer to study in Europe or English-speaking countries. . . . Until recently most of the students from [Ma'had Istiqaama] Tunguu [on Unguja island] who went to Oman would go to Algeria, but now it has changed so that the male and female Tungu students go to Algeria."[37]

Current Al-Hayat students and graduates in urban Ilala expressed ambivalence about spending time in the much quieter and more rural Pemba before moving to a very new cultural context in Algeria, where they received educational certificates that would be of uncertain value in the Tanzanian job market. (In Tanzania, competition and eligibility requirements—for example, the TOEFL exam—bar all but a handful of students from pursuing scholarships and opportunities to study abroad in English-speaking counties, such as the United Kingdom or United States.) Still, Al-Hayat presents a unique opportunity for students to receive a rigorous, mostly funded private-school education in a country that has the continent's fourth largest economy.

In addition, the frequency with which Ibadhi parents in Dar es Salaam send their children to the private Istiqaama school in Pemba is a testament to the mainland community's continued investment and participation in the social and economic life of the island. Further, the presence of mainland students at the school and Pemban students in Algeria speaks to the success of Istiqaama and local activists like Sheikh Muhammad in establishing local and global educational pipelines.

## Developing a Cross-Continental Educational Network

Beginning in the 1990s, around the same time Sheikh Muhammed developed the transnational educational network between Al-Hayat and Istiqaama, an Ibadhi Muslim educational and religious mission originating in the Mzab began recruiting East African Muslim students to study abroad at Al-Hayat. The recruits came to Algeria through Istiqaama in Tanzania, where the Ibadhi leadership viewed the collaboration with Al-Hayat as an opportunity to strengthen their ties to the global Ibadhi community and benefit from the expertise and organizational knowledge of more established Ibadhi institutions in Algeria.

To ensure that knowledge flowed in both directions, Istiqaama provided paid opportunities for Algerian teachers from Mzab to travel to Tanzania and Zanzibar and live in a culturally immersive environment while helping the schools to develop and teach their Arabic and Islamic programs.

Today, Al-Hayat recruits students from six "friendly countries," five of which are the African countries of Tanzania (including Zanzibar), Tunisia, Libya, Senegal, and Mali.[38] They also recruit students from Oman. Of the East African students who study in the Mzab, a majority come from the Istiqaama schools in Zanzibar and belong to the Omani diaspora. Algeria provides scholarship opportunities for Tanzanian students to study at universities in major cities located in the country's northern region, in Oran, Algiers, and Constantine. Al-Hayat covers tuition, room, board, and healthcare for their recruits from East Africa, but parents must purchase their students' flight tickets. The scholarships are strictly for study at the institute and do not guarantee entrance or support for study at Algerian universities on graduation. When students finish form 6 or grade 12 in Algeria, they must return to Tanzania and apply for the Ministry of Education scholarship to return abroad for college.

In a call for applications for the 2017–2018 academic year, the ministry announced that the government of Tanzania received forty scholarships for students to study in Algeria. There were three scholarships available for French study in the medical sciences and twenty-seven available for graduate degrees in the sciences. In addition, there was one scholarship for studies in transportation offered for both French and English speakers and religious affairs, presumably taught in Arabic. The main eligibility requirement for Tanzanian students applying for scholarships in the religious studies programs in Algeria is a certificate of completion for form 4 or grade 9 and a "good knowledge of the holy Koran."[39]

The University of Dar es Salaam does not accept certificates (*cheti*) showing the completion of secondary school from Algeria, so students must present evidence of the curriculum at the Hayat Institute to demonstrate that its standards of education match those of Tanzania. To accommodate its international graduates, the institute offers to print certificates and supporting materials in the language of the student's intended recipient. According to the students, it is much easier to receive scholarships to study in Malaysia, which recently signed a five-year memorandum of understanding with Algeria.[40]

When asked whether they felt their education abroad would position them well in an era of globalization, students in the Ilala mosque generally replied by saying that a knowledge of Arabic is not always useful outside of Algeria and that the emphasis on religion does not prepare them well for careers in business. As such, the Ibadhi youth who travel to Algeria from Zanzibar are now participants in a global Ibadhi movement aimed at reforming religious education to include secular subjects such as math, science, composition, and computer studies; and the college-educated Algerian teachers recruited to teach at Istiqaama in Tanzania are stalwarts of this reform, working closely with local Ibadhi leaders on curriculum development, girls' religious education, and the exchange programs between Zanzibar and Algeria. In addition to their religious and linguistic expertise, these teachers bring with them a vision of Ibadhi associational life and educational reform that is deeply informed by their own experiences growing up in a close-knit Ibadhi enclave in the Mzab Valley.

This cross-continental Ibadhi network driven by Istiqaama and Al-Hayat is an example of the new religious diplomacy between countries of the Global South that combines Islamic reform with socioeconomic development.

## Adapting to Life in North Africa

Students from Tanzania who are new in Algeria must rely on family members, friends, and fellow students who have studied there to help them transition to the new social and educational environment. As Fahmy, an eighteen-year-old philosophy and Arabic literature student in his fifth year at Al-Hayat and a fan of the twelfth century Andalusian philosopher Ibn Rushd (Averroes) said, "We teach our fellow [students] how to plan (*wanajipanga*). We have taken note of these [shared] ideas. We must create unity [among ourselves]."[41] He said that there was unity (*umoja*) among the residents of the Mzab because "they have their own [Ibadhi] religion." In contrast, he felt Tanzania lacked unity because people there adhered to so many different religions.

Perhaps to address this weak sense of Tanzanian unity in Algeria, the Association of Tanzanian Students in Algeria (ATSA) was developed in 2002. Headquartered in Algeria, the ATSA now has chapters in major cities across the country and holds formal elections for its leadership. The members of ATSA are university students on government scholarships. According to Haidar, a graduate of the Istiqaama Institute in Zanzibar, the ambassador has a special discretionary fund, part of which he uses to support the activities of the students.[42] Haidar said that he and other Zanzibaris met the ambassador in 2018 while attending an ATSA meeting at the Tanzanian embassy.

For some students, however, studying abroad in Algeria was considered an easy transition because it didn't require them to worry about things like finding Halal meat, as would be the case if they had studied in London. Muhammad, a twenty-two-year-old former student who attended secondary school in Arabic language (*al-thanawiyya*) at Al-Hayat, said that although it was difficult to find certain East African foods in Algeria, he enjoyed living somewhere with "four seasons."[43] He now sells clothes for a living and teaches at the Tandika Ibadhi mosque located in Dar es Salaam's district of Temeke. He explained that he did not have other options for study after graduation.

To address language barriers during their first year at Al-Hayat, all students from East Africa study Arabic along with a few other subjects; thereafter, all their courses are in Arabic except for French or English language courses. The students in Ilala agreed that a year of intensive Arabic was enough to prepare them for coursework in Algeria as they had already studied the language at Istiqaama. After hours, in their dorms and in between classes, however, they said they often speak Swahili with their East African peers. They also try to reproduce a sense of home by cooking *pilau*, *chapatis*, and sugar-covered donut bites (*visheti*).[44]

At the time of my visits to the Ilala mosque, I learned from members of the Istiqaama women's group that there were no female students from their community or from the school in Pemba who studied abroad at Al-Hayat.

However, girls who studied at the Istiqaama school and institute in Tungu, on Unguja Island, did go to Algeria on scholarship. The male students who attended Al-Hayat recalled that there was a separate "Madrasa al-Hayat for girls," where the focus is on the "domestic sciences," like home economics and sewing.[45]

## Haidar: The Unguja Route

When I met Haidar, who lives in Zanzibar Town and is not part of the Pemban group, he had just returned from his first year of study at Al-Hayat in Algeria.[46] Haidar was born in Rukwa, a region of mainland Tanzania. His father had earlier moved there for work from his hometown of Mwera in Zanzibar. As such, Haidar identifies as Zanzibari (Sw. *mtu wa Unguja*) and explains that he inherited his Ibadhi identity from his elders, whose direction he followed as a boy. He insists that while children ought to follow the leadership of their elders, only through studying can one obtain a deeper knowledge of their faith. After completing Form 4 in 2016 and spending a year in the advanced Arabic and Islamic Law (Shari'a) program at the Istiqaama Institute on Unguja Island, Haidar received an opportunity in 2018 to go to Al-Hayat in Algeria to continue his studies with the same focus. He explained that the leadership of Istiqaama and Al-Hayat, though independent of each other, shared the same objectives regarding the education of their communities' youth. "Because their goal is to provide expertise (*kutoa taaluma*) [and] skills for students," he said, "and to make students familiar with good Islamic behavior. That is the goal of all Istiqaamas. And to give aide also (*na kutoa misaada pia*)."[47]

The "good behavior" of a student and strong academics, serve as the primary criteria for teachers as they select who will benefit from study abroad in Algeria and Oman. East African students sent to Algeria and Oman represent their countries of origin as cultural ambassadors. Haidar explains that high marks on school or national examinations do not guarantee that one will receive a scholarship from Al-Hayat as might be the case for students who apply to study on government scholarships: "Over there [at Tungu], there are many things that they look for. Behavior (*tabia*), the behavior of a person, because even I am gifted, they look for behavior. So [it amounts to] good behavior, one's efforts, and the desire to [learn] more. Those students who go [abroad] and strive [to succeed] and are brave (*hodari*), they are the ones [endowed] with the opportunity, eh. So, the teachers themselves sit in a meeting, and they choose the students . . . so you receive the opportunity."

Before departing for Ghardaïa and starting their studies at Al-Hayat, students learn about their future home from the Algerians who teach Arabic and religion at Istiqaama. Haidar reflected, "So, if you go outside to study, you take lessons before entering the classroom (*unajifunza madarasa kabla darasani*). So, if you study well, you learn many lessons before entering the classroom. You learn how to live with others. I believe it was Sheikh Mustafa who informed us of the environment [in Algeria]."[48]

Haidar credited the Algerian teachers with establishing the collaborative relationship between the two institutes—the one on Unguja Island and the one in Ghardaïa—and said that it was because of their efforts that these student-teacher exchanges were possible.

Once they begin their studies, students like Haidar, who specialize in Arabic and Shari'a, find that there are few ways to supplement their religious education with more "marketable skills,"[49] such as speaking French and English and using computers. Moreover, while the students of Shari'a do participate in community events, dorm life, and school clubs, their classes are in a "special unit"—a college within the institute that separates them from their younger peers who study in the mixed curriculum of the madrasa. According to Haidar, "But in the classroom, our goal is specifically aimed towards Arabic and Islamic law. So, we did not have other studies in addition to those. I was hoping to study something like French—which, the secondary school students get the opportunity to study French and computer. And I have made that request, especially regarding the computer studies. They said they would work on it, inshallah."[50]

Students who study Shari'a generally end up in low-paying jobs (*kazi za chini*) when they return to Zanzibar, being best qualified to serve as teachers of Arabic and religion at private schools like Istiqaama that recognize their foreign certificates. Haidar already teaches these subjects as a volunteer at Istiqaama during his breaks. In keeping with the generally optimistic tone of his responses, however, he determined that when studying any given subject, a person must have both long- and short-term goals and consider what the benefit of a particular course of study has for their community: "So, when someone studies something, they should consider, 'What is my community missing in this area? If I go over there [to study], how important will my return be?' [The value of that is greater] than going to get something that people have already entered [into], have already studied. Eh, *that's* when you [decide to] go over there [to Algeria] . . . in search for something new [and] to address what is lacking. *That* is what is helpful."[51]

Haidar admitted feeling homesick, but he emphasized that he was self-motivated to study abroad and that this made it easier to garner confidence to overcome the challenge of being far from home. He recommended that any student opting to study in Algeria be flexible and open to change. "It is not that it is an easy thing; it is a *big* deal to reach your goals. [But over there] you study well, you sleep well, so those are the important things. The other stuff is manageable—you tolerate it."[52] Haidar aspires to obtain a master's degree in religion and Arabic but recognizes that this will not happen overnight and that, in the meantime, he should take advantage of being in a language-immersive school within an Arabic-speaking country. He explained,

> Without a doubt, that country is an Arabic country, so the language of the teachers will be at a higher level than here [in Zanzibar].... And those of us who have gone to study there see that ... eh, they are teachers that have studied in the *big* universities. Teachers that studied up to Medina, Mecca. This is not the case with the teachers that are here [in Zanzibar]. So, this guides the students. If he [the student] returns here, he will be different from the time he left to study. It is only natural that he would be different than those who study here.[53]

Arabic has been the primary language of instruction in Algerian government schools since the 1980s because most regions of the country had shifted from a bilingual French and Arabic system of instruction to a monolingual Arabic one by that time. The Arabization project of the post-colonial state aimed to replace spoken languages and dialects of Arabic with the standardized version of classical Arabic (*fuṣḥa*) taught in schools.

The suppression of the Berber language and identity led to fierce political protest against Arabization during the Berber Spring of 1980, which resulted in the Algerian government's recognition of Tamazight as an official language in 2001.[54] In my conversations with students in Dar and Zanzibar about their time abroad in Algeria, no one commented on the cultural specificities of the Mzab beyond highlighting its importance as a center of Ibadhi Islam. This suggests that students have limited interaction with the community around the Arabic-centric learning environment of the Al-Hayat and that the schools in the Mzab have adopted an apolitical stance like that of Istiqaama. The emphasis on Arabic-language immersion also positions Al-Hayat as an authority and competitor in the Algerian national education system and an international center for the study of Islam. Haidar explains that the Algerian teachers are experts in Arabic because they studied at major universities in

Algeria or traveled abroad to other centers of Islamic learning in places like Saudi Arabia. For Haidar, studying with such role models is motivating and transformative. It also sets him and his fellow travelers apart from their peers, who do not or cannot pursue such opportunities abroad.

### An Algerian Scholar on Pemba Island

In the short, published diary *Muthakirāt min A'māq Jazīra Zinjibār* (Memoirs from the Depths of the Island of Zanzibar), a young Algerian teacher named Qasim bin Ahmad al-Sheikh Balhaj recounts his travels from Algeria to Tanzania in 1998. He details his impressions of the East African Ibadhi community and the Istiqaama schools it runs in Zanzibar. Balhaj is one of the first Algerian teachers Ibadhi leadership recruited to build the Islamic studies and Arabic programs at the Istiqaama schools.

He first learned about the opportunity to teach abroad from two Algerian sheikhs in Al-Guerrara while he was teaching at a government primary school. His uncle Muhammad al-Sheikh Balhaj was the head teacher of Al-Hayat and served as mediator between his nephew and the two sheikhs responsible for developing collaborations with the Ibadhi communities in East Africa.

Balhaj cited two main motivations for wanting to teach abroad. First, he hoped to avoid the national service that was obligatory for all Algerian males nineteen years and older. Second, he desired to see and experience life in these other places whose histories he had studied. Balhaj and three "brothers" received invitations to teach in Zanzibar, although they did not depart together as planned.[55]

After boarding a flight that passed through the Cairo and Kampala airports in January 1999, Balhaj eventually landed in Dar es Salaam, where members of the Istiqaama Association were awaiting his arrival. Among those waiting was Maher (see chap. 2) of the Jabir bin Zayd Mosque in Dar es Salaam. Later that same day, Balhaj met Muhammad Tiwani, with whom he would eventually work at the Istiqaama institute in Pemba. Balhaj wrote the following about Tiwani: "And he is among those who came to Algeria more than once, accompanying the students of the Zanzibar mission. He welcomed me and I handed him the messages sent by their students to their families and books I had in my possession from Wadi Mzab. And I remember that evening he asked me to change my French clothes, which I brought and handed me Omani clothes instead. This is due to several considerations, some of which are my security."[56]

There is an expectation for foreign teachers employed by Istiqaama to conform to the norms of the Ibadhi and Arab diaspora in Tanzania, which involves wearing the Omani kanzu and kofia, eating African and Zanzibari foods, and gaining a familiarity with Swahili. For Balhaj, this resulted in his wistful reflection that he had transformed "to the extent that nothing remained of my Mozabiteity but my Algerianity."[57] As part of his cultural immersion and integration into the local Ibadhi community, the author stayed on the outskirts of Dar es Salaam at the home of a pious Ibadhi businessperson named Sheikh Ahmed al-Badri, who spoke Arabic fluently and had lived and studied in Oman. Four of the family's children studied at Al-Hayat.[58]

In Dar es Salaam, he remarked on the contrasts he observed, first juxtaposing the city's green suburbs against its clear blue sky and "the calm of its sea"[59] and then comparing the stark class inequalities and relative poverty of the African majority with the relative wealth of the city's (notably Indian) business elite. After acclimating to life there, Balhaj departed for Zanzibar and began his teaching appointment at the Istiqaama secondary school in Chake Chake, Pemba. He also visited the Istiqaama Institute on Unguja, which he referred to as "a fortress, for shaping generations."[60]

The total number of students in both schools in 1999 was one hundred thirty and their ages ranged from sixteen to twenty-five; most had attended government schools until middle or high school before leaving to enroll at Istiqaama. The secondary school in Chake Chake had eighty students, while the institute comprised a more selective population of fifty male youth representing Ibadhi communities across the region, including distant mainland cities such as Tabora, Mwanza, and Bukoba. Balhaj characterized the students as an emergent "elite that will be able in the future to turn the wheel of reform and change and development in this emerging homeland."[61] He remarked that the Ibadhi community in Zanzibar was in dire need of social and scientific reform, "especially concerning the Shari'a sciences and Islamic Studies and humanities in general."[62] Graduates of Istiqaama, he observed, would join the workforce or accept an assignment to serve as an imam in a town or village (whether on the islands or the mainland) that had a sizable Ibadhi population. Others would receive scholarships to study law, preach, or offer religious guidance in Oman.[63]

At the Istiqaama secondary school in Chake Chake, Balhaj joined a collegial group of young faculty that included Ibadhi and Shafi'i teachers "who were able to obtain Arabic-language lessons here and there in Zanzibar, Dar es Salaam, or others."[64] At the time of his appointment, the Istiqaama leadership opened a Quran school for girls that was in such demand that "the group was forced to close the registration doors days after they were opened due to overcrowding of the halls."[65] The two hundred enrollees were Ibadhi and Sunni girls aged five to twelve who came from all over the island. The school divided the girls into three levels of study based on their degree of education and made space for new classes at the boys' secondary school between the sunset and nighttime prayers. Balhaj marvels at the extra time and energy that his delayed Algerian colleague, brother Yusuf, invested instructing, supervising, and guiding the girls school curriculum. He attributes Yusuf's passion for the school, in part, to his prior experience working "in the field of girls' education" in Wadi Mzab, recounting that Yusuf quickly won their hearts so that they became "like his daughters."[66] Particularly popular among the female students were the classes dedicated to memorizing songs, hymns, and supplications, which familiarized them with the sound and pronunciation of Arabic. Yusuf recruited high-achieving students to assist with teaching and supervising the work of their peers in the classroom.

At the request of the local leadership in Chake Chake, Balhaj composed "a written program that carries a vision for the functioning of these schools, with vaccination recommendations according to the experience of the Mzabi school."[67] The program proposed separate learning materials and class periods on specific days of the week for the study of the Qur'an, the prophetic hadith, and Arabic, which also included praise poems and supplications. In the class period devoted to Arabic, for example, he suggested that the focus be on the correct pronunciation of the Arabic alphabet and recommended that teachers identify specific letters, such as the "qaaf" and the "daad," which were particularly "difficult for the Swahili tongue to pronounce."[68] With this foundation, students would be ready to transition to the study of "word formation, sentence structure, and training in reading and proper reading."[69] Students would retain what they learned through individual and group recitations, writing practice, and the use of "dictation, dialogue, and conversation."[70]

### Rachid: An Algerian Ibadhi Teacher in Zanzibar

After Balhaj's arrival, other Algerian teachers received appointments to teach at the Istiqaama Institute in Zanzibar. In 2016, I met with a teacher called Rachid, who began teaching at the institute in 2011. In addition to Tamazight and French, Rachid is fluent in formal Arabic, spoke some English, and was learning Swahili from his students and other staff members at Istiqaama. Our conversation took place in a combination of these languages.

We met during one of his free periods at school, and he wore the Algerian version of the prayer cap and robe that characterizes the teachers' uniforms. A native of Ghardaïa, he had moved to Zanzibar with his family a few years before. About ten years prior, he had developed an interest in East Africa while studying at the Emir Abdelkader University[71] of Islamic Sciences in Constantine, which sits near the border with Tunisia. There, he had specialized in communications and taken courses on the development of Islam in Africa. He had visited Tunisia often during his studies, and Ibadhi students from Tunisia and Libya would come to the Mzab to study at Al-Hayat.[72]

When students returned to their home countries after studying away in Algeria, many became respected Ibadhi scholars, following a long tradition of regional Ibadhi intellectual in North Africa. This was also the case for ʿAli Yaḥya Muʿammar (1919–1980), who was born around Nālūt, in Jabal Nafusa, and educated in the school of the ʿAzzābī scholar ʿAbdul bin Masʿud al-Kabawi before attending a primary school opened by the Italian colonial administration. Muʿammar also studied in scholarly circles (*ḥalqas*) in Jerba Island and the Mzab at Al-Hayat.[73] However, these North African Ibadhi exchanges halted for a time under the postcolonial leadership and long-standing authoritarian rule of Habib Bourguiba, who was succeeded by Zine al Abidine Ben Ali in Tunisia and by Muammar Ghadafi in Libya, both of whom did not look kindly on the Ibadhi communities in their countries. Rachid explained that all these figures were, "tough on the Ibadhiyya so ... [there was] no relation at that time, I think more than twenty-five years. Now after Bourguiba and after Ben Ali and Ghadafi, the relations [have changed]. They come to Algeria to visit, and people from the Mzab go to Libya and Tunisia for visits."[74] He was referring to the largely youth-led Arab Spring that sparked protests across North Africa in 2011 and resulted in both the overthrow of Ben Ali and in the capture and killing of Ghadafi by Libya's National Transitional Forces.[75]

While at university in Constantine, Rachid met some of the Algerian teachers from Istiqaama who put him in touch with the leadership in Zanzibar. Through them, he received an invitation to move to Unguja to teach Arabic and the Islamic sciences at Istiqaama in Zanzibar. He reflected that while Islamic education is quite strong there, the schools needed teachers who had both a better grasp of the Arabic language and greater organization as he was accustomed to in the Mzab.[76] From his perspective, Ibadhis were hardworking and very "strict" in their religious practice, and Ibadhi institutions in Algeria were "old." In contrast, the institutions of the Ibadhi community in Zanzibar were "young" and inexperienced in developing educational and social programs. "In Algeria it is more serious than here ... because in Africa you see everything is simple and the work isn't strict. But in Algeria ... [among] the Mozabite ... the organization is good, more than the African people."[77] He attributes this organization to the history of the Ibadhi institution of the imamate and the 'azzāba in Algeria.

Rachid's story reveals another side of Algerian-Tanzanian relations, one in which the largely Black African societies south of the Sahara are no longer just the "receiving nation" to which wealthier Arab states offer aide, educationals, and/or employment opportunities. Rather, the African societies of Tanzania and Zanzibar are also places of curiosity and opportunity for young North African Muslim scholars interested in expanding their horizons and contributing to the growth of Ibadhi communities elsewhere. Given these mutual interests and collaborative efforts, it was odd that Rachid made a separation between "Africa" and "Algeria," creating a curious distinction between the northern and southern regions of the continent. While unintended, the passive distinction recalls racialized French colonial policies that viewed the Islam of Black Africa (Islam Noir) as a more diluted form of Islam—one lacking solemnity in comparison with the more original and "strict" Islam practiced by the light-complexioned Arabs and Berbers of the north. Compounding this idea was the language of African "simplicity," which he attributed to the newness of Muslim organizational life in Zanzibar.

During his time at Istiqaama, Rachid advocated for the introduction of more technical skills and scientific research methods into the curriculum to improve student writing while also generating interest in preserving local histories. To start, he introduced a thesis requirement for graduating students, like the one already in place at Al-Hayat. He explained, "We began [the thesis requirement] two years ago, last year and the year before that. Previously, it was handwritten, but in the past year they started writing it by computer. I aim to make students' work more scientific ... [the student theses] are special for the culture for Zanzibar."[78] Rachid was familiar with social scientific methods from the extensive ethnographic research he did for his own postgraduate thesis (*mājastīr*) about a local radio program associated with an Ibadhi mosque in the Mzab region.

He observed, however, that there was little emphasis on research and writing in Zanzibari schools. As a result, recent works on Zanzibar are from the perspective of authors living in other countries. He cited as examples two well-known Arabic and Swahili histories of Zanzibar and the revolution, composed by writers of Omani heritage who now reside in Oman but maintain ties to Zanzibar.

Rachid and his family resided on the Istiqaama campus, living in one of the small bungalows built to accommodate teachers. The bungalows were arranged in a row beyond the classrooms and administrative buildings. "Life is good," he said reflecting on his time in Zanzibar. "It's very simple, but it is good, because people are very helpful and friendly. So, it is good for me, right now. It is good."[79] When I returned to Zanzibar in the summer of 2019, Rachid had already left Istiqaama, having accepted a teaching position in Oman.

Haidar and Rachid both express a desire for introducing social scientific research methods into the curriculums of Istiqaama and Al-Hayat to improve student writing and generate interest in preserving local histories. Both have used their knowledge and expertise to make a positive impact on their communities, showing that learning from and in a foreign context can be beneficial for both individuals and their Ibadhi communities.

## Conclusion

During the postcolonial period, Algeria and Tanzania have had a close and supportive relationship based, in part, on their shared history of colonization and liberation struggles in the 1950s and 1960s. For example, Algerian president Houari Boumediene provided military training and logistical assistance to other African countries, while Tanzania's first president Julius Nyerere supported nationalist movements such as the African National Congress (ANC) in South Africa and the Mozambique Liberation Front (FRELIMO).[80] They prioritized Pan-Africanism, self-reliance, and socio-economic development with an African and decolonial framework.[81] Although they did not fully achieve their economic and political goals, the shared socialist values of the two countries created a strong foundation for ongoing economic and political cooperation between the two countries which is little documented in scholarly works. For instance, the Algerian national oil company, Sonatrach, has partnered with Tanzania's natural gas industry, and there have been collaborations in sectors like agriculture, energy, infrastructure development, and trade.[82] Additionally, they are generally united in key issues affecting the continent, such as peacekeeping and supporting each other's causes in regional and international forums.

Through student exchanges, and academic and cultural programs such as those described in this chapter, Tanzania and Algeria have fostered mutual dependence and goodwill. Non-governmental educational partnerships like Istiqaama and Al-Hayat indirectly participate in this practice. Just as Istiqaama in Tanzania sends students to Oman to study Arabic and Islamic studies and subsequently recruits them as teachers and administrators after graduation, likewise, Algeria is a popular destination for Muslim students to study abroad. The branches of Istiqaama on Pemba play a significant role in connecting east and west through study abroad programs in Algeria and hiring Algerian teachers for Arabic and religious subjects. These connections hold religious and diplomatic power, aligning with past decolonization efforts that transcended borders and continents, relying on pan-African alliances and non-Western ways of knowledge, including socialist governance and Islamic learning. Istiqaama serves as a compelling example of the vital role that Muslim-minority and diaspora communities play in fostering informal diplomatic relations between countries of the Global South, providing new and underrecognized frameworks for cross-continental foreign policy.

**Notes**

1. Anne K. Bang, "Authority and Piety, Writing and Print: A Preliminary Study of the Circulation of Islamic Texts in Late Nineteenth- and Early Twentieth Century Zanzibar," *Africa* 81, no. 1 (2011): 89–107; Amal Ghazal, *Islamic Reform and Arab Nationalism: Expanding the Crescent from the Mediterranean to the Indian Ocean (1880s–1930s)* (New York: Routledge, 2014).

2. Jomier explained how anthropological studies of the Mzab "religious evolutions," both in the region and within Ibadhism, were "preoccupied more with the quest for Berber social structures and facts"; Jomier, *Une histoire*, 17.

3. Augustin Jomier, email correspondence with author, August 11, 2023. See also Cyrille Aillet, *L'ibadisme dans les sociétés de l'Islam médiéval: Modèles et interactions*, vol. 33, Studies in the History and Culture of the Middle East (Berlin: De Gruyter, Inc., 2018).

4. Paul M. Love Jr., *Ibadi Muslims of North Africa: Manuscripts, Mobilization, and the Making of a Written Tradition* (Cambridge: Cambridge University Press, 2018).

5. UNESCO World Heritage List, "M'Zab Valley," accessed October 27, 2020, https://whc.unesco.org/en/list/188/.

6. The town and city names are: El-Atteuf, Bounoura, Melika, Ghardaia, and Isguen.

7. Jomier, *Une histoire de L'Ibadisme en Algérie*, 14.

8. Rachid (Arabic and Islamic Studies teacher at Istiqaama), interview with author, Zanzibar, January 15, 2016.

9. Ghazal, "Countercurrents: Mzabi Independence, Pan-Ottomanism and WWI in the Maghrib," *First World War Studies* 7, no. 1 (2016): 81.
10. Majmūʿa min al-bāḥithīn, "Niẓām al-ʿAzzāba," 702.
11. Ibid., 703.
12. Augustin Jomier, email correspondence with author, August 11, 2023.
13. Ghazal, "Countercurrents," 81.
14. Institut Elhayat, "About," *Facebook*, n.d., accessed March 25, 2024, https://www.facebook.com/Institut.Elhayat/about.
15. Institut Elhayat.
16. Ghazal, "Countercurrents," 81.
17. Augustin Jomier, email message to author, August 11, 2023.
18. Institut Elhayat, "About."
19. Institut Elhayat.
20. Ibid.
21. Augustin Jomier, "Les réseaux étendus d'un Archipel Saharien. Les circulations de lettrés Ibadites (XVIIe Siècle-Années 1950)," *Revue d'histoire moderne & ontemporaine* 2 (2016): 26–27.
22. Amal N. Ghazal, "The Other 'Andalus': The Omani Elite in Zanzibar and the Making of an Identity, 1880s–1930s," *The MIT Electronic Journal of Middle East Studies* 5 (2005): 48.
23. Institut Elhayat, "About."
24. Institut Elhayat.
25. For more on the history of Islamic education in the Mzab, read: Jomier, *Une histoire de L'Ibadisme en Algérie*.
26. Institut Elhayat, "About."
27. Institut Elhayat.
28. Tiwani, *Qamusi-Ssalaa*, 86.
29. Tiwani, *Qamusi-Ssalaa*, 51.
30. Ibid., 48.
31. Nathalie Arnold Koenings, "For Us It's What Came After: Locating Pemba in Revolutionary Zanzibar," in *Social Memory, Silenced Voices, and Political Struggle: Remembering the Revolution in Zanzibar*, eds. William Cunningham Bissel and Marie-Aude Fouéré (Dar es Salaam: Mkuki na Nyota, 2018), 150.
32. Arnold Koenings explains that the Swahili term for "satiety" used by Pembans to describe the island's immense wealth from their clove harvests in the 1950s is *shibe* from "the verb *ku-shiba*, 'to be satisfied/well-filled'" (Koenings, "For Us," 154).
33. Ibid., 164.
34. Ibid.
35. Ibid., 174.
36. The students were not aware of any Tanzanian Shiʿa students studying at Istiqaama in Pemba or the Hayat Institute.

37. Suleiman (Istiqaama Youth Organization leader), interview with author, Dar es Salaam, June 2, 2019.

38. Preliminary scholarship on FBOs in Ghana, where Muslims are an economically marginalized minority, reveals a new expression of Ibadhi Islam under the Istiqaama Muslim Organization established in the town of Wenchi in the early 2000s. See: Mahmud Mukhtar Muhammed and Umar Wahab Sina, "Faith in National Development: A Review of the Activities of the Istiqaama Muslim Organisation of Ghana" (International Conference on Religion and National Development, Kumasi, Ghana: Kwame Nkrumah University of Science and Technology (KNUST), 2018). According to the authors of this study, Alhaji Umar Adam Suleman, a native of Wenchi, Ghana, originally founded this branch of Istiqaama in 1994, before its official registration as a faith-based organization (FBO). Like its counterparts in East Africa, this branch of Istiqaama maintains a network of Ibadhi schools across the country and receives support from the organization's headquarters in the Sultanate of Oman (pp. 11–14). The senior high school run by Istiqaama in Wenchi has over one thousand students, 95 percent of whom are Muslim and 5 percent of whom are Christian (15). It is unclear, however, how many of the Muslim students identify as Ibadhi. As in Tanzania, students at the Istiqaama senior high school in Wenchi receive scholarships to study the Shariʻa sciences in Oman.

39. "Scholarships Tenable in Algeria for the Academic Year 2017/2018," *DreamjobzSTZ*, accessed October 9, 2020, https://dreamjobtz.blogspot.com/2017/06/tcu-scholarships-tenable-in-algeria-for.html.

40. The aim of the memorandum is "to expand their cooperation in the field of higher education in a bid to turn Malaysia into an educational hub in the region." See Bernama, "Malaysia, Algeria Sign MoU to Expand Cooperation in Higher Education," *New Straits Times*, December 5, 2016, accessed March 28, 2024, https://www.nst.com.my/news/2016/12/194663/malaysia-algeria-sign-mou-expand-cooperation-higher-education.

41. Fahmy (Al-Hayat student), interview with author, Dar es Salaam, June 3, 2019.

42. Haidar (Istiqaama graduate and Al-Hayat student), interview with author, Zanzibar, July 5, 2019.

43. Muhammad (former student at Al-Hayat), interview with author, Dar es Salaam, July 3, 2019.

44. Institut Elhayat, "About."

45. Al-Hayat students and graduates (notes from group meeting), interview with author, Ilala Mosque, Dar es Salaam, June 3, 2019.

46. We met at a bus stop near the Amani soccer stadium and then wandered around a high-traffic neighborhood some miles outside Stone Town looking for a quiet, secluded place to sit for the interview. Eventually, we settled on some stairs behind the bleachers, the best of our options but not one without commotion.

A scrimmage was taking place between two local teams simultaneously, and we frequently found ourselves talking over intermittent outbursts of cheers and shouts from the fans. For this reason, the recording was exceptionally difficult to make out.

47. Haidar, interview with author, July 5, 2019.
48. Ibid.
49. Loimeier, *Between Social Skills and Marketable Skills*.
50. Haidar, interview with author, July 5, 2019.
51. Ibid., italics are mine.
52. Ibid.
53. Ibid.
54. Gilbert Grandguillaume, "Country Case Study on the Language of Instruction and the Quality of Basic Education: Policy of Arabization in Primary and Secondary Education Algeria," *UNESCO Digital Library*, Education for All Global Monitoring Report 2005, 2004, 1–57.
55. Bālḥāj, Qāsim bin Aḥmad al-Shaykh. *Mudhakirāt Min A'māq Jazīra Zinjibār* (Al-Jazā'ir: Manshūrāt al-Tabyīn/al-Jāḥiẓīyah, 2001), 10.
56. Ibid., 18.
57. Ibid.
58. Ibid., 20.
59. Ibid.
60. Ibid., 70.
61. Ibid.
62. Ibid.
63. Ibid., 71.
64. Ibid., 80.
65. Ibid., 80–81.
66. Ibid., 81.
67. Ibid., 82.
68. Ibid., 83.
69. Ibid.
70. Ibid., 83–84.
71. The university's namesake is the Algerian Muslim reformer Abdelkader bin Muhieddine (1808–1883), who led the resistance against the French colonial invasion of Algeria in the nineteenth century.
72. Rachid, interview with author, January 15, 2016.
73. According to M. H. Custers, he held numerous positions in educational institutions in Libya after his return in 1945 and "in the middle of the seventies he set up Jam'iyyat al-Fatḥ and Madrasat al-Fatḥ in Tripoli." See M.H. Custers, *Al-Ibāḍiyya: A Bibliography*, vol. 2, Ibāḍīs of the Maghrib (Including Egypt) (Maastricht, Netherlands: Universitaire pers, 2006), 221. 'Alī Yaḥyā Mu'ammar

is the author of *Al-Ibāḍīyah bayna al-firaq al-Islāmīyah* (*The Ibadiyya: Between the Sects of Islam*) and other works on the history and thought of Ibadis.

74. Rachid, interview with author, January 15, 2016.

75. Oliver Holmes. "Arab Spring Autocrats: The Dead, the Ousted and Those Who Remain." *The Guardian*, December 14, 2020, accessed March 28, 2024, https://www.theguardian.com/world/2020/dec/14/arab-spring-autocrats-the-dead-the-ousted-and-those-who-survived.

76. Ibid.

77. Ibid.

78. Ibid.

79. Ibid.

80. Geoffrey Barei, "Britain and Algeria, 1945–1965" (Doctor of Philosophy (History), London, University of London, School for Oriental and African Studies, 2003), 171.

81. See for example, Black Panther Pete O'Neil's description of his time in both places while in exile in Paul J. Magnarella, *Black Panther in Exile: The Pete O'Neal Story* (Gainesville: University of Florida Press, 2020).

82. See: "Algeria, Tanzania Sign Six Memoranda of Understanding," *Qatar News Agency*, August 2, 2023.

# 5

## Ibadhi Migrations, Religion, and Commerce in the Lake Region

In June 2019, I took a two-day road trip starting from Mwanza, a boulder-rock port city on the southern shores of Lake Victoria, to visit several of the semi-arid, agricultural towns and villages where many Omani-Ibadhi families from the region had settled. The primary purpose of the trip was to retrace the steps of these enterprising arrivals who had come to Mwanza after first disembarking in coastal towns like Zanzibar. I was accompanied by Mariam (see chap. 1) and two of her sisters. One sister was about to graduate from high school and the other had recently returned to Tanzania from Abu Dhabi and was helping run the family café. I had been staying with their family in Mwanza that summer and through them was able to hire the driver and develop an itinerary that would enable us to connect with representatives of Ibadhi mosques and Istiqaama in each town we would visit. The phone introductions made to Ibadhi leaders in each place prior to our arrivals by their paternal uncle, the branch chairman of Istiqaama in Mwanza and owner of a major construction company, proved critical in dispelling any misgivings our hosts in each town might have had about my intentions for interviewing them.

In a boxy sedan owned and driven by a taxi driver who was occasionally in the employ of the family, we retraced the routes taken by the largely young, poor, and almost all male ancestors of the Ibadhis I had met in Mwanza. Most of the emigrees were petty traders or skilled workers who came from the desert interior region of Oman. At the time they left, interior Oman was ruled by an Ibadhi imam based in Nizwa. Ibadhi migrants would depart from the oasis towns and villages, where they were born and raised, heading first to the cosmopolitan seaports of Muscat and Sur located along the Arab/Persian Gulf. When the monsoon winds would allow, they would follow generations of Omanis before them who had boarded dhows or steamships to head south to Mombasa and Zanzibar. Having made it to the Swahili coast, the later migrants would find work through extended Omani family networks until they could save or borrow enough capital from relatives or Indian creditors to board another vessel that would transport them from the islands to other coastal towns like Dar es Salaam, Tanga, and Bagamoyo. There most would continue to "buy time,"[1] as historian Thomas McDow has noted of such migrations, working often as petty traders until they could afford to travel, or until an opportunity would present itself that would enable them to establish themselves in interior places and spaces. Some of them went to Mwanza and from there spread south through the territory of the Sukuma and Nyamwezi peoples to small trading centers.

I argue that colonial-era (ca. 1890–1950) Ibadhi migrations from coastal centers like Zanzibar to urban and rural places on the mainland enabled the growth of the religious and economic networks and towns that would become the basis of Istiqaama's economy, leadership, and branches in the greater Lake Region of northwestern Tanzania. When these later Ibadhi migrations began, Zanzibar was much more prosperous than Oman and still ruled by an Ibadhi sultan. My Ibadhi contacts in Tanzania tend to characterize Oman at that time as underdeveloped and drought-ridden, constantly embroiled in sectarian conflicts and divided between interior imamate and coastal sultanate rule. In the 1960s, after Zanzibari and Tanganyikan independence from European colonial rule—and following the Zanzibar Revolution—a series of failed socialist projects in the late 1960s and early 1970s further quickened an economic downturn at the very same time that the newly oil-rich Oman was rapidly growing its own economy under Sultan Qaboos. While Ibadhi migrations between the two countries never stopped, its dominant direction changed, with people of Omani heritage traveling to their ancestral homeland from Tanzania in search of asylum, citizenship, marriage partners, and/or better economic prospects in new industries like Oman's Petroleum Development Organization (PDO). The economic strains engendered by the idealist socialist project in Tanzania also stimulated a growth in internal migrations, with many Ibadhi rurally based families and youths closing their modest shops (*dukas*), boarding up their homes, and leaving their mosques in the hands of local caretakers and clients as they departed to try their luck in the country's urban centers.

This chapter shows how Istiqaama plays the part of a go-between—similar to the classic Swahili middleman or cultural broker in the nineteenth-century trade between the coast and interior—in the heritage conservation and economic activities of Ibadhis in Tanzania. Some of these Ibadhis are nationals and residents of Oman who are returning to the original towns and villages in which their ancestors settled in order to rediscover and preserve their heritage. These efforts can be seen both in physical renovations of historic Ibadhi sites and the development of new spaces, all under the guidance of Istiqaama. Additionally, the conservation of the Ibadhi-built environment is tied to other ways in which Ibadhis are documenting their heritage across Tanzania. This includes Omani TV series like *Min al-Sawāhil* (From the Coast), which nostalgically showcases Omani life and culture along the coast through interviews and site visits to farms, homes, and schools, the collection of Arabic manuscripts from private libraries and archives, and the sharing of personal histories and artifacts related to early settlers in the region. Prior to embarking on our road trip, following in the footsteps of my travel companions' ancestors, I had heard many stories about the first ancestor to arrive in colonial Tanganyika, Mzee Zahor from the Al-Farai clan of Oman. While the earliest Omani migrants traveled by foot along caravan trails, Mzee Zahor seems to have traveled to the interior after the establishment of the German colonial cross-country train system, so sometime in the late nineteenth and early twentieth century. Men such as Zahor and the Afro-Arab families they established were forebears who played a significant role in shaping the heritage and communal identity that Istiqaama is now dedicated to preserving.

## Early Migrations from the Coast: People of the Foot and People of the Rail

Most accounts of people of Omani-Arab descent in the Lake Region focus on "big men" traders in the nineteenth century who owned and operated massive caravans between there and the coast, staffed with porters carrying goods, food, tents, and large harems.[2] This chapter, however, focuses more on the stories of lesser-known Ibadhi-Omanis in the interior and their descendants' rise to success from poverty in the decades following independence from German (1885–1918) and then British (1916–1961) rule. Colonial-era Omani migrants who traveled across the East African mainland did so by train, unlike their precolonial forebears who arrived in the Lake Region from the coast on foot or caravan. The more ambitious and successful among them became caravan traders to interior spaces that would later become major commercial cities of the interior, like Tabora (roughly nine hundred miles from the coast) or Ujiji farther west and bordering Lake Tanganyika. These were key centers of ivory and slave trades, the latter dependent on the violent capture and exploitation of African peoples, many of whom originated from central Africa. In 1873 the British colonial government abolished the slave trade in Zanzibar, but the institution of slavery did not itself end until 1897.[3] In the twentieth century, when cross-country trains became available, newer waves of Omani traders from the coast disembarked at Tabora and then continued their journeys to cities like Mwanza on Lake Victoria or to remote interior villages.

I documented these stories through interviews with members of Istiqaama in the towns and villages of Sukumaland, often over a cup of Arabic coffee and dates, or accompanied by a guided tour of historic Ibadhi mosques and newer Istiqaama schools and family-owned factories. While primarily from the perspective of people of Omani ancestry in Tanzania, these interviews revealed how deeply intertwined African, Arab, Asian, and even European, histories were in the region.[4] They also showed the role of Istiqaama and local Ibadhi communities in setting standards of piety, intra-Muslim cooperation, and development in contemporary communities separated by miles of farmland and savannah. This chapter begins at the end of the nineteenth century with a brief history of Omani migrations and explaining the effects of the European colonial expansion on community, migration, religion, economy, and diaspora in the broader Lake Region of eastern Africa. The discussion then sheds light on the Omani diaspora's role in agriculture and industry in postindependence Tanzania and how these economic endeavors provided the financial and social foundation for Istiqaama's institutions and branches on the mainland.

## Mzee Zahor and the Trope of the Traveling Arab Confectioner

For his part, Mzee Zahor, the relative of my traveling companions, got his big break after meeting a Sukuma chieftain named Majebere in the coastal town of Tanga. He had arrived in the coastal city from Zanzibar and made a modest living practicing his trade as a confectioner of Omani sweet meats (*halwa*). According to Zahor's descendants in Mwanza, Chief Majebere so enjoyed the taste of the sweets that he invited him to travel with him back to his headquarters and establish a halwa shop there in what is now the remote city of Lalago (population under twenty-three thousand), part of the Maswa District in the semiarid Simiyu region about three and a half hours southeast of Mwanza by car. Simiyu borders the southern edge of the Serengeti and includes the Maswa Wildlife Game Reserve, which is made up of "rolling hills covered in thickets and rock outcrop known as kopjes ... interspersed with seasonally dry rivers containing permanent water holes."[5] The residents of this area are not strangers to wildlife, and the region has historically been a site for hunting and poaching wild game, a lucrative practice in which some of my Ibadhi interlocutors admitted their families were once involved. Zahor agreed on the condition that he would receive the protection of the chief as he journeyed toward the Lake Region. He then boarded a German train to Tabora and from there to the fishing village of Kagei (also known as Kayenze) outside of Mwanza, which was a historic point of encounter between African chiefs, Arab and Indian traders, and European missionaries and explorers. In Kagei, another Omani emigrant received Zahor and offered him a place to pray, rest, and acclimate to the new environment, hosting him in an Ibadhi mosque built for worship, communal gatherings, and travelers. The still-in-use, one-story mosque reflects the typical austerity of historic Ibadhi architecture,[6] without a minaret or outward or interior ornamentation. Like on the islands, this mosque was intended primarily for the use of local Omani families and their visitors. It continues to serve as a community center (Ar., *bayt jam'iyya*) for local Omani residents and travelers.

Zahor eventually left Kagei to settle in Lalago. He established a shop and acquired land through his marriage to one of Chief Majebere's daughters. Like the Omani diaspora in Tanzania, the Sukuma are patrilineal, and in some cases "practice polygamy, exchange bride wealth, and traditionally viewed land ownership as communal, with private family right of usufruct to specific plots of land."[7] It was typical for Omani immigrants of the Lake Region to marry Sukuma or Nyamwezi women, in part as a way of securing land rights and protection when they first arrived. Later in the 1970s and 1980s, foreign missionaries and aid workers in the region noted that emigrants from Oman would have one Arab wife born into an Omani family and one or more African wives.

Having established a social safety net and secured land for cultivation, Zahor became a farmer and in time purchased an ox-drawn plow (Sw., *machini ya n'gombe*) that helped him increase his annual yield. His labors served as the foundation of later economic activities of his descendants, who would eventually leave Lalago and settle in larger towns and regions where there were better economic prospects. These descendants would come to play an important role in the leadership of the Istiqaama Muslim Society in the postindependence period.

**Figure 5.1**: Historic Ibadhi Mosque, Kayenze Village, Mwanza Region, 2016. Photo by author.

Zahor's story is a typical account of Ibadhi migrations to the northwest, though his successes were relatively modest in comparison to other Omanis such as Thani bin Amir al-Harthi, who was himself a confectioner who had left his hometown in Nizwa due to the drought. In recounting Thani's career, McDow writes, "Less than twenty years later, he was one of the wealthiest traders in Kazeh, an ivory depot on the East African plateau, over four hundred miles from the Indian Ocean."[8] Trading caravans involved a cast of characters from diverse socioeconomic and ethnic backgrounds—different from the coast, where social stratification was well defined. The mobility and interdependence of the caravans meant that "ethnic and status hierarchies"[9] were in a state of constant formation. The constant interactions between the coast and interior, however, did inspire those of means to build "new settlements that looked like Indian Ocean towns and spread Swahili language and culture,"[10] so much so that the basic design of the Swahili house or Ibadhi mosque one would encounter in Zanzibar found their replicas in interior towns.

**Figure 5.2**: Omani House and Shamba (Farm), Kayenze, 2016. Photo by author.

## Anglo-German Colonial Rule in Victoria Nyanza (1890–1961)

The greater Lake Victoria region was not initially part of the Anglo-German Agreement of 1866, which separated mainland Tanzania (then Tanganyika) into two spheres of influence: one English and the other German.[11] In the 1880s, the European powers dispatched representatives from their chartered companies to serve as administrators in the resource rich and populous Lake Region, which was strategic because of its "location on the head-waters of the Nile."[12] In a subsequent act of imperial hubris in 1890, the same powers signed a treaty that enabled German forces to send a military expedition led by Emin Pasha, a former Ottoman governor in the upper Nile who had been driven out of southern Sudan during the Mahdist rebellion in 1889.[13] The two main military bases of the German colonial regime were in Bukoba, located on the southwestern shores of Lake Victoria, which from 1890 to 1894 was the main administrative center. Mwanza, at the time, "was the seat of the government for the south and east lake region under the control of non-commissioned officers."[14] In imposing their rule on local African communities, the military formed dubious treaties with Sukuma and Nyamwezi rulers or used brute force to bring the African rulers and their subjects to heel. In their attempts to establish a system of indirect rule, the colonial officers appointed governors called *liwalis* (often those claiming Arab or coastal Swahili origin) to govern in their place.¹⁵

In 1901, the construction of the British-funded Kenya-Uganda Railway facilitated the transport of passengers and goods from the coastal port of Mombasa to the port town of Kisumu on the banks of Lake Victoria. The railway, together with the steamers brought to the lake in 1904, stimulated what historian Buluda Itandala refers to as a "commercial invasion," bringing "new traders from the coast."¹⁶ Among them were Indians, Arabs, and Africans who served as intermediaries in the burgeoning illicit ivory trade.¹⁷ When they arrived, they set up shops where they would trade money and cloth for local resources, such as agricultural and animal products, produced by African farmers and pastoralists. Traders from the Arabian Peninsula and the Persian Gulf regions, especially, Oman, Yemen, and the Swahili-speaking communities of the coast, began to establish shops in rural areas far from Mwanza and Bukoba, notably in the regions and towns now known as Shinyanga, Simiyu, and Meatu. The gradual diversification of the economy in the interior decreased African participation in the caravan trade with the coast, and Mwanza grew as a regional center of trade connecting Tanganyika to the powerful kingdom of Buganda to the north across the lake.¹⁸

The presence of foreign traders in the lake region further enabled the German colonialists to transform Sukumaland from an economy of subsistence farmers and pastoralists to a peasant cash crop economy, based largely on the production of cotton. The drive to mass produce cotton for sale to Europe only intensified after Germany's defeat in World War I, after which the British government seized the African territories formerly under German control and formed a mandate called the Tanganyika Territory in 1920. It was in this context of colonization, capitalist enterprise, a transportation boom, and diminishing sovereignty of African rulers (*batemi*) in eastern Africa that new waves of Omani-Ibadhi traders began to arrive.

## Cotton Production and African Economic Organization

Cotton growing and textile production began thousands of years ago in East Africa, but the practice ceased in the mid-1800s because it became more cost efficient to import cloth from Europe. When the German colonizers reached the southern region of Lake Victoria in the 1880s, they found that cotton production had continued at a small scale and "German companies and settlers started growing cotton."¹⁹ Later in the early 1900s, in British-controlled

Uganda, the government had also begun to test grow Egyptian cotton in what would become the metropolitan centers of Entebbe and Kampala. In his autobiography *Dream Half-Expressed* (1966), Indian agriculturalist merchant and trader Nanji Mehta detailed how he made his fortune as an enterprising merchant from Gujarat. The book is at times paternalistic in its account of Mehta's interactions with African people, yet from his narrative, we learn the process by which Indian shop owners established themselves around Lake Victoria, gradually diversifying their businesses by experimenting with various forms of crop production. Mehta planted his first crop of Indian cotton behind the shop he had established in the forest several miles away from his main business in what was then the village of Kamuli. With the success of the crop, he "arranged with the native African people to gin it by hand" and used the fluffy white product for "stuffing beds and pillows" for sale.[20]

In 1909 a European, Indian, and African co-owned company called the Uganda Company Ltd. was formed to gin the cotton for export to England. As government interest and experimentation in cotton growing increased so did that of Indian merchants and African farmers. Expanding his business enabled Mehta to import more goods from Bombay and invest his profits from the sale of the goods into a network of rural shops, including one by the source of the Nile in Jinja, "two at Kamuli and two in the heart of the forest."[21] Privately owned Indian, German, and British companies and the colonial government of Uganda began to establish ginneries around the region, and Indian agents there "purchased unginned cotton from African farmers and dispatched it to the ginners."[22] Low paid African workers transported the cotton from the farm to the factories, workers who later had the added burden of paying the per capita tax that the government would later levy against the native population.[23]

Similar developments were underway in Tanganyika. As the cotton industry grew there, the colonial government noticed a shortage in the production and harvesting of the crop. To push forward with their economic agenda, they "decided to force the local population to grow cotton on plots,"[24] under oppressive labor conditions. The harsh policies eventually resulted in the Maji Maji rebellion against German rule, although ultimately unsuccessful and resulting in the death of many Africans involved is the most celebrated example of resistance European colonial rule in Tanzanian history.[25] The practice of forced labor in Tanganyika intensified under British rule during World War II and new sites of cotton production developed across the region as part of the Sukuma Land Development Scheme.[26] The largest growth in cotton production in the southern Lake Region occurred between the 1940s after the British took control at the end of World War I and the 1980s, under Julius Nyerere's postcolonial African government. In the late 1940s, African farmers in Tanganyika found that some of the ginning companies were cheating on the weight of their cotton at posts where the Lint and Seed Marketing Board had set the price. Following their protest, the growers established local scales for weighing the cotton before taking it to the regional markets. Local cooperative societies developed in rural Tanganyika for weighing and marketing.[27] The societies merged into the Lake Province Growers Association, which sent a delegation across the lake to Uganda to learn more about cooperative organization there. By the early 1950s, the colonial government had recognized the societies and appointed an officer to facilitate their operation.

Anthropologists Gottfried and Martha Lang attributed the success of the societies to preexisting Sukuma social and political organization into chiefdoms, village councils, strong and wide-reaching kinship networks, and mutual aid programs for crop cultivation and production.[28] By 1960, the societies had formed into unions that "owned and operated a total of 6 of the 19 ginneries in the areas."[29] They stored and bagged the raw cotton, recorded weights and paid the growers, while the unions transported cotton to the ginneries, where it was then dispatched to train depots.[30] The federation of unions set the policy for the sale of cotton and provided farm education and hostels for members of the cooperative societies.[31]

These societies proliferated widely but eventually showed signs of corruption and lost the faith of farmers. By the time President Nyerere began relocating rural people into villages as part of the postcolonial *Ujamaa* policies, the cooperative structure had disintegrated in favor of village committees in which membership was not voluntary and in which people did not have the expertise to cultivate cotton or set up lines of credit. In the mid-1980s, after the Tanzanian Cotton Authority failed to gain the trust or motivation of farmers to produce high-quality cotton, societies reemerged. "They were not voluntary, had no independent sources of finance and so depended on the government and donors, had management appointment by the government and were, ultimately, political rather than economic organisations [sic]."[32] A variety of financial and bureaucratic problems occurred to plague the new cooperatives, and farmers found themselves without pay for up to two years. The cotton remained in storage, unginned, for several seasons while its price depreciated. Towns like Lalago, the base of Chief Majebere,

**Figure 5.3**: "Jeshi la Vijana" (Youth Army) Stamp, Zanzibar and Tanzania, 1967. Ujamaa era stamp depicting villagization and agricultural reform. From the collection of Adam Gaiser.

were once the center of the cotton boom and major sites of Arab settlement, gradually lost their prominence as the cooperative societies became defunct. Though intended to create national solidarity through shared labor and resources without regard to ethnic or linguistic differences, the resulting effect was economic isolation, a scarcity of resources, and a thriving black market of imported goods in which Omani descendants became key middlemen. Those involved in this trade were generally from less well-established families, as Indians and Arabs of means had begun to migrate to major urban centers like Mwanza, Shinyanga, or Tabora—or "back" to Oman in the 1970s—to establish large shops and businesses in proximity of the government, ports, and larger markets. The Arab arrivals distinguished themselves from their South Asian counterparts by marrying into African families and establishing what are today some of the regions oldest surviving mosques and centers of rural Muslim life. The kinship ties, spirituality, religious architecture, and diverse industries, such as factories, cotton ginneries and construction companies, bind these physically distant Afro-Arab Ibadhi communities today. Familial, religious, and economic institutions are also the foundations of the Istiqaama charitable and educational networks in northwestern Tanzania.

The success of Istiqaama in Tanzania can be attributed to several main factors. The Omani diaspora, like other trading communities, has settled in a vast geographic area across Tanzania since the late nineteenth century. Like Mzee Zahor, after disembarking from Zanzibar or the cities of the coast, the ancestors of my Omani-Ibadhi interlocutors first journeyed to major commercial centers or post cities of the interior, such as Tabora, Mwanza, Bukoba or Ujiji, before being redirected by their predecessors to the remote towns and villages where other Omani-Ibadhi were settled. There they would be welcomed by kinsmen at the small community mosques that were multipurpose, serving as spaces for prayer and community gatherings, travel lodges, and soup kitchens. Mosque communities would assist newcomers in meeting local authorities, establishing their trades, and navigating the new linguistic and cultural contexts of their place of settlement. Traders sought protection and aid from local African authorities, such as the Sukuma chiefs, through marriage and gifts, and these cross-cultural bonds remain integral for the relative success of the Omani diaspora in Tanzania today. The branch and national leaders of Istiqaama tend to be male members of well-established Omani families who maintain good relations with Tanzanian state authorities and the broader African business community, and in many cases, they also have Omani citizenship or international economic networks. Donors from Oman contribute to Istiqaama projects in regions where they maintain personal ties, for example, in the villages their parents were born and where there exists a family house or a community mosque and graveyard. For these transnational philanthropists, supporting Istiqaama is also a way of preserving East Africa's Ibadhi heritage, which many see as an extension of Oman's heritage. Lalago, the now sleepy town where Mzee Zahor settled, is one of those places that Istiqaama has earmarked for restoration.

### Ibadhi Religious Education and Practice in the Rural Northwest: The Case of Lalago

At the center of the Lalago town square stands a colorful statue of President Nyerere, wearing the iconic "Kaunda suit."[33] The monument signals the town's full integration into postindependence Tanzania following the Arusha Declaration of 1967, which set out to define a particular brand of African socialism, or *ujamaa*. When we arrived in Lalago from Mwanza, most of the town's residents were out for the day with their livestock. They had taken the animals, along with their prepared foods and wares for sale, to attend the country's third largest auction. Most of the residents are subsistence farmers, though they sell or trade their surpluses.

Before the 1970s when Lalago's Ibadhi community began to leave for Oman or bigger cities, there were some fifty families from the Omani Al-Busaidi and Al-Aduani tribes living in Lalago. At that time, there were only two roads in the whole town. One street served as the parking lot for large machinery and vehicles, while the main street comprised a series of shops established by the first generation of Omani settlers in the town who specialized in the sale of clothing and fabric. When we arrived, we were greeted by the caretaker of the Ibadhi mosque, Mzee Idris, an elderly man of Somali heritage who grew up with the descendants of Zahor al-Farai in Lalago. He had been notified of our arrival by the chairman of Istiqaama in Mwanza and had prepared a mini tour of the sleepy town center. My companions greeted him with warmth, remembering him from visits to Lalago as young children. The Somali community in Lalago were neighbors of the Omanis for generations and bonded over their shared faith in Islam, trading interest, and newcomer status. Mzee Idris himself grew up on the same street as Zahor's relatives and was thus, as Mariam put it, "Ibadhi cultured," as this was the dominant expression of Islam in his community at the time.[34] With some exceptions, Ibadhi identity in rural Tanzania was historically determined through one's paternal Omani ancestry, regular attendance at Ibadhi mosques, or marriage into or close association with Omani-Ibadhi as in the case of Mzee Idris. Though not Omani, he is accepted as a member of Istiqaama through another form of kinship: his family's close association with the Al-Farai clan of Oman in Lalago. One of the ways Ibadhis are identified in Lalago is through the annual distribution of Ramadan dates shipped from Oman or the United Arab Emirates, which are delivered by Istiqaama to families affiliated with the Ibadhi mosque. Each Ibadhi family receives five boxes of dates that bear the label of Istiqaama. Mzee Idris explained, "Our family names are specified on those five boxes. That's how we understand who is [and who is not] Ibadhi."[35] Aside from the annual shipments of dates, the arrival of aid in the form of food, textbooks, and clothing is not a regular occurrence in rural towns and villages.

The town's first houses were thatched mudbrick ones (Sw., *makuti*) but were gradually rebuilt with corrugated iron roofs, cement blocks, and mortar with installation of running water and electricity. Taking us past the abandoned Omani homes on the desolate street across from the mosque, and now under

**Figure 5.4**: Storefronts of Omani Abandoned Shops, Lalago, Simiyu Region, 2019. Photo by author.

its care, Mzee Idris explained former Omani residents of Lalago either sold or designated their homes and stores as religious endowments (*awqāf*) when they relocated to Oman or regional urban centers in the 1970s.[36]

The small Ibadhi mosque in Lalago sits across the main street from a series of boarded up "ghost houses" (Sw., *magofu*), which are a favored nesting place of the local bat population. Istiqaama has plans to renovate the houses into schools and health care centers and designate the shops as part of a waqf (religious endowment), the proceeds of which would go toward the upkeep of the new buildings on their completion. Mzee Idris explained that leaders from the organization's headquarters in Dar es Salaam had come by to measure and take pictures of the vacant Arab family homes to assess their market value. The rural town has both private and government primary and secondary schools. Before the Istiqaama boarding school opened in Shinyanga, located about 78 kilometers southwest of Lalago, Ibadhi youth in rural areas would study the

Qur'an in the mosque, a practice that continues today under the guidance of a Sunni teacher. Mzee Idris pointed to a corridor in the Lalago mosque where the classes take place and recalled that the teacher did not spare the rod when students got out of hand or failed to master a lesson.

The teacher who served the mosque at the time of our visit to Lalago did not have the same reputation for harsh punishment. Mzee explained that while he can teach Qur'anic recitation and basic language and is familiar with Ibadhi teachings, he has not had much advanced religious education neither in Tanzania nor abroad. "He did not go to Muscat, he did not go to university... truthfully, he has not gone anywhere, but he knows how to recite Quran. He has studied the principles of Ibadhism and understands them. So, he went to secondary school and completed Form 2. And as it came to pass, he ended up in a corner, and he did not continue."[37] The statement highlights the role and limitations of the mosque teacher in Lalago, emphasizing his knowledge in Qur'anic recitation and basic teachings of Ibadhism, despite not having advanced religious education. This indicates a gap in formal training but also underscores the importance of practical knowledge and understanding of the community's beliefs.

The Ibadhi community in Lalago had been without a mosque teacher for a year before the recent hire. His initial compensation was room and board and irregular salary of donations, which eventually became unsustainable for a young man living far from home and no prospects of stable future employment. Mzee explained, "But he does well by us, what I mean is, he leads prayer and teaches the children over there [in the mosque]. So, the Istiqaama leadership in Mwanza told us to wait, when we have succeeded [in securing funds] we will tell you. However, we continued to fundraise little by little among ourselves. It was not an open practice; everyone was just giving him something secretly, not openly. Therefore, no one knew how much you gave him."[38]

He recently approached the mosque community to receive regular payment, and they were able to fulfill the request after the Omani Ambassador to Tanzania visited Lalago with an Ibadhi delegation from Mwanza. The ambassador agreed to pay the teacher a salary of 150,000 TZS per month or $64.32 for one year, a modest amount but certainly a boost until the year came to an end and the same problem arose. While they made requests for more support, Mzee feared that in the interim the teacher would find the financial insecurity of his position unsuitable and decide to leave with little notice. Compounding the issue of low teacher pay is a problem of student retention and uneducated parents who earn low incomes and see little point in sending their children to school when they could be earning money for their families by hawking eggs or peanuts to passengers at bus stops.

While male members of the Ibadhi and Sunni community attend prayers there regularly, the old Ibadhi mosque has not yet expanded to include a women's section. Its male members usually gather at the Sunni Friday mosque (Sw., *msikiti wa ijuma*) just a few streets away for weekly congregational prayers. This situation highlights gender disparities within the Ibahdi community, reflecting broader societal norms and practices. In this community, women are actively involved in domestic roles and grassroots religious activities, but they have limited visibility in public spheres or leadership roles (see chap. 6). Additionally, there seems to be uncertainty or conflicting sentiments within the Ibadhi community regarding the obligation to accommodate and participate in Friday prayers, though space is made available by their Sunni neighbors.

Mzee Idris mentioned Mufti Al-Khalili's return to Tanzania in the 1990s as the moment when the Ibadhi community began to participate in the congregational prayers. "When he came, he counseled all the men here to pray the Friday prayer. That they should be doing Friday prayer, not the travel prayer. They had prayed the traveling prayer (*ṣalāt al-safar*) the whole time. Up until some of them laid to rest, they continued to pray the travel prayer."[39] In the ritual primer *Talqīn as-Ṣibyān* by the celebrated Ibadhi scholar Nūr Al-Dīn al-Sālimī (1869–1914), the author details the prescriptions of the travel prayer: "If you happen to be traveling, you are obligated to shorten [the prayer] (*idha kunta musāfiran wajaba 'alayka 'an taqsura*). [You should perform] two prayer cycles (*raka's*) for each of the afternoon prayers (*az-zuhr*), and the evening prayers (*al-'asr*) and the final night prayer (*al-isha al-akhīra*). So, you would pray two cycles for the *zuhr* prayer, and two cycles for the *'asr* prayer and two cycles for the *'isha* prayer."[40]

Al-Salimi explains that the person performing the travel prayer could perform each of the three required prayers for travel at their prescribed time during the day. Alternatively, if it is more convenient, the traveler can combine the second and third prayers of the day and the two afternoon prayers and the final night prayer with the one that would usually precede it at sunset (*al-Maghrib*).[41] Given the long mercantile and commercial history of Oman in the Indian Ocean region, it is unsurprising that most Ibadhi *fiqh* manuals contain a section that details the obligations for prayer when traveling to accommodate voyagers.

Ibadhi elders in Lalago prayed Safar well into the 1990s, and this practice continued among the youth in rural communities who sought to emulate their local leadership. The practice distinguished Ibadhis from non-Ibadhi Muslims and was used to replace the Friday prayers, which could not be performed in the absence of a just imam. The roots of the Safar prayer date back to the period of Umayyad Islamic rule (661–750), when Ibadhis lived as a persecuted minority under the first caliphate. As discussed in chapter 2, modernist Ibadhi scholars such as Nur al-Din al-Salimi argued for the reestablishment of the Friday prayers, a stance later adopted by postrevolution Ibadhi thinkers in Oman and Zanzibar, such as Mufti al-Khalili and his acolytes Muhammad and Khalfan al-Tiwani in Pemba. Even for those Ibadhis who had married and built families with African women, who spoke KiSukuma and other regional languages fluently, and who had not returned to Oman in decades—or even visited the country—the absence from their ancestral homeland remained palpable and necessitated a continuation of the Safar prayer.

While we sat for coffee and dates served by his Somali wife on the verandah of the family's one-story home, Mzee Idris explained the sense of impermanence and preoccupation with the homeland felt by past generations of Omanis in Lalago. "They were thinking they would return [to Oman] . . . For example, one man was named Ali Hassan, he used to stay over there [in one of the abandoned homes on the street]. He prayed Safar until he left and went [to Oman]. He died after one year. He stayed for one year; right mama [turns to his wife who nods]? He died, but he returned home."[42] Despite the deep ties to their ancestral homeland in Oman, many Ibadhis in Lalago felt a sense of longing and impermanence. The stories of these individuals reflect a complex relationship with both their Tanzanian and Omani identities, highlighting the enduring connection to their ancestral lands despite geographical distance.

Mzee Idris added about Ali Hassan, "He prayed [in congregation] at home, over there." When asked why the elders did not adhere to modern Ibadhi teachings, such as the reforms of Mufti Al-Khalili, Mzee, he replied that they lacked local guidance in these matters. "There was no one there to tell you, you had no one to explain the matter to you."[43] The experience of Ibadhis in Lalago sheds light on the dynamics of religious leadership, community traditions, and shifting practices of the Omani diaspora in the rural northwest. It also hints at the authoritative influence of external figures like the Omani mufti in guiding and shaping the religious practices of the community in the postcolonial period.

Ibadhis in the Lake Region are generally in agreement with the scholarly opinion that Omanis historically spent little time proselytizing, focusing instead on ensuring their social and economic survival outside of Oman. My interlocutors frequently insisted that conversion of Africans to Islam came later (Sw., *walisilimisha watu baadaye*) and that even then, those who became Muslim tended to be family members, slaves, or other closely related persons. The dominant narrative is that conversion was not forced (Sw., *hakuna lazima*) and that the Arabs did not teach Islam, because theirs was a madhab exclusive to Arabs (Sw., *madhheb ya waarabu tu*). According to Mzee, "In Ramadan people would fast and others [non-Muslim Africans] admired the practice so they emulated [them]."[44] Converts to Islam often received Muslim names from their Arab connections, and Islamic education mainly focused around Qur'an recitation with limited emphasis on content or meaning.

In addition to underscoring that Islamic learning primarily took place within families and that Omanis prioritized teaching their own rather than spreading the faith beyond their community, Mzee highlights the current Ibadhi community's role under Istiqaama in reviving religious practices, particularly during Ramadan.[45] He elaborated, "Indeed, it is our job to encourage people to follow religion, to come pray. During Ramadan we encourage them, and Ramadan is like that throughout Tanzania, you could say.... Here there are drunkards, but when Ramadan arrives, they are not drunk, and they pray the five prayers. During that time, we don't have any trouble encouraging people. Everyone understands completely that during this month, everyone must try praying to get into heaven [after the resurrection]. Everyone prays that maybe in the future things will get better, but it is like that."[46]

Mzee acknowledged that, unlike in the past where such practices did not necessitate elaboration for their ancestors, the Ibadhi community now actively promotes ritual obligation during Ramadan. The emphasis on religious observance highlights the community's commitment to supporting one another's spiritual growth and well-being, as well as its efforts to preserve traditions that are in danger of being neglected or forgotten.

Lalago was formerly a ward in the Shinyanga District, but now it is part of the Simiyu. Most of the aid that trickles down comes from the district headquarters of Istiqaama in the district capital of Meatu. At the time of our conversation, the Ibadhi mosque in Meatu was only five years old and had been built with a women's section to accommodate the city's growing population. According to the Meatu leadership, the construction of the mosque began in 2002 and 85 percent of the funding came from donations secured by the chairman of Istiqaama in Mwanza. As elsewhere, the leadership is primarily composed of successful businesspeople who volunteer their time to handle mosque affairs and supervise the distribution of any aid and building projects sponsored by Istiqaama. "These leaders, each one has his own business. One has a garage, and he is the chairman.... The secretary, his work is to repair phones and he has a shop to repair phones. Meaning they all run private businesses."[47]

While Istiqaama chairpersons and secretaries in major cities may assist rural communities in finding teachers for their mosques, they do not generally pay the salaries of these hires, so local actors struggle to raise these funds. They meet once a month and have smaller meetings throughout the week where they connect with subcommittees of education, parents, and youth. The youth are responsible for volunteering at Ibadhi weddings, funerals, and other celebrations and somber occasions held for the community at the mosque.[48]

The leaders of Istiqaama are Ibadhi men, elected for their piety and standing in the community and their achievements in business and strong connections to Oman. They claim that the reason they were able to integrate so well into local economies and family structures is because they did not discriminate between Africans and Arabs and focused their attention on trade instead of focusing on Islamic outreach (*da'wa*). Those mainland Africans who became Muslim, they explain, did so because they observed the strict Ibadhi adherence to Islamic traditions of prayer and fasting and in time began to model what they characterized as righteous behavior. Rather than impose their religion on outsiders, they converted through example.

Overall, the dedication and collaboration of business savvy rural Istiqaama community leaders play a crucial role in sustaining and advancing the Ibadhi community's religious and social activities. The need for continued support and funding for vital services such as mosque teaching positions highlights the ongoing challenges faced by those communities in securing resources for valued religious education and community engagement activities. Despite these challenges, their commitment to support one another reflects a strong sense of unity and shared responsibility within rural Ibadhi communities.

### Religious Competition in the Rural Northwest

Despite the long history of Arab Muslim settlement in the greater Lake Region, Islam never became dominant,[49] as local populations continued to practice their ancestral traditions and converted to Christianity in large numbers influenced by well-resourced mission schools and churches. Ibadhis are believed to have shown little interest in proselytizing their faith, preferring instead to establish themselves economically. Mzee explained, "When those Christian foreigners entered, they proselytized, they informed people of their faith ... [they would say] come pray! And the people would go to them. But the [Omani] elders just looked on."[50]

The first church to gain a significant following in the southern Lake Region was the Roman Catholic Church, but today other denominations are gaining large followings. Commenting on the matter with some amusement, Mzee noted "the Seventh-day Adventists have come, so and so has come, there are others who pray all night long, all day long."[51] The increase in public expressions of piety in rural Tanzanian communities at times leads to tensions between Muslim and Christian neighbors over noise (competing calls to prayer and preaching through loud speakers) and unequal access to resources and development within the respective religious communities.

Ibadhis today see the dominance of Sunni Muslims and Christians in the southern Lake Region as a byproduct of their Omani elders' reluctance to propagate their religious traditions within the communities where they settled, choosing instead to focus their energies on managing their shops and trades. Other Muslim traders such as the Yemenis who settled in the interior did promote Islamic education and practice in their new communities. However, they offered no equivalent to the modern schools and health care centers that played a large role in the expansion of Christian ideas and institutions in rural areas in Tanzania. Itandala suggests that the Sukuma people living in the lake zone "managed to resist" the spread of Christianity through the first decade of the twentieth century because their social and political institutions remained relatively intact despite German rule. "Up to 1909, missionary activity in Usukuma was still confined to the White Fathers stations at Bukumbi, Nyegexi, and Mwanza town and the CMS station at Bulima, in Nasa, where converts to Christianity were still very few, possibly because the new religion was too contrary to Kisukuma social and religious practices such as polygamy, ancestor worship and *bufumu*."[52]

Until the establishment of the Istiqaama schools in the 1990s, there had been little effort to train an indigenous African Ibadhi leadership that could expand the faith beyond the closed network of Omani families. This contrasts with the various Christian missions in the lake zone, which long ago replaced European and American with culturally Sukuma churches, priests, and deacons. Through the rise of indigenous African churches, some of the more recent Pentecostal movements have proven attractive to elders and youth alike in rural Tanzanian communities.

The majority Christian population of Lalago has grown exponentially since the establishment of the St. Francis Xavier Catholic Parish in the neighboring town of Gula in 1949. The early community consisted of "a church, rectory, and primary school" built in the image of local Sukuma houses, which were primarily mudbrick with flat grass roofs.[53] Under the leadership of ordained and lay American missionaries from the Maryknoll society, the Catholic presence in the region grew gradually over the subsequent decades, with parishes built approximately twenty-five miles apart. Typically, their parishes were built on the outskirts of the town rather than at the center, as this was where the Arab communities would build their mosques. The most detailed written accounts of the religious and social life of people living in the rural towns during the transition to independence in Tanzania between 1950 and 1970 are from missionaries associated with the American Catholic missionary society, Maryknoll. They include observations of local Arab communities and their various economic engagements in Lalago, which they called "an Arab village." In his account, Father Frank Breen observes, "The parish was situated on a hill three miles from the town of Lalago, which in the 1950s could accurately be described as an Arab village. Arabs who were involved in the slave trade had been relocated to Lalago and all commercial enterprise in the town was in Arab hands, except for one bar owned by an African. Over the years, Arab traders and lorry-owners proved to be cordial neighbors to the priests and cooperative in responding to business requests."[54]

Like the Arab Muslim traders who had already established a commercial center in Lalago, by the time of the missionaries' arrival, the Catholic newcomers built their institutions with permission and land grants from Chief Majebere. The chief had been "appointed" by the British colonial administration "to be paramount king in all of Sukumaland."[55] In return, he pressured the priests to build "a dispensary and eventually a hospital" in his kingdom, which they eventually did, having great success in attracting patients and providing medical services and medications competitive with those available at the more distant government hospitals.[56] One missionary described the chief as "65 years old, tall and regal-looking, had six wives and about 40 children."[57] The account suggests that, contrary to acting as a mere pawn to the foreign authorities in the region, Chief Majebere knew how to get what he wanted from the various foreigners in his domains and he was not adverse to pomp and circumstance. As historian Thomas Spear has observed, historical scholarship on African rulers during this colonial period focuses too much on the ways in which "they were exploited, manipulated and transformed by colonial and local authorities and not enough on internal African politics and the agency that chiefs exerted in using the resources at their disposal to respond to their subjects' desires for the future. To mobilize African ambitions, colonial rules had to appeal to both the past and the future, to what Africans had been as well as what many wished to be, and to provide a means of deploying tradition to attain modernity and vice versa."[58] These appeals, which were made to both government officials and missionaries, were often expressed in demands for modern institutions of education, health care, and even worship.

While Lalago's Arab community did engage in farming, most began as traveling salesmen or shopkeepers, selling imported fabrics, bicycles, household wares, grain, and cooking oil made from local products like pressed cotton seed. Successful Omani traders would buy farming equipment, such as tractors, and hire out their tilling services to the African farmers. They also hunted and sold wild game and ivory and invested in diamonds from local mines. They invested the wealth extracted from these endeavors into cars, buses, and trucks for the long-distance transport of passengers and wholesale items to towns and markets from as far away as Arusha near Mt. Kilimanjaro.

While cotton production continues in Lalago and the surrounding farming communities in the Lake Region of Tanzania today, high government taxes and frequent draught and flooding results in low yields and delays in sales. Mzee Idris explained that while buyers are eager to purchase the cotton, they feel constrained by the taxes and demands of regional authorities. To adjust to these strictures, farmers began to diversify their crop production to include sunflower seed (Sw., *alizeti*), peas (*choroko*), and sorghum (*mtama*). As part of the fallout of the unstable cotton industry, residents of Lalago struggle to meet their basic needs and cite hunger and alcoholism (*ulevi*) as endemic concerns. The cotton season had opened on May 21, but a month later, during our interview, the crop remained in storage. Mzee informed me that they were eagerly awaiting a "money car" (Sw., *gari ya pesa*) from the major agribusiness company, Olam, which is one of two major buyers.[59]

Mzee attributed the economic decline to the departure of prominent businesspersons and farmers from Lalago due to the frustration caused by the ebbs and flows of an unreliable cash economy. "The [Omani] elders left when the cotton business had started to go backwards. It did not used to be that way; the policy became such that a person from whom cotton was purchased was not paid until his death. What I mean is, you would go ahead and sell your cotton only to be reassured of payment [by the buyer] the day after tomorrow, [then again] the day after tomorrow. By the time you cultivate the next crop, you have not been paid for the previous one."[60]

Those who did not leave for Oman moved in waves to Mwanza to look for better business opportunities, leaving the town's two "Arab streets" empty. Among those who left is the owner of a major construction company in Mwanza who employs several former residents of Lalago, the Arab-owned juice factory is also a key regional employer.

## Ibadhi Heritage and Industry in Rural Tanzania

Juma, an Ibadhi owner of the Jambo Juice Factory in Shinyanga, explained that his Arab ancestors came to East Africa from the city of Barzman in the Sharqiyya region of Oman as adults to escape political and economic strife and a desert drought that resulted in widescale food scarcity. Zanzibar appealed to the island's Arab immigrants because of its ample rainfall from the biannual monsoon showers, which stimulated the growth of fruit and other produce unimaginable for a desert emigrant accustomed to drought and perpetual food shortages. Moreover, in Zanzibar they found a stable business environment that enabled even those emigrants who possessed little or no capital to seek employment in Stone Town or establish a shop or farm in the countryside. As Juma put it, "They came to help themselves here [in East Africa]."[61] He related that only a few residents of Barzman made the trip to Zanzibar, those that did first settled on the islands and married women from there, like Juma's grandmother who was from Pemba Island. Eventually some left Zanzibar for the East African mainland. The house of his emigrant ancestors still stands in Barzman under the care of extended family members in Oman.[62]

Juma's maternal grandfather was from Lalago. However, his mother and father married in the nearby village of Imalaseko, part of the greater Shinyanga region. The Ibadhi community there was close-knit and consisted of over twelve families, all of whom followed "Arab traditions" brought over from Oman and Zanzibar. The small town neighbors the world-renowned game parks of Serengeti and Ngorongoro. Juma grew up in the 1960s and 1970s, before the populations of the towns had grown and the boundaries of the parks became more formalized. The Sukuma name Imaleseko means "when you get there, there is no more laughing," which is a reference to the village residents' caution against making loud noises that would attract the attention of lions out on the prowl. The only Ibadhi mosque in Imalaseko was

**Figure 5.5**: Jambo Factory and Semitruck, Shinyanga, 2019. Photo by author.

built sometime in the 1930s, "when the king [or sultan] was still in Zanzibar,"[63] and the Omani community's youth studied religion in a madrasa while also attending the government school for primary and secondary education. Juma has four brothers and three sisters. After he and one of his brothers completed their secondary education in the village government school, they decided to leave school to go into the family trucking business.[64]

In the 1970s and 1980s, several Arab families in northwestern Tanzania used the capital earned from their petty trade (*biashara ndogo ndogo*) centered on small-scale farms, shops, and from working in the mines to buy trucks for the transport of agricultural produce, primarily cotton, from the fields to the ginneries and markets. Juma's family used their trucks to buy cottonseed oil and then sell it in the regional towns and cities. Once they saved enough money, they opened a wholesale store and began to distribute sugar and oil to local markets. In time he and his brother applied for small bank loans to build two cotton ginneries and opened an oil mill to press the cottonseed. They formed a group to manage their modest cotton trade and began to explore new areas of trade and investment.⁶⁵ Their success inspired the brothers to purchase Chinese-made, water-purification equipment and bottles, expanding their business to include the sale of potable water. Eventually, they decided to increase their water production and traveled to Germany to purchase the necessary equipment. They found a German company willing to lend them a line-one machine for purifying water and making soda. After a while they were able to acquire additional lines for making juice and soda. The company began by selling their bottled beverages to small local businesses. They saved and reinvested their profits into new industries along the way and eventually formed Jambo Food Products Ltd in 2013. The company claims to have grown in sales by 15 percent annually with their products sold in stores around the country.⁶⁶ According to a report by Africa Outlook, a print and online magazine designed for business executives, the Jambo Group is now a conglomerate of oil mills, ginneries, petroleum products, spinning mills, cargo transportation, and food products. Moreover, it is "one of the largest manufacturers of carbonated soft drinks, fresh juices, and the processing and bottling of water within East Africa, based in Shinyanga, Tanzania."⁶⁷ The company's slogan is "life in every drop," and they present their business as having a humanitarian mission of providing safe and clean water and other quality beverages and foods at prices affordable for Tanzanians.⁶⁸

The business remains family owned, and on our stop in Shinyanga, they invited me and my travel companions to dine in their walled and gated compound that stretches several acres from the juice and soda factory, across the main road into town. In the dryness and heat of summer, the expansive driveways, fountains, and well-watered gardens of date palms and other tropical and subtropical plants gave the appearance of an upper-class family home in Muscat, Oman. After lunch with the family matriarch, we made our way across the highway to the well-maintained factory complex, where a fleet of now three-hundred lorry trucks⁶⁹ stood by to take shipments of juice, soda, and water to buyers of the product and the company's various clientele.⁷⁰ Above the iconic Mercedes three-point star on some of the trucks reads the Sukuma word *Jamukaya*, meaning "a place for everyone," which signifies the company's efforts to market their product as born of local efforts but intended for universal consumption. One truck depicting high-resolution images of a new cola reads, in Swahili, "jivunie kizozi kipya" or "be proud of the new product," again signaling that this is an unapologetically Tanzanian product and the community it serves are shareholders in its success. The factory has "the capacity for production of more than 72,000 bottles each hour."[71] Already providing products to 60 percent of Tanzania, the company plans to add another hundred trucks to its fleet to reach neighboring countries in East and Central Africa, specifically Rwanda, Burundi, and Uganda.[72] Obstacles that the company may encounter in its expansion are increased regulation on the use of plastics in production and not transferring the burden of tax increases onto their customers.[73] Because of the company's origins in Shinyanga, much of its customer base is in the broader Lake Region.[74]

According to Juma, the mosques in Lalago and Imaleseko were built by the same Arab ancestor in the 1930s, which indicates how deeply intertwined the social and religious lives of rural Ibadhi communities are, even though the journey between the towns was thirty kilometers or more and carried out on foot. Juma is one of the all-male twelve trustees of the Ibadhi mosques in Shinyanga. The board is responsible for electing the chairperson, the secretary, and the treasurer of the regional branch. They also appoint the leadership of all the Shinyanga Ibadhi schools and provide supplies and equipment when donor funding and school budgets fall short. The board also plays the role of mediators in disputes that occur at the mosques or schools. These include the modest old Ibadhi community mosques built by their Omani ancestors and the newly constructed Ibadhi Friday mosques in the region, some of which are renovations of replacements of preexisting mosques. Due to its geographical proximity to Mwanza and the strong family ties that exist between Omanis across the northwest, they frequently collaborate with the other branches of Istiqaama, though they are self-sufficient in their sources of funding and decision-making. Juma explained, "You know, Ibadhi Omanis or Istiqaama are one family. They come from the same place, have their customs, their relationships, they live together and that becomes something like brotherhood (*kama ni ndugu*). Unlike other countries where they [Ibadhi Omanis] do not interact well with one another, the Omanis over here know each other; they interact and understand each other."[75]

Alongside their government education, Juma and his siblings studied religion from both Shafi'i and Ibadhi perspectives in a madrasa built by the community a short distance from the mosque in the center of Imaleseko. Istiqaama built another madrasa open to all Muslim students regardless of madhab affiliation in the town that forms part of the network of twelve Ibadhi schools, according to Juma's estimate, and mosques in the greater Shinyanga region. In addition to the smaller madrasas that emphasize religious education, there is an Istiqaama boarding and day school that follows the

**Figure 5.6**: Istiqaama Shinyanga Secondary School, 2019. Qur'an atop religious studies textbooks and exam sheets. Photo by author.

government curriculum of secular and religious studies on the outskirts of Shinyanga city and only a few kilometers from the juice factory. Prior to the rise of Istiqaama and the proliferation of Ibadhi schools in towns and villages in Shinyanga, Juma explained, the religious education they received had been minimal. The push to revive religious education among Ibadhis came as "a force from outside" because before Istiqaama "the elders used only their own strengths" to persuade the youth to adopt the traditions of their ancestors.[76]

While the Istiqaama leadership in Tanzania are tight-lipped about exact amounts and sources of funding, all agree that assistance from Oman is critical for the organization's developmental goals in the short and long terms.

According to Juma and my other interlocutors in Mwanza and Shinyanga, the Istiqaama leadership in Oman rewards local initiative by contributing to the furtherance of grassroots building projects. "Istiqaama of Oman is the one who helps here in Africa, we could say Tanzania itself awaits the Shinyanga model. You are building the mosque and they over there contribute." He continued, "They [Oman] don't start anything... it goes from zero to above (*zero kuja juu*)."[77] Two types of Omani donors contribute to Istiqaama's projects in Tanzania. The first are those who are from there or whose parents are from there but left to live in Oman and who contribute directly to the organization's projects in their hometowns. The second are those donors who send their contributions to the Istiqaama headquarters in Muscat and let the leadership there decide how and where to send the funds and gifts. Juma explained that Istiqaama fills in where the government and foreign aid organizations fall short. Their proximity to local Omani-Ibadhi communities, born of over a century of established transregional kinship bonds and ethnoreligious fraternity, ensures a relationship of trust that is often missing between local and foreign development actors in postcolonial African societies. This trust enables both sets of actors to avoid government bureaucracy and politics that may slow the transfer of funds and the shipment of resources from Oman to Istiqaama communities in Tanzania.

Moreover, the expectation from Oman that development begin in local communities—and with local start-up funds—ensures community control of development. The direct line between Istiqaama's leadership in Oman and Tanzania has the potential to eliminate corruption and misuse of funds, as donors frequently travel overseas to the communities they support to check on the progress of projects. The donors from Oman do not dictate specific guidelines for the construction or maintenance of the building projects but they do insist on "good leadership." Juma explained, "Basically, if they see that there is leadership in the community, and it works, they contribute." When asked why some branches of Istiqaama appear to have made more advancements in education than others, Juma replied that this was an issue of each community's history, its leadership, and the scope of its projects.[78]

In regions where Ibadhi leadership was strong, like Zanzibar, Tanga, and Dar es Salaam, Istiqaama could easily adapt to existing practices of patronage that included building spaces of worship, founding schools, recruiting teachers locally and from abroad, and establishing soup kitchens for those in need. He insisted that favoritism was not the issue; rather, some Ibadhi communities have always been more organized than others. "While we are talking about primary schools, they are talking about secondary schools, they are talking about universities, and they are talking about sending fifty students to Oman to study education (*elimu*). So, you cannot compare them."[79] The Shinyanga Ibadhis are a close-knit and united community, but there is only one congregational mosque in the regional capital that is several kilometers from those who reside in surrounding towns. This contrasts with Unguja Island on Zanzibar, for example, where there are large new Ibadhi mosques in towns and villages far from outside of Stone Town, such as Fuoni and Mwera.

In addition to assisting with the construction of mosques and schools in Shinyanga, donors from Oman send food and dates during Ramadan, sewing machines, clothes, and other resources according to the specific needs of the community. According to Juma, "They also help educate disadvantaged children and orphans, finding them and bringing them to the schools where they should study. They dig wells and help widows at home with daily living allowances."[80]

## Conclusion

Major trading centers like Tabora and Mwanza, the former capital of German East Africa in the northwest, would become national branches of Istiqaama in the postcolonial period. What this chapter has shown, however, is that rural towns and villages in the broader lake regions of Mwanza, Shinyanga and Simiyu were home to the entrepreneurial Ibadhi families who would raise the founders of lucrative Tanzanian industries, like cotton ginneries, juice factories, and construction and transportation companies. Almost always starting from humble origins, these now affluent figures would become the current leaders of Istiqaama. One tends to find new Istiqaama schools and mosques only in towns where there is an old mosque or row of homes built by early Omani settlers. Affluent Swahili-speaking Omani nationals are now returning to the homes of their parents or grandparents in Tanzania with schemes to repair their family homes or invest in the building of new or renovation of existing mosques, schools, and dispensaries. Istiqaama serves as the middleman in such interactions as individuals and groups of donors from Oman generally reach out to the Istiqaama's branch leaders in their region of interest. In turn, Istiqaama families host them during their stay in Tanzania and may arrange a tour for them of historic Ibadhi settlements and mosques, like my own journey.

African and Arab kinship networks and merchant capital merged to create the economic and social foundations that support the branches of Istiqaama in northwestern Tanzania. The Ibadhi-Omani story intersects with the histories of migration and commerce of other ethnic minorities and diaspora groups in the broader Lake Zone, such as Hindus and Muslims from Gujarat, India. The Ibadhi experience there has been shaped by a unique colonial and agricultural past and the complex African and non-African, Muslim and non-Muslim, social relations that existed and continue to exist.

## Notes

1. Thomas E. McDow, *Buying Time: Debt and Mobility in the Western Indian Ocean* (Athens: Ohio University Press, 2018).

2. See for example Stuart Laing, *Ivory, Slavery and Discovery in the Scramble for Africa* (Dar es Salaam: Mkuki na Nyota, 2017), 63–70.

3. See Elisabeth McMahon's book, for example, which describes how emancipation enabled the formerly enslaved to integrate into island social and cultural life in Pemba: Elisabeth McMahon, *Slavery and Emancipation in Islamic East Africa: From Honor to Respectability* (Cambridge: Cambridge University Press, 2013).

4. The interconnectedness and interdependency I speak of here does not imply absolute harmony.

5. See Tanzania Wildlife Management Authority (TAWA), "Maswa Game Reserve," n.d., accessed March 27, 2024, https://www.tawa.go.tz/attraction-details/maswa-game-reserve.

6. Stéphane Pradines, *Historic Mosques in Sub-Saharan Africa: From Timbuktu to Zanzibar* (Leiden, Netherlands: Brill, 2022), 281; Abdul Sheriff, "Mosques, Merchants, & Landowners in Zanzibar Stone Town," in *The History and Conservation of Zanzibar Stone Town* (ZanzibAr. Dept. of Archives, Museums & Antiquities, 1995), 46–66.

7. "Maryknoll History in Tanzania, Part Five A: Shinyanga Diocese, 1954–1963," n.d.

8. McDow, *Buying Time*, 86.

9. Ibid., 87.

10. Ibid.

11. Buluda Itandala, "African Response to German Colonialism in East Africa: The Case of Usukuma, 1890–1918," *Ufahamu: A Journal of African Studies* 20, no. 1 (1992): 3.

12. Ibid., 4.

13. Ibid.

14. Ibid., 7.

15. Ibid., 5. See also Jonathon Glassman, *FEASTS AND RIOT: REVELRY, REBELLION, AND POPULAR CONSCIOUSNESS ON THE SWAHILI COAST, 1856–1888* (Ann Arbor: University of Michigan, 1995).

16. Itandala, "African Response," 23.

17. Ivory smuggling continues today, though the Tanzanian government has recently made a public show of cracking down on those they deem the "ring leaders" of this exploitative practice. The scandal involved the so-called Ivory Queen, a Chinese businessperson named Yang Fenglan and was widely covered in the national newspapers and television during the years of my fieldwork in Tanzania, which suggests that Arab and African traders, or men for that matter, no longer have a monopoly on the ivory trade. "Yang was accused of operating one of Africa's biggest ivory-smuggling rings, responsible for smuggling $2.5m (£1.9m) worth of tusks from some 400 elephants." The Tanzanian government has cracked down on poaching in recent years, leading to a steady increase in the number elephants. The government continues working toward a "zero poaching" policy across the country. See: No Author. "Chinese 'Ivory Queen' Yang Fenglan Jailed in Tanzania," BBC News, February 19, 2019, accessed March 30, 2024, https://www.bbc.com/news/world-africa-47294715.

18. Itandala, "African Response," 23–24.

19. Andrew Coulson, "Cotton and Textiles Industries in Tanzania: The Failures of Liberalisation," *Review of African Political Economy* 43, no. S1 (2016): 44.

20. Nanji Kalidas Mehta, *Dream Half-Expressed; an Autobiography* (Bombay: Vakils, Feffer and Simons Private LTD., 1966), 98.

21. Ibid., 100.

22. Ibid., 110.

23. Ibid.

24. Coulson, "Cotton and Textiles," 44.

25. Ibid., 44.

26. Coulson writes of this spike in production "more than 50,000 bales (10,000 tonnes) were produced in 1941" alone. Ibid., 45.

27. Gottfried O. Lang and Martha B. Lang, "Problems of Social and Economic Change in Sukumaland, Tanganyika," *Anthropological Quarterly* 35, no. 2 (1962): 90.

28. Ibid., 93.

29. Ibid., 91.

30. Ibid.

31. Ibid., 92.

32. Coulson, "Cotton and Textiles," 47.

33. A safari-style suit, often in a gray, khaki, or olive hues, made popular by Zambia's first president Kanneth Kaunda and worn by other African nationalists and presidents of the 1960s and 1970s, such as Julius Nyerere.

34. Very little has been written about Somali communities in precolonial Tanzania or the conditions under which they migrated to and settled in the broader Lake Region. Literature on Somali history in Tanzania tends to be documented by human rights organizations and focuses on Somali refugees and their struggle to attain Tanzanian citizenship in towns like Chogo in northeastern Tanzania, follow-

ing the civil war in Somalia in the 1990s and the fall of the socialist leader Siad Barre's regime. See Brendan Bannon and Eveline Wolfcarius, "Somali Bantus Gain Tanzanian Citizenship in Their Ancestral Land" (The UN Refugee Agency (UNHCR), June 3, 2009), March 27, 2024, https://www.unhcr.org/news/somali-bantus-gain-tanzanian-citizenship-their-ancestral-land.

35. Mzee Idris (Ibadhi Mosque caretaker), interview with author, Lalago, June 17, 2019.

36. Mzee Idris, interview with author, June 17, 2019.

37. Ibid.

38. Mzee Idris, interview with author, June 17, 2019.

39. Ibid.

40. ʿAbd Allāh ibn Ḥumayyid Al-Sālimī, *Talqīn Al-Ṣibyān Mā Yalzamu Al-Insān* (Masqat: Maktabat al-Jīl al-Wāʿd, 2015), 36.

41. Ibid., 36–37.

42. Ibid.

43. Ibid.

44. Mzee Idris, interview with author, June 17, 2019.

45. Istiqaama Mwanza (male community leaders), interview with author, Mwanza, April 25, 2016.

46. Mzee Idris, interview with author, June 17, 2019.

47. Ibid.

48. Fieldnotes, Meatu, June 20, 2019.

49. Notably absent from the oral histories I collected on this trip, and in my other conversations with Ibadhis in Tanzania, was any mention of Sufism or the role of Sufi teachings in local communities. Given that the impact of Sufism has been widely documented in the historical studies on the spread of Islam beyond elite circles of mostly Arab groups and their kin in Tanzania, I found it curious that Sufi communities never came up as having any bearing on Islam or the work of Istiqaama. This is unlike Salafism and Wahhabism, which were often presented as a threat to the identities of Ibadhi youth and a counternarrative to Omani ideals of religious tolerance and Istiqaama's ideals of intra-Muslim cooperation.

50. Mzee Idris, interview with author, June 17, 2019.

51. Ibid.

52. Itandala, "African Response," 25.

53. Father Frank Breen, "Maryknoll History in Tanzania, Part Five A: Shinyanga Diocese, 1954–1963," in *Maryknoll History in Africa: Tanganyika 1946 to early 1960s*, v. 2. (Maryknoll, NY: Maryknoll, n.d.), https://maryknollafrica.org/category/our-downloads/.

54. Ibid.

55. Ibid.

56. Ibid.

57. Ibid.

58. Thomas Spear, "Neo-Traditionalism and the Limits of Invention in British Colonial Africa," *The Journal of African History* 44, no. 1 (2003): 27.

59. Most of Tanzania's cotton comes from small-scale farming in the semiarid region of northwestern Tanzania. Growing cotton does not require large amounts of water nor high-quality soil, "but it is labor-intensive, and requires effective marketing and transport" (Coulson, "Cotton Textiles," 42). Soil exhaustion and drought cause runoff that affects the growth of otherwise resilient crops. Where the soil is not productive, farmers use fertilizers and pesticides, but these are expensive and are taken out of the farmers' final sale price. Moreover, the long-term use of chemical sprays may present health risks for the farmers and their communities. Today, cotton is first processed in local ginneries using a roller gin "which separates the cotton lint (the fiber) from the seeds on which they grow." In Tanzania, the ginnery keeps seeds of the desired varieties for distribution to farmers for planting the next crop. The excess seed is processed to extract cooking oil and the remaining cake is fed to livestock as a protein source.

60. Mzee Idris, interview with author, June 17, 2019.

61. Juma (Jambo factory CEO), interview with author, Shinyanga, June 18, 2019.

62. Ibid.

63. Ibid.

64. Ibid.

65. Phoebe Calver, "Jambo Food Products: Life in Every Drop," *Africa Outlook*, 2020, accessed March 15, 2024, https://issuu.com/outlookpublishing/docs/jambo-food-products-ltd.

66. Ibid.

67. Ibid.

68. Ibid.

69. Tom Wadlow, "Jambo Food Products Ltd 2020: Quenching Africa's Thirst," *Africa Outlook*, December 25, 2019, accessed March 15, 2024, https://www.africaoutlookmag.com/company-profiles/1217-jambo-food-products-ltd-2020.

70. Africa Outlook reports that other trucks such as those made by "Scania, Iveco, Mitsubishi and Man" are being replaced with a reliable fleet of Volvo trucks, which could easily be a multimillion-dollar investment. During my visit to the site in 2019, there were several Mercedes trucks as well.

71. Calver, "Life in Every Drop."

72. Wadlow, "Quenching Africa's Thirst."

73. Ibid.

74. "The group's success puts it in competition with the Bakhresa Group, an in-ternational food and beverage company under the name of Azam based in Dar es Salaam, which was founded and ran by a Yemeni Tanzanian named Said Sa-lim Awadh Bahkresa. Azam also owns a national football league, a television channel,

and the high-speed ferries that carry passengers from Dar es Salaam and Zanzibar daily. Born to a Hadrami Yemeni family in Zanzibar in 1949, Mr. Bakhresa purportedly "dropped out of school at the age of 14 to become a potato mix salesperson, before he got involved as a restaurant operator in the 1970s" (Media Council of Tanzania. "The Bakhresa Family," Media Ownership Monitor Tanzania 2018, accessed March 15, 2024, https://tanzania.mom-gmr.org/en/owners/individual-owners/detail/owner//the-bakhresa-family/). In thirty years, he expanded his holdings well beyond Tanzania and became the wealthiest man in Tanzania and one of the wealthiest in Africa.

75. Juma, interview with author, Shinyanga, June 18, 2019.
76. Ibid.
77. Ibid.
78. Ibid.
79. Ibid.
80. Ibid.

# 6

## Gendered Righteousness

*Ibadhi Women and Their Local Networks*

Every year, Ibadhi families registered with Istiqaama in Tanzania receive a copy of the organization's calendar. On each month's page is a high-quality color photograph depicting male members of the organization at one of its national branches. In most of the images, they are standing in front of mosques, schools, clinics, or donated wells and water tanks. In other images, the men are attending events hosted by Istiqaama, such as Qur'an recitation competitions and meetings that bring together branch leaders from all over the country.

The December 2019 page, for example, displays images from the organization's 2018 annual meeting at the Serena Hotel in Dar es Salaam. The focal point is a picture depicting members of the organization's national board seated on a stage at the front of a conference room while Hamad Masauni, the deputy minister of Tanzania's home affairs and a member of Parliament, addresses the audience from the dais. The chairman of Istiqaama, who is the CEO of a multimillion-dollar Tanzanian transportation organization called SuperDoll, sits in the middle of the panelists on the stage. To his right is Nassor al-Farai, vice chairman of the national board, leader of the Mwanza branch, and owner of the Great Lakes Construction Company. Flanking them are other delegates (*wajumbe*) of Istiqaama.

The members of the Tanzanian Ibadhi delegation are clothed in the Omani national dress. The plaques in front of them show the Tanzanian and Omani flags side by side, publicly signaling the transnational character of the organization and the leaders' roles as cultural attachés entrusted to serve the interests of both countries. Behind them is a tricolor banner of red, green, and white, the colors of the Omani flag, announcing both the event and the two

**Figure 6.1**: Istiqaama Calendar Page, May 2019. Annual Istiqaama conference at the Serena Hotel in Dar es Salaam. Photo credit and permissions: Istiqaama Tanzania, Salum Seif Alhinai, executive secretary of Istiqaama.

countries' shared objective of "working together toward our [mutual] progress (Sw., *mshikamano kwa maendeleo yetu*) (See fig. 1)."

Aside from its obvious purpose, the calendar serves as a type of annual report, informing Ibadhis in Tanzania—and anybody else who happens to see it—about Istiqaama's good works. It also encourages increased contributions and participation in the charitable initiatives represented in the images. Finally, the calendar serves as a reminder of where the authority lies and how this authority is entangled with the politics of class, language, racial purity, patrilineal descent, citizenship, and gendered divisions of labor within the organization. Flipping through the months, one notices a public image of Ibadhi Islam in Tanzania that is notably male, Arab, well-to-do, and Omani. Strikingly absent from the calendar are women, leading one to assume that they have little role to play in Istiqaama's philanthropical initiatives, decision-making, public worship, and efforts at public diplomacy.

As such, this chapter argues that the absence of women in Ibadhi public life in Tanzania is part of Istiqaama's larger efforts to maintain an image of righteousness. Importantly, although this image is patriarchal, it is also indicative of a source of tension within the organization: wanting to project an Ibadhism that is strict in its moral commitments (which includes secluding women from the public eye) and yet also tolerant and progressive (at least behind the scenes, where women happen to be active as educators, entrepreneurs, caregivers, and community liaisons). This two-sided dimension of righteousness portrayed in the Istiqaama calendar is intended to engage not only Tanzanian Muslim publics but also any pious publics and donors in Oman who make decisions about whether, or how, to support the organization's efforts.

That the exclusion of Ibadhi women from public life in Tanzania is seen as a form of righteousness could be explained conveniently as the product of patriarchal Omani gender norms; however, my conversations with urban Ibadhi women in Mwanza revealed a more complex reality. More than demonstrating deference to male leadership, being absent in Istiqaama's mosques and public advertisements is a way for women to project their distinctive Ibadhi identity. By adhering to norms regarding patrilineage, racial and ethnic purity, marriage, and citizenship, women can demonstrate their Omani-ness in the postcolonial African environment in which they live—something that is critical to one's sense of belonging in the diaspora.

Urban Ibadhi women are aware of their relatively privileged social status in Mwanza. This privilege derives from their family origins in a diaspora historically known for its ties to the Islamic and Arabic-speaking world, its religious conservatism, relative economic success, and strict adherence to consanguineous marriage. Like their male counterparts in Tanzania, however, they inhabit a "dual ontology," caught in a continual struggle to adhere to "historical cultural identity on one hand, and the society of relocation on the other."[1] In some way, then, maintaining a righteous public image as an Ibadhi woman necessitates working behind the scenes.

Further, the need to demonstrate belongingness in the Arab diaspora becomes more acute for those Tanzanian-born Ibadhi women who come from mixed-race backgrounds, who do not speak Arabic or hold Gulf citizenship, who marry into Ibadhi-Omani families, or whose fathers are not Omani. In the diaspora, being Arab is not the same as being Omani; the children of a Yemeni father and an Omani mother, for example, are not considered Omani. Moreover, although being Ibadhi is at the heart of one's sense of belonging in Tanzania, converting to Ibadhi Islam does not make one an Omani.[2]

## Ibadhis and Scholarship on Muslim Women's Piety

Scholarship on gender and sexuality and Islam focuses largely on women's piety, authority, dress, and charitable giving in the context of the Islamic revival that gained momentum during the 1990s and early 2000s.[3] The case studies in this area tend to center on charismatic women leaders in Sufi orders or the more Salafi-oriented da'wa movements. They show how pious women in urban centers like Cairo, Egypt, demonstrate agency in the teaching and learning of Islamic texts, practices, and "forms of bodily comportment considered germane to cultivation of the ideal virtuous self."[4] For women in these situations, the main issue is not about challenging patriarchal norms like male-only mosque leadership, women's seclusion, and unequal access to public spaces of worship. In fact, their religious devotion has effectively resisted the efforts of nonreligious political authorities to confine religion to personal matters and has also challenged Western liberal beliefs regarding the suppression of Muslim women.[5] The power of this piety movement lies in its appeal to women across different social classes, with those from lower-income backgrounds playing a critical role in defining the parameters of participation or nonparticipation in public religious life and spaces. Further, the rise of social media and new generations adept at online activism have enabled women in places like Turkey to challenge patriarchal "cultural norms around privacy and intimacy,"[6] norms that regard the domestic sphere, not the mosque, as the primary site of women's ethical formation. In these contexts, women are actively campaigning for equal access to mosque spaces where they may gather, study, and pray with the same ease and frequency as men.

Conversely, although the Ibadhi women I spoke with in Mwanza expressed frustration about not having their own spaces in which to gather, study, prepare meals for major events, celebrate weddings, and perform community duties (like washing the bodies of the deceased), their access to mosque space for daily or congregational prayer was not a primary concern. Moreover, their absence from the mosque and decision-making circles neither precluded their participation in other areas of community life nor prevented them from creating new, more inclusive spaces of learning and worship by drawing on their own business networks and financial resources. In fact, when describing their activities, Ibadhi women in Mwanza used a language of self-reliance. Such language reflects a recognition of their own marginalization within the national organization and in public spaces like community mosques; but it also reflects the entrepreneurial spirit of their pious works.

## The Istiqaama Women's Group

In 2011, women from Ibadhi families in Mwanza came together to create a women's organization that was independent of the national Istiqaama one but bore the same name: Istiqaama Women's Group. By 2016, when I first met the group, they had recruited approximately fifty members.

The group has a president, vice president, and treasurer responsible for collecting the membership fee of TZS10,000 (US$4) at every meeting, which occurs on the third of each month. They deposit the funds into a communal bank account. The group also collects sadaqa through local community networks and personal connections and supporters in Oman. The donations, which they generate independently of the men's organization, serve as a form of economic security for the group members and as capital for the group's various philanthropic initiatives.

After reaching fifty members, the group opted to apply for a permit from the Tanzanian Ministry of Home Affairs so that they could purchase property collectively and enjoy recognition as a registered association. (Acquisition of the permit was contingent on having an adequate number of members to prove that any funds or land obtained was for collective rather than individual benefit.) In April 2016, they received the permit from the ministry and began to formalize the organization's work.

The president of the group is Shireen, Mariam's mother (see chaps. 1 and 5); curiously, she was the only non-Ibadhi (she is Yemeni) and non-Omani member of the group, but she had a husband belonging to a prominent Omani family in Mwanza and his mother was Sukuma. The family's five children identified as both Sukuma and Omani and sometimes referred to themselves as "Afro-Arab." Through marriage, Shireen became familiar with the religious and social practices of the Ibadhi community, and her demonstrated leadership skills and experience in local business led to her election as the group's leader. Extensive experience as a business owner and manager also qualified her well for the position. In their youth, she and her husband had owned a local nightclub in Mwanza and played a role in the housing-construction industry. Pictures from that time show a beaming and fashionably dressed young mother wearing skirt suits with shoulder pads and a face of carefully done-up makeup.

Her days of running the nightclub behind her, Shireen now operates a café in Mwanza that serves breakfast (from 8:30 a.m. to 10:30 a.m.) and lunch following the afternoon prayers (from 1:00 p.m. to 3:00 p.m.). On the menu are Swahili favorites such as *chapatti*,[7] *maandazi*,[8] samosas, and a hearty lunch of rice or *ugali*[9] with a choice of red meat or chicken, cooked bananas, and avocado juice. Accordingly, Shireen's clothes are now more conservative, both at work and in public. Her stylish suits having been replaced with long-sleeved, loose-fitting, full-length dresses (*diras*) decorated with colorful geometric patterns or floral designs. A long hijab, often matching in color, covers her hair and frames a light-tan face that at once projects compassion and the shrewdness of a seasoned businessperson and pillar of her community. Like other Istiqaama women, she wears a black robe over her clothes and headscarf, appearing more conservative than the café's casually dressed, mostly non-Ibadhi and non-Arab female staff and clientele.

The importance of correct dress in town, especially near the mosque, was apparent when I visited the café with Mariam and her sisters. We followed their mother's example by covering up our pants trousers and T-shirts with loose-fitting robes. This was partly because the café sits in the direct line of vision of the Ibadhi congregational mosque and its outdoor bench (*baraza*), where kanzu-clad men meet to chat following each of the five daily prayers, sometimes enjoying dates with coffee poured from a thermos into tiny porcelain cups. The mosque baraza, located as it is at the center of town and in full view of passersby, is a place where one goes to observe and to be observed—a site from which righteous behavior is both conveyed and monitored.

The original location of the café had been on the first floor of the building complex that houses several other businesses, which are part of the mosque's waqf. The rent collected from the businesses in the complex funnel back into the Istiqaama treasury for maintenance of the mosque and community development. Connecting the building on one of the higher floors is an interior passageway that simplifies access to the mosque's prayer hall for members of the local business community while also enabling the mosque leadership close oversight of the activities that take place in both. The café has since been moved to its current location, which is larger and sits across the street from the mosque.

Located in Mwanza's business district, the city's Ibadhi mosque is easily identifiable by its two towering minarets, a blue, marble-tiled facade, large archways, and heavy wooden doors with engravings, like those found on the homes of past Arab and Indian elites, landowners, and merchants in Zanzibar. A plaque on the front wall of the mosque informs visitors that Mufti Al-Khalili laid its foundation stone on June 1, 1995, clearly signifying the mosque's adherence to the religious authority of Oman. Locals refer to it in Swahili as "msikiti wa waarabu" or "the Arab mosque."[10]

**Figure 6.2**: Ibadhi Congregational Mosque (est. 1995), Mwanza, 2016. Photo by author.

Within walking distance, there is a Khoja Ismaili Jamaat Khana, an Ithnashari Shiʿa Mosque, and a Memon Mosque, all forming a constellation of houses of worship that is reminiscent of the mercantilism of the coast. While the buildings look rather different from Swahili stone houses, they too signal this lakeport city's cosmopolitanism and the mobility of its populations while simultaneously delineating communal and ethnic boundaries through its built environment. These boundaries are somewhat relaxed, however, when some mosques open their doors for congregational prayers or during encounters at shared spaces of business and sociality, such as Shireen's café in the center of town.

The largely male customer base that frequents the café during its peak breakfast and lunch hours is comprised of mosque attendees and local businesspeople. This puts Shireen in a unique position to navigate both male and female spaces in the local Ibadhi and broader Muslim communities, which is notable considering the Ibadhi mosque does not have a women's section; neither do women serve on its board nor attend meetings in the sebleh, where announcements are made and matters concerning the community are discussed.

There is no universal prohibition against women performing prayers at mosques in Tanzania. In fact, the practice is quite common among Sunni women across the country. This is due in part to a longer history of congregational prayer within some of these communities, in addition to an earlier emphasis on building mosques and prayer spaces large enough to accommodate these worshippers and the gendered division of space. Another possible reason for the greater participation of Sunni women in mosque life is that most adherents to Sunni Islam are African, with only small minorities being Arab (mostly Yemeni) and Asian.[11]

Regardless, members of the Istiqaama Women's Group in Mwanza hold various views on the lack of an Ibadhi female presence in the mosques and at community meetings. During a meeting at the home of a group member, Shireen explained, "Ibadhis [in Mwanza] don't a have a place for women to pray like the Sunnis, so they pray at home. In Muscat and other places [however], they do build areas for women."[12] One of the women commented that a well-known sanctimonious elderly male figure, who apparently tends to avoid interactions with women, had once informed the community that if women came to the mosque, "they would cause trouble." In recounting this familiar story, the women all laughed, after which the group's treasurer cited a prophetic hadith that states women receive greater rewards in the afterlife if they pray at home (Sw., *ni thawabu zaidi kuswali nyumbani*). The treasurer went on to explain that women do perform the *tarāwīḥ* prayers at the Ibadhi Friday Mosque during Ramadan and that this is a meritorious practice.[13]

From Shireen's perspective, Ibadhi women's exclusion from the mosque is a matter of space. The mosque's designers, whether consciously or not, neglected to include a space for women to pray in seclusion, and this explained their absence from mosque life. She suggested that Ibadhi women in Tanzania lag behind their counterparts in Oman in matters of prayer because women in Oman have benefited from the state's modernization campaigns, including the building of Friday mosques in every major city of the sultanate. An important feature of these mosques is the inclusion of sizeable women's sections, which suggests an increased emphasis on accessibility in Omani women's participation in public piety. (See chap. 2.)

The different perspectives on women's mosque participation in Mwanza raise important questions about the gendered and intergenerational politics of space in the new Ibadhi mosque movement. For now, however, the net result is the same: women are not privy to much of the discussion or decision-making that happens in the mosque. Rather, they may hear news or ask about the meetings in conversations at home with a husband, brother, or father. In these same informal conversations, moreover, women may mobilize their male kin to ask Istiqaama for support on a particular matter. Indeed, it was in this way that the Istiqaama women in Mwanza began to address women's access to religious education and space.

Since then, according to Shireen, the group has acquired two plots of land. They are in the process of changing the title deed of the latter from individual to collective ownership. One of these two plots will support the girls' school, which aims to increase women's influence in the mosque and school system. The other plot will be used for the construction of a mosque that will be open to all madhabs and will include a women's section.

Another notable achievement of the group occurred during Ramadan in 2015, when the women raised TZS4,000,000 (US$1,597) to install waterpipes at the girls' school so that students would be relieved of the tiresome task of collecting water from a source a mile off site.[14]

Before the formation of the women's association, however, no organized community initiatives like this existed. "We had to start from scratch," Shireen explained. "We made food, mats, and other things to sell to sustain [ourselves], the initial costs [of] which were high."[15]

As homemakers and owners of small businesses, the women's group does not have access to the kinds of social and material capital generated by the male leadership; neither do they travel to and from the Gulf for business and study with the same frequency as their spouses, fathers, brothers, and uncles. Ibadhi women are thus more likely to collaborate with and to assist non-Ibadhi individuals and groups in Mwanza. For this reason, just as mosque attendance and public prayer are the important barometers of men's participation in the religious life of Istiqaama, alliance building with non-Ibadhis, social events like fundraisers, self-help initiatives, women's study groups, and home visits tend to be the measures of women's pious works.

The group's current activities focus on providing support to individuals in the community during major life events, such as funerals. The women also have a storage area with their own equipment, including funeral palls. In the event of a death in the family, the women host guests in their homes, share cooking and serving equipment, and prepare meals for visitors. Moreover, each woman donates TZS10,000 (US$4) on the first day of the funeral to cover Ibadhi mourning and burial expenses. If the husband of one of the group's members were to die, she would be given approximately TZS400,000 (US$160) toward her living expenses.[16]

The group also provides support to those in need during Ramadan. A form is distributed to each member to declare a donation to provide for Mwanza Muslims who cannot afford the meal to break the fast *(iftari)*. In 2015, the women managed to collect TZS600,000 (US$240) for this purpose.[17]

The Ibadhi Women's Group has also devised independent strategies for overcoming obstacles that women and girls face in education and religious participation. Shireen explained, "Like Istiqaama Mwanza, we [women] want to sustain ourselves; we women are not dependent on men *(hatutegemee wanaume)*."[18]

This idea of self-reliance (Sw., *kujitegemea*) has a distinct political and social history in Tanzania. In popular and political discourse, kujitegemea often appears alongside another term, *ujamaa*, usually translated as "national unity" or "familyhood." Ujamaa also refers to the socialist ideology and policies associated with the independence party and mass movement that TANU (the Tanganyika African National Union) established in 1954.[19] The implementation of these dual concepts of ujamaa and kujitegemea in the process of nation building was essential for shaping a socialist state based on the African principles of communitarianism. The idea of ujamaa centered on the notion of "self-reliance"—that people should build their futures for themselves—and on "the full participation of all Tanzanians in developing the nation. This took the form of communal labor in the rural sector and communal ownership of land and nationalization of the private sector and of public services," said Shireen.[20]

Shireen and the other group members, now in their late fifties and early sixties, are part of this ujamaa generation, and it is possible that their familiarity with the principles of the movement influenced their own vision of work and progress as it connects to self-reliance. Jessica Ott has suggested that the Swahili term *umoja*, or unity, which is closely related to ujamaa in the sense of the collective responsibility that it engenders, has become an "increasingly gendered" political form of discourse.[21] Using the framework of "collective conviviality," Ott demonstrates how "*umoja* avoids directly confronting patriarchal social structures, which raises questions about its potential to ensure gender justice."[22]

In practice, Shireen emphasized that the women's association works together with and supports (Sw., *tunashirikiana na tunakaa nao*) the initiatives of the men's organizations and said that the close personal relationships between the members of the two Istiqaama groups enable them to depend on each other for the implementation of their various initiatives. However, it is difficult to ascertain to what degree this support flows both ways; the women suggest that little of the funds generated by the Mwanza branch of Istiqaama under the male leadership trickles down into their own treasury, leaving them largely dependent on their own initiative and ingenuity in fundraising.

During my fieldwork in 2016, one of the leaders of the men's organization in Mwanza said that Istiqaama was in the process of revising its constitution to include the women's group in its leadership structure. As of July 2022, however, the women had yet to receive official recognition from the national Istiqaama organization. Recognition by the larger organization would undoubtedly expand the women's sphere of influence and enable them to apply for funds from the Istiqaama treasury.[23] On the other hand, their incorporation into the larger organization could diminish their power to make decisions regarding the distribution of funds and undermine their leadership vis-à-vis the more established men's organization.

Formally recognizing the women's group might also enable Istiqaama to reach a larger segment of the Omani and Muslim population in Mwanza because of the unique capacity of the women's organization to use smart phones and new media to mobilize other Ibadhi women around educational and charitable initiatives in Mwanza and Oman. The women communicate largely through WhatsApp, which enables them to mobilize quickly in the event of an emergency, such as a sudden death in the community.

Finally, incorporation of the women's group might motivate the development of other forms of organization and empowerment among Ibadhi women in Tanzania, including under Istiqaama.

## A Women's Institute in Mwanza

Apart from the various services they provide within their own community, Ibadhi women in Mwanza have developed collaborations with various Sunni and Shi'a Muslim charities in the city, especially with women of Yemeni heritage. I had the opportunity to visit a number of these charities with Mariam and her mother, the most memorable of which was a residential school for a women's institute in Nyamanaro. On the road to the Mwanza airport, Nyamanaro is a town that has undergone rapid development in the past ten years, as evidenced by the new and half-finished houses and shops lining the main road leading to the school. The ride was initially very rough, but we noticed that road construction was underway. Dusty potholes gave way to a smooth dirt road and, as we neared the educational institute's campus, a newly paved highway. As we approached the school, a large property of at least one acre came into view. Around it was a concrete and iron fence connected by a black gate at the entrance.

We met the institute's founder, Sara, in her office. Volumes of hadith and other Islamic texts, including a Swahili translation of the authoritative Sunni hadith collection *Sahīh al-Bukhārī* lined the bookshelves, along with framed certificates from the government legitimizing the property and school, including a certificate of recognition (Sw., *shahada ya taasisi*) from the National Muslim Council of Tanzania, BAKWATA. The back room stored an open and empty deep freezer and the remaining office furnishings and equipment were modest, including black-and-white checkered floors, two light-blue plastic chairs, a computer monitor, and a photocopier, among other things. The photocopy machine had been a donation from the Amana Bank, which is well regarded by Muslims in the region. The bank donated several items to the school when they first opened and continues to support the ma'had in various unspecified ways. Other local charities, such as The Table and Desk Foundation (TDCF), which was started by South Asian Shi'a emigres from Mwanza who now live in the United Kingdom, donated several tanks to the school for water storage.[24]

The women's institute comprises dormitories, classrooms, administrative offices, a computer lab, a community garden, and a lengthy workshop room that looks like an industrial garment factory with neatly organized rows of small desks topped with black, vintage sewing machines. The massive wall that surrounds the property maintains the privacy of the female teachers and residential students.

Sara is a petite Afro-Yemeni woman who single-handedly runs the school with occasional support from private donors and her dedicated core of teachers. Her inspiration for founding the school came after she attended a lecture by a local celebrity known for delivering compelling sermons in town. The dā'iyya, or preacher, had recounted her experience visiting the fishing towns and villages that surround the lake and expressed her dismay at the impoverished situation of the children there, who had few opportunities for education or social mobility. Moved by her story, Sara gathered five other Sunni women to establish the school, which got its start in a rented house in an area called Ghana, north of the permanent campus. The purpose of the school was, and continues to be, to provide girls from low-income families with an inexpensive and safe learning environment where they also receive regular meals. It bothered Sara that when girls completed Form 4,[25] they could not find employment; in addition, several of them got pregnant after graduating or became infected with HIV. She said, "It hurt me very much. So, I saw that it was better to have religion, to get that knowledge first."[26]

At first, the ma'had enrolled only fifteen girls because many feared they could not afford to attend, but the number of students has grown steadily each year since, totaling seventy-five by the time of my visit in the summer of 2019.

At that time, the school had four teachers whose courses focused primarily on the study of Arabic, the Qur'an, and basic Islamic texts and ritual practices. Another four teachers taught in the vocational studies section, which included courses focused on home economics, such as cooking, embroidery (Sw., *kudarizi*), and sewing. The school hoped to provide more, however, and had registered to receive training from the Information and Communication Technology Commission (ICT) and the Vocational Education and Training Authority (VETA), which the Tanzanian government created in 1994 to "ensure quality vocational skills, providing, regulating, coordinating, promoting, and financing vocational education and training for national socio-economic development."[27] With ICT and VETA accreditation, the school could supplement the current curriculum with vocational training and grant students government-recognized certificates to help them gain work or start businesses in the fields in which they excel. This would help the school achieve its goal of enabling women from the villages to employ themselves (Sw., *wajiajiri*) when they return home after graduation. Until then, Sara says the school tries to find resources related to a graduate's specialization (such as a sewing machine), which they then give to the graduate before she leaves the school.

In its early years, to secure donations, the six founders often threw fundraising or self-help events called *harambees*, or parties (*haflas*), where community members participated in games and activities, watched short skits, and bought homemade food and treats. The events helped, but the money earned barely covered maintenance costs, teacher salaries, and the food and supplies needed to keep the school running. At one point, Sara's partners began to waver as they were aging and tired of operating the school on a volunteer basis without a steady source of income. They suggested closing the school and relieving themselves of the responsibility.

"I said no," Sara told me. "I still had the will to do it. Therefore, in 2017, we had a big *harambee*, just as we used to. I had seen that they were defeated. And thank God we received the money to build this [new] campus."[28]

The plot they purchased already had two buildings, which they preserved to use as classrooms and dormitories. They were able to add more brick buildings with corrugated iron roofs using the harambee funds. The sewing machines, which have increased in number from four to thirty-six since the school opened, were purchased at a discount for about TZS60,000 (US$24); a collection of embroidery machines was added as well.

Further development occurred a few months prior to our visit, in October 2018, when construction began on the privacy wall surrounding the institute. A wealthy Egyptian businessperson who lives in a neighboring lake district provided the funds and oversaw the construction. Sara and her colleagues had heard that there was someone in town who liked "to do religious works," so they wrote him a letter requesting support for the wall the next time he was in Mwanza for business. After visiting the school and measuring the plot, he agreed to build the wall using his own contractors as he preferred not to make a cash donation. By December 2018, work on the wall was complete, worth a total of TZS80,000,000 (US$31,942).

In more recent years, due to the sharp economic downturn experienced by many middle- and upperclass Tanzanians and businesses, women's organizations have limited their use of harambees to raise funds for charitable causes, recognizing that the financial burden and time required to plan the events would likely not result in the necessary returns. Because most students do not pay full tuition or room and board, the teachers and administrators have had to devise new ways for them to contribute to their education and care at the school.

"This year we have a different system of receiving students," Sara said. "That is, every student must come [to school] with food. Because things have become hard."[29] She went on to explain that because they cannot depend on tuition money, they are asking students to bring food from home, both at the start of each school term and after each break, so that they can contribute to the meals. Most of the students come from farming or fishing backgrounds on the lake belt, which includes the regions of Musoma, Pala, Dida, and Shinyanga, so their contributions come mainly in the form of produce like corn, beans, and other nonperishables. These items boost the school's consistent, but varied, monthly contributions from committed patrons. "Although it is not enough," Sara said, "*alhamdullilah*, it pushes us along."[30]

The school does set a monthly budget with the help of a volunteer accountant from BAKWATA. The budget is then used to determine how much support to request from patrons each month, and this has helped resolve some of the economic issues.

Another change they have made is requiring parents to make monthly visits to the school to see their children because in the past, some parents would not visit their children for a whole year. Sara worried that the girls who were not visited would become disconnected from their roots and family networks. Further, she was concerned that parents were abusing the boarding policy, using it as a form of long-term childcare. Under the new policy, if parents do not visit for two months in a row, their children are sent home. Regular visits from family members also enable a steady flow of donations in kind, although this may put an economic strain on parents who are responsible for several other children at home or who find it difficult to leave their farms or pay for transport into town.

The school's economic position has been further challenged by the current political administration. Contrary to the desire of the women founders, the school is subject to the authority of BAKWATA. The founders had tried to register with the government as an independent organization, as the Istiqaama Women's Group had, but they could not afford the registration fees. "So, when you don't register with the government," Sara explained, "you must register with something, so that you don't get in trouble. So, we have registered with BAKWATA.... We are under the umbrella of BAKWATA."[31] She went on to explain that they would be "freer" if they could register as a nongovernmental organization rather than as a religious one, but she said they would never be allowed to fully cut ties with BAKWATA "because that is how the government wants it."

When I asked how the school benefited by registering with BAKWATA, she suggested that it gave them some form of legitimacy and protection—particularly important in the era of President John Pombe Magufuli (1959–2021), whose administration put Muslim charities under high surveillance. Sara said that after the wall was funded, she was jailed by the government for nine days and the Egyptian who built it was also arrested and investigated. Both were suspected of operating with terrorist organizations such as Al-Qaeda.

Sara explained that the school's other board members had been persistently absent during the time of her arrest, so when the government came to investigate the campus, they were suspicious that she was the only person managing the school. She suggested that there was a racial dimension to the division of labor in women's groups in Mwanza—one where "White" Arab woman (*weupe*) had a reputation for not showing up to help as they were not used to doing activity outside their domestic duties. This often caused the work to fall on one person—and during the school's surveillance, that one person happened to be Sara.

The school administrators are now very careful about writing down the names of donors and keeping receipts for major donations and tracking communication with donors on social media, in case such an investigation was to happen again. Regardless, the surveillance impacted the group's *haflas* as people want to see registration before they participate. Registration with the government as a school was not possible for two years, until August 2019, as President Magufuli had set out to investigate all Islamic charities; therefore, if someone wanted to donate to the group during this time, they had to do so secretly.

In addition, the school found that donors they could formerly rely on for regular funds or supplies were scared off by the arrests and surveillance. For example, a Somali businessperson who used to donate soap, sugar, and oil each month stopped the deliveries because of political concerns. This created a problem, Sara explained, because they had come to depend on the supplies and had not created space in their budget for purchasing them.

BAKWATA is ineffective in protecting Muslim groups from this surveillance and harassment; it also does not have a unified vision of how to help those under its charge as it oversees such a large number and variety of Muslim groups, often with very disparate objectives.

## The Khairia Sunni Women's Group

Taking their name from the Arabic word that can mean both virtuous and charitable, the Khairia Sunni Women's Group was formed in the year 2000. The members are from mixed backgrounds, identifying primarily as Yemeni, Omani, and Indian, and most come from families that have been in Mwanza for generations. The group began with twenty-five members, and by the time of my interview with their chairperson, Mona, in 2019, their numbers were up to thirty-five. When we met in her second-floor apartment off a main street surrounded by shops and businesses in Mwanza Town, Mona explained that most of the members were "housewives" who, in addition to their domestic duties, engaged in small businesses (Sw., *biashara ndogo ndogo*) out of their houses. Since the group began, its members have dispersed, with some living in other towns and cities like Dar es Salaam.

Group members' main source of pride is their educational and health initiatives, most notably the madrasa they have been running since 2003, when the original patron passed away and gifted it to them. The school initially had 161 students, which decreased to 120 when students or their families started to move away. The youngest students are three years old. Monthly membership fees are TZS32,500 (US$13) per member, and payments go toward teacher salaries and maintenance, but tuition is free.

The group also provides childcare for families in the neighborhood, and they would like to build a nursery on the plot that they had purchased next to the school for this sole purpose, but the space is too small. So, instead, they plan to build a two-story social hall to generate revenue for the school.

Like Istiqaama, the group has extensive kin networks outside of Mwanza Town, which means they often receive proposals and requests from rural communities to assist in developing programs and resources that benefit women in those places. Their current projects include volunteering at the major Sunni Friday Mosque in Mwanza, doing things like donating carpets and helping with cleanup following prayers and events. In addition, for Eid al-Fitr, they rent a school space like that of the Thaqafa School and charge entrance fees to provide games, toys, and a jumping castle for children. They also host a Qur'an competition for boys and girls every year during Ramadan.

Also like the Istiqaama Women's Group, their meetings take place in different locations and are usually hosted by one of the group members. The meetings, which occur on the last Saturday of every month, are both social and professional, with discussions often focused on creative ways to change attitudes around social issues. The women also determine what causes to raise money for during events and their annual party, or hafla.[32] Although they would like to develop their own event ideas, Mona explained that many of their ideas were borrowed from women's groups in Kenya. They especially favor event ideas that elicit the power of storytelling through drama because they see this as a means of transmitting lessons to several people at once.

At their annual haflas, they dress in character and enact social dramas with various themes that teach lessons of Islam. One such drama, for example, is a cautionary tale about not valuing one's parents. It tells of an educated child who travels away from home in search of work but does not tell their parents; when the child loses the job and returns home for the support of their mother, they find that she has passed away. Other dramas center on themes of charity, prayer, and the example of the close companions of the Prophet Muhammad (the Sahaba). For the haflas hosted by male-led Muslim groups like the main Istiqaama organization, they buy electronic products and other goods from local businesses and then auction them off at higher prices.

The funds raised at the haflas support a variety of projects. One such project is to assist students who develop financial difficulties midway through their studies abroad in neighboring countries like Kenya. The group was also able to secure a building to perform the ritual washing of bodies in preparation for burial, although this was done in conjunction with additional financial support from the Istiqaama Women's Group.

Other fundraising activities include trivia nights, with faith-related questions and awards for the winners, and a *fete fete*—essentially a bazaar at which community members can set up stalls in a designated area to sell various goods. The latter event is not very profitable, as each table is TZS10,000 (US$4) to rent and there are other setup costs; but they provide enjoyment and leisure for women and children while also giving community members an opportunity to meet.

Adding to the economic challenges faced by Khairia is their members' lack of financial independence as most do not have a steady source of expendable income and cannot always pay the membership fees or financially contribute in other ways.

Mona explained that younger people, due to their many other responsibilities, are more likely to contribute monetary resources to support the group's initiatives than attend meetings or participate in event planning; moreover, the group struggles to recruit younger members as many young women often leave Mwanza when they get married or study abroad.

Since the younger cohort tends to be less involved in pious work and volunteering, they often are not present, meaning those who are left to carry out the work become tired and overcommitted. For their work to be successful, Mona said, members must be more financially self-sufficient and committed to showing up and sharing responsibilities within the group.

Sustainable income is a constant source of concern for the group's leadership, as is the youth's apparent lack of time and interest in carrying on their grassroots initiatives that revolve primarily around fundraising for causes such as religious education, supporting orphans and other children at risk, caring for the dead, and helping families in times of economic hardship and crisis. Mona explained, "All we hope for is to get more funds to build the social hall so that we can generate income that is sustainable; income is quite a challenge because we do not get much support from external sources. We have seven madrasa teachers, and we need to be more sustainable [to support them]."[33]

Although it is recognized as a religious society by the government, the Khairia Women's Group has managed to avoid registering with BAKWATA and sees little value in doing so as it would mean decreased autonomy without any additional financial assistance. As Mona put it, BAKWATA itself needs funding.

## Conclusion

The collaborations between the Istiqaama Women's Group and other Muslim associations I observed in Mwanza tended to occur primarily between middle- and upperclass Yemen Sunni and Omani Ibadhi in Mwanza, suggesting that while women in these communities may adopt an ethic of Muslim unity, this unity is in some sense confined to class and caste identities that exclude the majority of the town's residents. Moreover, as Shireen's marriage demonstrates, the two Arab diasporas are bound by kinship ties and cultural familiarity and their relative prominence in business. Members of both communities have family on the coast and abroad and frequently send their children to neighboring countries or the United Arab Emirates and Oman for study.

When studying religious institutions, especially those of religious minorities, it is easy to look to the most public-facing members for answers about what it means to belong to the group and what makes the group unique. But the official narratives rarely give way to nuances in group identity formation; neither do they tend to highlight how religious agency operates on the margins, which is often more flexible than what is found at the center. In the case of the women's organization in Mwanza, such flexibility can be found in its leader, who is not Ibadhi but Shafiʻi, and not Omani but Yemeni—a demographic that would probably not be found in a leader of the larger, and perhaps more rigid, men's organization. Incidentally, being outside the public eye and doing this more grassroots-type work is what enables such flexibility, which suggests that how women both engage the public and present themselves publicly matters in postcolonial Muslim contexts such as Istiqaama in Tanzania.

The absence of publicly available information on or advertising of Ibadhi women's activities in Tanzania further underscored the importance of examining gender dynamics in religious organizations. By looking beyond the public-facing figures and official narratives of Istiqaama, I was able to discover the crucial role that women play in shaping sustainable community institutions and support networks. Their more flexible work schedules, creative funding schemes, and extensive social networks enable them to engage in important grassroots work focused on caring for vulnerable members of the community, particularly women and girls, in real time.

The case of the Istiqaama Women's Group in Mwanza reveals a complex and nuanced picture of how gender operates within the context of a conservative diaspora religious organization. While the official narratives and public image of Istiqaama may center around male leadership and activities, my observations showed that women play a crucial role in the day-to-day operations of the organization, particularly in local community building and support work. They do not view their work as a challenge to male authority but as a locally focused and more modest supplement to the grander transnational projects enacted by well-connected male elites in their community. As this role suggests, the two groups—men's and women's—cannot exist without each other, but there is undoubtedly a very gendered dynamic to the role of each. While the role of the male is to be the public face of Istiqaama, the role of the female is to be a local face—and a driving force in the organization's work in specific parts of Tanzania.

## Notes

1. Bill Ashcroft, Gareth Griffiths, and Helen Tiffin, eds., "Diaspora," in *The Post-Colonial Studies Reader* (New York: Routledge, 1995), 425.

2. The Istiqaama women's organization in Mwanza practices religion and charity in ways that secure their own and their families' place within an exclusive Omani diaspora. At the same time, the group draws on their own expertise, social networks, and community resources to ensure the economic security of vulnerable members of their community and empower disadvantaged women and girls beyond the diaspora. Scholarship on Islam in East Africa tends to focus on the Swahili-speaking coastal regions with very little work on Muslim women and gender in mainland towns and villages.

3. Adeline Masquelier, *Women and Islamic Revival in a West African Town* (Bloomington: Indiana University Press, 2009); Britta Frede and Joseph Hill, eds., "En-Gendering Islamic Authority in West Africa," *Islamic Africa*, 5, no. 2 (2014).

4. Saba Mahmood, *Politics of Piety: The Islamic Revival and the Feminist Subject* (Princeton: Princeton University Press, 2004), 2.

5. Ibid.

6. Oguz Alyanak, "When Women Demand Prayer Space: Women in Mosques Campaign in Turkey," *Journal of Middle East Women's Studies* 15, no. 1 (2019): 126–27.

7. A fried flatbread, usually served with stew or beans.

8. A spiced donut.

9. A doughlike staple made of corn flour, millet, or sorghum.

10. In Swahili, *"Jiwe la msingi la Masjid Ibaadh Mwanza limewekwa na Mufti wa Sultanate of Oman Sheikh Ahmed bin Hamed Al-Khalili, Tarehe 6-1-1995. 4-Shaaban-1415 hijriya."*

11. In a study of Muslim women in Mombasa, Kenya, Margaret Strobel explains how a self-perceived sense of social backwardness motivated Omani Arab women in the city's old town to establish their own, largely ethnicity-based, collectives and self-improvement organizations in the 1950s. The first Arab women's association in Mombasa (the Arab Women's Institute) emerged, in part, as a response to criticisms lodged against members of this ethnic group by their more organized Asian counterparts. The institute was at first more concerned with the politics of prestige that depended on reinscribing social hierarchies by maintaining a selective membership (mostly Omani Arabs) with a conservative agenda focused on enhancing the social image of the group. In protest to the institute's exclusionary practices, the more ethnically diverse and inclusive Arab Muslims Cultural Association emerged in its place. This new association eventually dropped the "Arab" part of its name to appear more inclusive. See Margaret Strobel, *Muslim Women in Mombasa, 1890–1975* (New Haven, CT: Yale University Press, 1979), 184–87.

12. Istiqaama Women's Group, interview with author, Mwanza, April 26, 2016.

13. Ibid.

14. Shireen (president of the Istiqaama Women's Group), interview with author, Mwanza, April 25, 2016.

15. Ibid.

16. Ibid.

17. Istiqaama Women's Group, interview with author, April 26, 2016.

18. Shireen, interview with author, April 25, 2016.

19. See David Westerlund, *Ujamaa Na Dini: A Study of Some Aspects of Society and Religion in Tanzania, 1961–1977* (Stockholm: Almqvist & Wiksell International, 1980).

20. Istiqaama Women's Group, interview with author, April 26, 2016.

21. Jessica Ott, "Umoja: A Swahili Feminist Ethic for Negotiating Justice in Zanzibar," *Feminist Anthropology* (2022): 1.

22. Ibid.

23. Shireen, interview with author, April 25, 2016.

24. This organization has a relatively large budget of £291,647 as of December 31, 2020, accessed March 15, 2024 "About Us." *The Desk and Chair Foundation.* https://www.tdcf.org.uk/about-us/.

25. Form 4 signals the end of the ordinary four-year high school track.

26. Sara (founder of the women's ma'had), interview with author, Mwanza region, June 15, 2019.

27. Vocational Education and Training Authority, "About Us" (United Republic of Tanzania: Ministry of Education Science and Technology), accessed May 25, 2022, https://www.veta.go.tz/about-us.

28. Sara, interview with author, June 15, 2019.
29. Ibid.
30. Ibid.
31. Ibid.
32. Mona (leader of the Khairia Women's Group), interview with author, Mwanza, December 6, 2019.
33. Ibid.

# Conclusion

The book's cover image, which was taken in 2019, shows a wall and fence enclosing acres of land meant for the construction of a modern Istiqaama high school on the outskirts of Mwanza. As of 2024, nearly five years later, the school has still not been built on "Ibadhi Street," which is paved and marked with black lettering on a yellow street sign in anticipation of its establishment, like signs found in the city center. This deliberate naming of an Ibadhi space in a mainland town before the actual building of the school is a nod to past Ibadhi pioneers and settlers in the northwest and represents the community's hopes for future development and role within Tanzanian society. However, these aspirations for the state-of-the-art school have been put on hold indefinitely as the community struggles with economic challenges caused by the COVID-19 global pandemic as well as, perhaps, a national climate wary of Gulf and Islamic organizations and institutions.

The chapters in this book show how nostalgia, or a longing for a virtuous Ibadhi past, influences Ibadhi revivalism and identity politics today. Grassroots expressions of Ibadhi identity, like the Istiqaama school, nationalist movements, and state-building projects, are discussed. Reclaiming a specific historical narrative helps unite the Omani diaspora community, giving them a sense of heritage and identity despite external pressures and historical traumas. The Ibadhi community in Tanzania seek to honor their past while dealing with current challenges, illustrating the complex and diverse nature of nostalgia, as explained by cultural theorist Svetlana Boym, in shaping identity.

At the same time, the existence of "Ibadhi Street" in Mwanza implies a more tolerant religious environment in Tanzania compared to Oman. While Oman valorizes religious tolerance and political neutrality, public declaration of sectarian identity is not permitted for mosques and schools, even if the majority of attendees may be Ibadhi. In contrast, the street sign and fence at the high school in Mwanza—along with the Istiqaama logos and plaques commonly found in Ibadhi mosques that provide information about their history, founding, and namesakes of religious authorities such as Imam Jabir ibn Zayd or Mufti al-Khalili—indicate that while it is not obligatory to be Ibadhi to attend the school, doing so implies accepting the moral and communal boundaries imposed by Ibadhism. These boundaries are being redefined in the postcolonial era through neoliberal reforms that have enabled the privatization of religious institutions in Tanzania since the 1980s and the renewal of ties between Tanzania and Oman.

Visible examples of Ibadhi-Omani influence in Tanzania also form part of a local initiative undertaken by Ibadhi actors in the country and other parts of East Africa, such as Uganda, Kenya, and the countries of Central Africa, where Omanis settled—not discussed in this book but important to keep in mind for future scholarship in this area. The aim of this initiative is to revitalize the religious practices of the Omani diaspora by establishing sustainable educational and economic institutions. These efforts are made possible through the resources and moral support provided by the transnational Istiqaama community. The Tanzanian branches of this community are dedicated to preserving various elements of Ibadhi tradition, achieved through the restoration and expansion of Ibadhi heritage.

Examples of these preservation efforts include the conservation and expansion of old Omani family mosques in Zanzibar and the mainland, along with the construction of new and larger Friday congregational mosques. Additionally, the development of the Istiqaama school system discussed in chapter 3 is an essential aspect of these endeavors. Both the Omani state and Istiqaama in Muscat and Tanzania collaborate on a global scale by combining public Islamic outreach (daʿwa) and reform through education, heritage conservation, and charitable initiatives within an Ibadhi framework.

Chapter 4 showed that through their engagement with Islamic reformism, the Ibadhi community in Tanzania seeks to assert their distinct identity within the larger Muslim community in Tanzania while also highlighting their unique connections to religious communities in Oman and Algeria. This reformism is not only a means of religious revitalization but also a way to assert their social and economic influence within Tanzania.

Furthermore, this reformism is not solely focused inward, but also outwards towards promoting religious tolerance and unity among Muslims in

Tanzania. By emphasizing the principles of inclusivity and diversity within Islam, the Ibadhi community in Tanzania aspires to foster better interreligious relations which will also secure their own place as a religious minority within the country's predominantly Christian and Sunni Muslim religious landscape.

Ibadhis are greatly influenced by both past and present Ibadhi and Omani national discourses on religious tolerance and unity among Muslims. The memory of the Islamic sultanate in Zanzibar, as well as the revolution, also plays a part in this. Additionally, these efforts are driven by a desire to maintain and strengthen the diplomatic relationships between Tanzania and Oman since the revolution in 1964.

Istiqaama works to address suspicions that it is promoting Omani neoimperialism and soft power in postcolonial and postrevolution Tanzania. They do this through two interconnected strategies. Istiqaama is a community of mainly Swahili and Arabic speakers who practice Ibadhism. They are a religious minority operating both within and outside the boundaries of the nation-state. They achieve this by using their extensive Afro-Arab diaspora networks in Tanzania and Oman. Istiqaama also connects Ibadhi religious communities on the so-called Swahili coast and the East African interior by establishing local branches of the association in major Omani settlements across the country. In the past, trade interests linked the Omani diasporas on the coast and the inland regions.

As chapter 5 showed, those living farther inland, like in Mwanza or Shinyanga, conducted their economic activities independently from the sultanate in Zanzibar. They relied more on the cooperation of local African authorities. This resulted in a less rigid religious authority structure within the mainland Ibadhi communities and they integrated better with the predominantly non-Muslim or Sunni African communities in the northwest. However, their isolation from the coastal region meant that the Ibadhi communities in the interior did not benefit as much from the patronage practices of the sultans and Arab ruling elite. This also led to the assumption that Ibadhi merchants in northwestern Tanzania practiced a more localized form of Islam and were not actively spreading their religious teachings beyond their own circles. Before this book, there was no comprehensive scholarship that showed how the different histories of colonialism, economic enterprise, and integration and/or segregation from non-Arab communities have influenced the current state of Ibadhi religious activity in various regions of Tanzania today.

This book opens possibilities for further research in several areas. For instance, future work could examine the nature of the state's collaborations with Istiqaama in Oman Tanzania mainland, and Zanzibar. How have state actors perceived the increasing influence of diaspora religious networks and their role in revitalizing local economies and religious institutions through the introduction of new spaces for worship, congregation, and business across the country? What challenges do minority religious groups, which receive substantial internal and external funding, pose to Muslim authorities such as BAKWATA and the office of Zanzibar's mufti, who represents Islam on behalf of the state?

Muslim diaspora organizations like Istiqaama provide a unique opportunity to understand the impact of distinct local politics and social history in Oman, mainland Tanzania, and Zanzibar on the role of Muslim women in the public sphere and grassroots organizations in each location. Moreover, examining the long-term sustainability of cultural conservation projects within Muslim communities in East Africa and the Gulf can help identify challenges and opportunities for preserving and redefining cultural heritage over time. Research into gendered strategies for ensuring the continuity of cultural traditions and practices can provide valuable guidance for the various cultural brokers involved in such conservation efforts.

In this book, I have examined the representation of Ibadhi religious practices in Tanzania, specifically focusing on Istiqaama and its educational and charitable institutions. This book makes an important contribution to the academic discussion on contemporary Muslim politics, emphasizing how Muslim individuals establish and convey religious authority through new and existing institutions. It illustrates how religious patronage, which may on the surface seem apolitical, actually holds important symbolic authority that can both ease and aggravate tensions between postcolonial states and former colonial powers. While this phenomenon has been extensively researched in relation to countries colonized by Western powers, little research has been done on how similar power dynamics play out in countries that were also under the imperial influence of non-Western powers. My analysis focuses on the role of religious authority and grassroots activism in this process. This book offers insights into the religious practices of the Omani and Ibadhi communities in postcolonial and postrevolution Tanzania, underscoring the rise of new forms of transnational knowledge exchange between the countries of East Africa and the Gulf, and East and Northwest Africa.

# GLOSSARY

al-tasāmuḥ—religious "tolerance"; Ibadhi generosity or prudent association with non-Ibadhis. See also: *walāya*.
'abaya (Ar.); buibui (Sw.)—long, loose overgarment, usually black, worn by Muslim women.
'ulama'—classically trained Muslim scholars.
uṣūl (al-fiqh)—sources of the Islamic legal tradition.
Ahl al-Ḥaqq w'al-Istiqāma—the People of Truth and Righteousness; Ibadhi self-designation.
Al-Busaidi Dynasty—the ruling family of Oman based in Muscat; the royal household of the Zanzibar sultanate (1830s–1964).
islāḥ—reform.
al-Nahḍa—lit., "the awakening"; the Ibadhi and Omani "renaissance."
al-shūrā—the principle of consultation; the council that elects the leader of the Ibadhi imamate.
al-taʻaṣṣub—religious fanaticism or sectarianism.
furū' (Ar.); matawi (Sw.)—"branches" of religion.
musliḥ, pl. muslihīn—Muslim reformer.
bara (Sw.)—mainland Tanzania (Tanganyika).
Zanzibar archipelago—a group of islands in the western Indian Ocean that, with its two main administrative centers, Unguja Island and Pemba Island, forms part of the United Republic of Tanzania.
baraza (Sw.)—concrete bench part of the exterior wall of a classical Swahili home; a meeting place.
bidʻa—unlawful or reprehensible innovation to Islam.
daʻwa—Islamic outreach or missionary activity.

**Omani diaspora**—people of Omani ancestry who live in Tanzania, specifically those who practice Ibadhi Islam.
**dishdāsha (Gulf Ar.)**—ankle-length (typically white) Islamic shirt worn by men in the Arabian Gulf.
**diwān**—chief administrative office; the sultan's cabinet of officials.
**dāʻī/ dāʻīyya; pl. duʻāt**—Muslim missionaries or preachers; one who performs daʻwa.
**duka (Sw.)**—small shop or kiosk.
**elimu (Sw.)**—secular education.
**fiqh**—Islamic jurisprudence.
**firqa**—sect of Islam.
**ifṭār (Ar.), futari (Sw.)**—the meal that breaks the fast every day at sunset during Ramadan.
**hafla**—party or celebration.
**ḥalqa (Ar.)**—Islamic study circle.
**harambee (Sw.)**—"pulling together"; community self-help events.
**hijab**—cloth head covering worn by Muslim women.
**Ibadhi/Ibadhiyya**—a branch of Islam and school of law (madhab) found primarily in Oman, North Africa, and among the Omani diaspora in East Africa that predates and is neither Sunni nor Shiʻa. Modern Ibadhi thought centers of principles of just religious rule, consultation, strict religious observance, and religious tolerance.
**ijāza**—certificate of achievement; diploma from a traditional Islamic school.
**imām**—prayer leader or religious sovereign.
**imamate**—Islamic theocracy; sovereign polity of the imam.
**jāhiliyya**—the age of "ignorance" before the revelation of the Qurʾan and the prophecy of Muhammad.
**Jamiʻi Zinjibar**—the Zanzibar Congregation Mosque (a.k.a. Masjid Sultan Qaboos)
**jamʻiyya**—association, organization, or society.
**jumʻa**—Friday congregational prayers, typically held at a mosque and includes the weekly sermon (*khuṭba*).
**jumuiya (Sw.)**—community or association.
**qabīla (Ar.); kabila (Sw.)**—tribe or clan; genealogical affiliation usually determined by patrilineage.
**kanuni (Sw.)**—lit., "rule" or "doctrine"; common law in Tanzania.
**kanzu (Sw)**—ankle-length (typically white) shirt worn primarily by Muslim men in East Africa.
**khalīfa**—caliph or successor of Prophet Muhammad; historical leader of a caliphate.
**khawārij**—lit., "those who separated"; an early Islamic secessionist movement, sometimes called a sect, which emerged during a dispute over who should lead

the Islamic caliphate following the Battle of Siffin in 657 CE; precursor to the Ibadhi movement.
**khayr**—charitable deeds.
**khilāfa**—lit., "successor state"; caliphate.
**kitmān**—lit., "secrecy" or "concealment"; one of the four stages of religion in Ibadhism that obliges Ibadhis to hide their teachings and practices in the face of persecution.
**kofia (Sw.)**—round embroidered cloth hat with no brim worn by Muslim men in East Africa.
**kuamsha (Sw.)**—to awaken.
**kujitegemea (Sw.)**—to depend on oneself, self-reliance.
**ma'had**—Islamic educational institute.
**madhab, pl. madhāhib (Ar.); madhehebu (Sw.)**—school of Islamic law.
**madrasa**—religious school or place of higher education.
**Mapinduzi ya Zanzibar**—the Zanzibar Revolution (1964).
**mawaidha (Sw.)**—advice or counsel, often delivered as a lecture or sermon.
**mawlā**—a "client" or protected person and convert to Islam who was incorporated into an Arab family or tribal network.
**mihrab**—recess in the wall of a mosque that marks the direction of prayer towards Mecca.
**msikiti (Sw.)**—mosque.
**masjid jāmi' (Ar.); msikiti wa ijumaa (Sw.)**—Friday Congregational Mosque.
**mtemi, pl. batemi (Sw.)**—Bantu African ruler or chief.
**muezzin**—person who performs the call to prayer.
**mufti**—Muslim jurist who issues a legal opinion (*fatwa*).
**mwalimu (Sw.)**—secular or religious teacher; respected member of a community.
**niẓām al-'azzāba**—network and council of Ibadhi Muslim scholars in North Africa.
**qadi**—a judge in Islamic law.
**qunūt**—supplicatory prayer recited while standing. A debated practice in Islamic traditions.
**Quran**—the Islamic book of revelations received by the Prophet Muhammad.
**al-ru'ya**—the beatific vision; the doctrine pertaining to seeing God in the afterlife.
**ṣadaqa**—voluntary almsgiving; charity.
**ṣaḥāba**—the close companions of the Prophet Muhammad.
**al-salaf**—lit., "the predecessors"; referring to the pious first generations of Islam.
**Salafism**—a global Islamic interpretive tradition that aims to purify the faith by following the pious ancestors of Islam and rejecting unlawful innovations, Islamic revivalism.
**ṣalāt al-safar**—the travel prayer.

**sebleh**—meeting space or community gathering in Omani culture.
**shahāda**—the Islamic proclamation of faith that states, "There is no god but Allah, and Muhammad is the messenger of Allah."
**Shari'a**—lit., "path" or "way"; Islamic law.
**sharīf, pl. shurafā'**—descendant of Prophet Muhammad; patrician individuals or families often endowed with exceptional religious authority.
**Shi'a**—one of the two main branches of Islam that rejects the authority of the first three caliphs and regards 'Ali ibn Abi Talib and his male descendants as the true successors of Prophet Muhammad.
**Sufism**—a mystical and devotional branch of Islam. Its practitioners aim to seek spiritual truth and establish a direct and personal connection with God. Sufism is divided into different orders (*tariqas*), each with its unique teachings, practices, and lineages. However, certain Sufi rituals and practices, including forms of meditation involving song and dance, recitation of poetry, and the honoring of saints, are criticized by some Muslim scholars and fundamentalist movements like Wahhabism. These critics consider these practices as unauthorized innovations (*bid'a*).
**Sunni or *ahl al-sunna wa al-jama'a***—those who adhere to the customs of Prophet Muhammad (the Sunna); one of the two main branches of Islam and the religious affiliation of the majority of Muslims in the world.
**ta'āyush**—peaceful coexistence.
**tabia (Sw.)**—good behavior; obedient.
**ta'līm**—lit., "teaching" or "education."
**taqiyya**—religious dissimulation or denial of religious beliefs and associations in times of persecution.
**taqwā**—Muslim piety or religious consciousness.
**tarāwīḥ**—special prayers performed nightly at a mosque during Ramadan that include recitations of long portions of the Qur'an.
**tarbiyya**—moral education; guidance for a good upbringing.
**tawhīd**—Islamic conception of monotheism; the idea that God has no partners.
**Turāth (Ar.); Urithi (Sw.)**—heritage.
**Ujamaa (Sw.)**—"familyhood" or "brotherhood"; a postcolonial African socialist ideology focused on social and economic development during the leadership of Tanzania's first president, Julius Nyerere, between 1964 and 1985.
**Ummah**—the Muslim community.
**umoja (Sw.)**—unity.
**ustaarabu (Sw.)**—lit., "becoming an Arab"; gentility; civilized behavior.
**visiwani (Sw.)**—the island region off the coast of Tanzania that includes the Zanzibar archipelago and its two main islands of Unguja and Pemba.
**Wahhabism**—movement of Islamic puritanism based on the teachings of the eighteenth century scholar Muḥammad b. 'Abd al-Wahhāb from Najd.

**walāya and barā'a**—association and dissociation; the Ibadhi obligation to practice association with other Ibadhis and dissociate with but also tolerate non-Ibadhis.

**wamanga (Sw.)**—underprivileged Omani Arabs who emigrated to East Africa especially during the first half of the twentieth century.

**waqf; awqāf**—Islamic endowment.

**Zakat**—almsgiving; one of the five pillars of Sunni Islam.

**Zinjibāris**—term used to refer to the Swahili-speaking diaspora of Omani heritage in the Sultanate of Oman.

# BIBLIOGRAPHY

Abdel Haleem, M. A. *The Qur'an: A New Translation*. Oxford: Oxford University Press, 2016.
Abusharaf, Rogaia Mustafa. "The Omani-Zanzibari Family." *Hawwa* 16, no. 1–3 (2018): 60–89.
Ahmed, Chanfi. "Networks of Islamic NGOs in Sub-Saharan Africa: Bilal Muslim Mission, African Muslim Agency (Direct Aid), and Al-Haramayn." *Journal of Eastern African Studies* 3, no. 3 (2009): 426–37.
Aillet, Cyrille. "L'ibâḍisme, Une Minorité Au Cœur de L'islam." *Revue des mondes Musulmans et de la Méditerranée* 132, no. 132 (2012): 13–36.
———. *L'ibadisme dans les sociétés de l'Islam médiéval: modèles et interactions*. Berlin: De Gruyter, 2018.
Akhtar, Iqbal. "Negotiating the Racial Boundaries of Khōjā Caste Membership in Late Nineteenth-Century Colonial Zanzibar (1878–1899)." *Journal of Africana Religions* 2, no. 3 (2014): 297–316.
Al-Ismaili, Ahmed. "Ethnic, Linguistic, and Religious Pluralism in Oman: The Link with Political Stability." *AlMuntaqa* 1, no. 3 (2018): 58–73.
Al-Khalili, Shaykh Ahmad b. Hamad. *Al-Ḥaqq Al-dāmigh*. Al-Ṭabʿah 2. Sulṭanat ʿUmān: Maktabat al-Ḍāmirī, 1992.
———. *The Overwhelming Truth: A Discussion of Some Key Concepts in Islamic Theology*. Ruwi, Sultanate of Oman: Ministry of Awqaf and Religious Affairs, 2002.
Al-Rāshidī, Mubārak bin ʿAbd Allāh. "Al-Imām Abū 'Ubayda Bin Abī Karīma al-Tamimī Wa Fiquḥu." PhD diss., Zaytuna University, 1996.
Al-Riyami, Nasser Abdulla. *Zanzibar: Personalities & Events (1828–1972)*. Muscat, Oman: Beirut Bookshop, 2012.
Al-Sayfī, Muhammad ibn ʿAbd Allah ibn Saʿīd. *Al-Ibāḍiyya Fī Zinjibār Wa Mā Jāwarhā Min Duwwal Sharq Ifrīqiyya*, vol. 6. Masqat: Unknown, 2013.

Alyanak, Oguz. "When Women Demand Prayer Space: Women in Mosques Campaign in Turkey." *Journal of Middle East Women's Studies* 15, no. 1 (2019): 125–34.

Anderson, Benedict. *Imagined Communities: Reflections on the Origin and Spread of Nationalism*. Revised ed. London: Verso, 2016.

Antoun, Richard T. *Muslim Preachers in the Modern World: A Jordanian Case Study in Comparative Perspective*. Princeton, NJ: Princeton University Press, 2014.

Asad, Talal. *Genealogies of Religion Discipline and Reasons of Power in Christianity and Islam*. Baltimore: Johns Hopkins University Press, 1993.

Ashcroft, Bill, Gareth Griffiths, and Helen Tiffin. "Diaspora." In *The Post-Colonial Studies Reader*, part 16 (multiple authors), 425–59, London and New York: Routledge, 1995.

Atia, Mona. *Building a House in Heaven: Pious Neoliberalism and Islamic Charity in Egypt*. Minneapolis: University of Minnesota Press, 2013.

Azri, Khalid Al. "Change and Conflict in Contemporary Omani Society: The Case of Kafa'a in Marriage." *British Journal of Middle Eastern Studies* 37, no. 2 (2010): 121–37.

Bālḥāj, Qāsim ibn Aḥmad al-Shaykh. *Mudhakirāt Min Aʿmāq Jazīra Zinjibār*. Al-Jazāʾir: Manshūrāt al-Tabyīn/al-Jāḥiẓīyah, 2001.

Bang, Anne K. "Authority and Piety, Writing and Print: A Preliminary Study of the Circulation of Islamic Texts in Late Nineteenth- and Early Twentieth Century Zanzibar." *Africa* 81, no. 1 (2011): 89–107.

———. *Sufis and Scholars of the Sea: Family Networks in East Africa, 1860–1925*. Indian Ocean Series. London: Routledge Curzo, 2003.

———. "Teachers, Scholars and Educationists: The Impact of Hadrami-ʿAlawī Teachers and Teachings on Islamic Education in Zanzibar ca. 1870–1930." *Asian Journal of Social Science* 35, no. 4/5 (2007): 457–71.

Bang, Anne K., and Knut S. Vikør. "A Tale of Three Shambas Shāfiʿī-Ibāḍī Legal Cooperation in the Zanzibar Protectorate: Part I." *Sudanic Africa* 10 (1999): 1–26.

Bannon, Brendan, and Eveline Wolfcarius. "Somali Bantus Gain Tanzanian Citizenship in Their Ancestral Land." *UN Refugee Agency (UNHCR)*, June 3, 2009: https://www.unhcr.org/news/somali-bantus-gain-tanzanian-citizenship-their-ancestral-land.

Baptiste, Enki. "Des vallées du pays ibadite aux littoraux du sultanat: une histoire patrimoniale des manuscrits ibadites omanais." *Arabian Humanities* 15 (2022).

Baraza la Wawakilisshi Zanzibar, "Ripoti Ya Kamati Teule Ya Kuchungwa Upotevu Wa Nyaraka Uliotokea Katika Taasisi Ya Nyaraka Na Kumbukumu Za Taifa Zanzibar." Accessed March 28, 2024. https://testing.zanzibar assembly.go.tz/files/documents/select_report/RIPOTI_KAMATI_TEULE_NYARAKA.pdf.

Becker, Felicitas. *Becoming Muslim in Mainland Tanzania, 1890–2000*. Oxford: Oxford British Academy, 2008.

———. "Islamic Reform and Historical Change in the Care of the Dead: Conflicts over Funerary Practice among Tanzanian Muslims." *Africa* 79, no. 3 (2009): 416–34.

———. "Obscuring and Revealing: Muslim Engagement with Volunteering and the Aid Sector in Tanzania." *African Studies Review* 58, no. 2 (2015): 111–33.

Benabdallah, Lina. 2021. "Spanning Thousands of Miles and Years: Political Nostalgia and China's Revival of the Silk Road." *International Studies Quarterly* 65 (2): 294–305.

Berkey, Jonathan P. 1995. "Tradition, Innovation and the Social Construction of Knowledge in the Medieval Islamic Near East." *Past & Present* 146 (1): 38–65.

Bernama, "Malaysia, Algeria Sign MoU to Expand Cooperation in Higher Education." New Straits Times, December 5, 2016, https://www.nst.com.my/news/2016/12/194663/malaysia-algeria-sign-mou-expand-cooperation-higher-education.

Binte-Farid, Irtefa. "'True' Sons of Oman." In *Gulfization of the Arab World*, edited by Marc Owen Jones, Ross Porter, Marc Valeri, 41–56. Berlin: Gerlach, 2018.

Bishara, Fahad. *A Sea of Debt: Law and Economic Life in the Western Indian Ocean, 1780–1950*. Cambridge: Cambridge University Press, 2017.

Bissell, William Cunningham. *Social Memory, Silenced Voices, and Political Struggle: Remembering the Revolution in Zanzibar*. Dar es Salaam: Mkuki na Nyota in association with French Institute for Research in Africa, 2018.

Bolton, Caitlyn. "Making Africa Legible: Kiswahili Arabic and Orthographic Romanization in Colonial Zanzibar." *American Journal of Islamic Social Sciences* 33, no. 3 (2016): 61–78.

Bourdieu, Pierre. *The Field of Cultural Production: Essays on Art and Literature*. New York: Columbia University Press, 1993.

Boym, Svetlana. *The Future of Nostalgia*. New York: Basic Books, 2001.

Breen, Father Frank. "Maryknoll History in Tanzania, Part Five A: Shinyanga Diocese, 1954–1963," in *Maryknoll History in Africa: Tanganyika 1946 to early 1960s*, v. 2. Maryknoll, NY: Maryknoll, n.d.: https://maryknollafrica.org/category/our-downloads/.

Brennan, James. "Blood Enemies: Exploitation and Urban Citizenship in the Nationalist Political Thought of Tanzania, 1958–75." *Journal of African History* 47, no. 3 (2006): 389–413.

Burgess, G. Thomas. *Race, Revolution, and the Struggle for Human Rights in Zanzibar*. Athens: Ohio University Press, 2009.

Calver, Phoebe. "Jambo Food Products: Life in Every Drop." *Africa Outlook*. 2020. Accessed March 15, 2024. https://www.africaoutlookmag.com/company-profiles/785-jambo-food-products-ltd.

Chidester, David. *Savage Systems: Colonialism and Comparative Religion in Southern Africa*. Charlottesville: University of Virginia Press, 1996.

Cooper, Frederick. *From Slaves to Squatters: Plantation Labor and Agriculture in Zanzibar and Coastal Kenya, 1890–1925*. New Haven, CT: Yale University Press, 1980.
Coppola, Anna Rita. "Oman and Omani Identity during the 'Nahḍahs': A Comparison of Three Modern Historiographic Works." *Orienta Moderno* 94, no. 1 (2014): 55–78.
Coulson, Andrew. "Cotton and Textiles Industries in Tanzania: The Failures of Liberalisation." *Review of African Political Economy* 43 (2016): 41–59.
Crenshaw, Kimberlé. 1991. "Mapping the Margins: Intersectionality, Identity Politics, and Violence Against Women of Color." *Stanford Law Review* 43 (6): 1241–99.
Custers, M. H. *Al-Ibāḍiyya: A Bibliography*, vol. 2, Ibāḍīs of the Maghrib (Including Egypt). Maastricht, Netherlands: Universitaire Pers., 2006.
Desplat, Patrick, and Dorothea Schulz, eds. *Prayer in the City: The Making of Muslim Sacred Places and Urban Life*. Germany: Biefeld University Press, 2012.
Dolezal, Luna. "Shame, Vulnerability and Belonging: Reconsidering Sartre's Account of Shame." *Human Studies* 40, no. 3 (2017): 421–38.
Doumato, Eleanor Abdella, and Gregory Starrett. *Teaching Islam: Textbooks and Religion in the Middle East*. Boulder, CO: Lynne Rienner, 2007.
Dubois, W. E. B. *The Souls of Black Folk*. New York: Vintage / Library of America, 1990.
Dubuisson, Daniel, and William Sayers, trans. *The Western Construction of Religion: Myths, Knowledge, and Ideology*. Baltimore: Johns Hopkins University Press, 2003.
Durkheim, Emile. *The Elementary Forms of Religious Life*. New York: Free, 1995.
Eickelman, Dale F. "Mass Higher Education and the Religious Imagination in Contemporary Arab Societies." *American Ethnologist* 19, no. 4 (1992): 643–55.
———. "The Modern Face of Ibadism in Oman." In *Studies on Ibadism in Oman*, edited by Angeliki Ziaka. Hildesheim, Germany: Georg Olms, 2014.
Ersilia Francesca. "Ibadi School of Law." *The Oxford Encyclopedia of the Islamic World: Digital Collection*. Oxford: Oxford University Press, 2022.
Estim Construction Company Limited. Accessed March 15, 2024. https://estimconstruction.co.tz/portfolio/jaameh-zinjbaar-zanzibar-mosque/.
Euben, Roxanne L., and Muhammad Qasim Zaman. "Sayyid Qutb 1906–1966." In *Princeton Readings in Islamist Thought: Texts and Contexts from al-Banna to Bin Laden*. Princeton and Oxford: Princeton University Press, 2009.
Fair, Laura. *Pastimes and Politics: Culture, Community, and Identity in Post-Abolition Urban Zanzibar, 1890–1945*. Athens: Ohio University Press, 2001.
Fanon, Frantz and Philcox Richard. *The Wretched of the Earth*. New York: Grove Press, 2004.
Francesca, Ersilia. "Ibāḍī Law and Jurisprudence." *Muslim World* 105, no. 2 (2015): 209–23.

Frede, Britta, and Joseph Hill. "Introduction: En-Gendering Islamic Authority in West Africa." *Islamic Africa* 5, no. 2 (2014): 131–65.
Gaffney, Patrick D. *The Prophet's Pulpit: Islamic Preaching in Contemporary Egypt*. Berkeley: University of California Press, 1994.
Gaiser, Adam R. *Sectarianism in Islam: The Umma Divided*. Cambridge: Cambridge University Press, 2023.
———. *Shurāt Legends, Ibāḍī Identities: Martyrdom, Asceticism, and the Making of an Early Islamic Community*. Columbia: University of South Carolina Press, 2016.
———. "Imāmate in Khārijism and Ibāḍism." In *Encyclopaedia of Islam, THREE*, edited by Kate Fleet, Gudrun Krämer, Denis Matringe, John Nawas, Devin J. Stewart. Leiden, Netherlands: Brill, 2017.
———. "Khārijīs." In *Encyclopaedia of Islam, THREE*, Edited by Kate Fleet, Gudrun Krämer, Denis Matringe, John Nawas, Devin J. Stewart. Leiden, Netherlands: Brill, 2020.
Geertz, Clifford. *The Interpretation of Cultures: Selected Essays by Clifford Geertz*. New York: Basic, 1973.
Ghazal, Amal N. "Countercurrents: Mzabi Independence, Pan-Ottomanism and WWI in the Maghrib." *First World War Studies* 7, no. 1 (2016): 81–96.
———. *Islamic Reform and Arab Nationalism: Expanding the Crescent from the Mediterranean to the Indian Ocean* (1880s–1930s). New York: Routledge, 2014.
———. "The Other 'Andalus': The Omani Elite in Zanzibar and the Making of an Identity, 1880s–1930s." *MIT Electronic Journal of Middle East Studies* 5 (2005): 43–58.
Gilsaa, Søren. "Salafism(s) in Tanzania: Theological Roots and Political Subtext of the Ansār Sunna." *Islamic Africa* 6, no. 1–2 (2015): 30–59.
Glassman, Jonathon. *Feasts and Riot: Revelry, Rebellion, and Popular Consciousness on the Swahili Coast, 1856–1888*. Ann Arbor: University of Michigan, 1995.
———. *War of Words, War of Stones: Racial Thought and Violence in Colonial Zanzibar*. Bloomington: Indiana University Press, 2011.
Gooding, Phillip. *On the Frontiers of the Indian Ocean World: A History of Lake Tanganyika C. 1830–1890*. Cambridge, Cambridge University Press, 2022.
Goshey, Emily. "Eternal Punishment in Modern Ibādī Discourse: A Moral Argument." In *Local and Global Ibadi Identities*, vol. 13, Studies on Ibadism and Oman, 2019, edited by Yohei Kondo and Angeliki Ziaka, 327–42. Hildesheim: Georg Olms Verlag, 2019.
Grandguillaume, Gilbert. "Country Case Study on the Language of Instruction and the Quality of Basic Education: Policy of Arabization in Primary and Secondary Education Algeria." *UNESCO Digital Library, Education for All Global Monitoring Report 2005*, 2004, 1–57.
Guner, Ezgi. "NGOization of Islamic Education: The Post-Coup Turkish State and Sufi Orders in Africa South of the Sahara." *Religions* 12, no. 1 (2021): 24.

Guo, Shibao. "From International Migration to Transnational Diaspora: Theorizing Double Diaspora from the Experience of Chinese Canadians in Beijing." *International Migration & Integration* 17 (2016): 153–71.

Haefali, Evan. "The Problem with the History of Toleration." In *Politics of Religious Freedom*, 105–1. Chicago: University of Chicago Press, 2015.

Hall, Stuart. "Introduction: Who Needs 'Identity'?" In *Questions of Cultural Identity*, 1–17. Los Angeles: Sage, 2011.

———. "The Work of Representation." In *Representation: Cultural Representations and Signifying Practices*, 13–64. Edited by Stuart Hall. London: SAGE Publications Ltd, 1997.

Hall, Stuart and David Morley, *Essential Essays. Volume 2*. Durham: Duke University Press, 2019.

Hanely, Will. "Grieving Cosmopolitanism in Middle East Studies." *History Compass* 6, no. 5 (2008): 1,346–67.

Harvey, Graham. *Food, Sex and Strangers: Understanding Religion as Everyday Life / Graham Harvey*. Durham, NC: Acumen, 2013.

Heilman, Bruce E., and Paul J. Kaiser. "Religion, Identity and Politics in Tanzania." *Third World Quarterly* 23, no. 4 (2002): 691–709.

Hillewaert, Sara. *Morality at the Margins: Youth, Language, and Islam in Coastal Kenya*. New York: Fordham University Press, 2019.

Hirschkind, Charles. *The Ethical Soundscape: Cassette Sermons and Islamic Counterpublics*. New York: Columbia University Press, 2006.

Hoffman, Valerie J. "Ibadism: History, Doctrines, and Recent Scholarship." *Religion Compass* 9, no. 9 (2015): 173.

———. "Oman: Country Overview," vol. 3, *World Encyclopedia of Religious Practices*, 2006: 173.

———. "The Articulation of Ibadi Identity in Modern Oman and Zanzibar." *Muslim World*, 2004.

———. *The Essentials of Ibadi Islam*. Syracuse: Syracuse University Press, 2012.

Holmes, Oliver. "Arab Spring Autocrats: The Dead, the Ousted and Those Who Remain." *The Guardian*, December 14, 2020. Accessed March 28, 2024. https://www.theguardian.com/world/2020/dec/14/arab-spring-autocrats-the-dead-the-ousted-and-those-who-survived.

Hurd, Elizabeth Shakman. *Beyond Religious Freedom*. Princeton: Princeton University Press, 2016.

Ibrahim, Abdullahi Ali. "The 1964 Zanzibar Genocide: The Politics of Denial." In *Africa and the Gulf Region: Blurred Boundaries and Shifting Ties*, edited by Rogaia Mustafa Abusharaf and Dale F. Eickelman, 55–73. Berlin: Gerlach, 2015.

Ingrams, W. H. *Zanzibar: Its History and Its People*. London: Stacey International, 1931.

Institut Elhayat, "About," Facebook, n.d. Accessed March 25, 2024. https://www.facebook.com/Institut.Elhayat/about.
Iqrā': Lil Saff Al-Rabi' Al-Ibtidā'i, al-Taba'a al-'ashira, Ministry of Education in Oman: Istiqaama Muslim Community of Tanzania, 1997, 47.
Janson, Marloes. *Islam, Youth, and Modernity in the Gambia: The Tablighi Jama'at*. New York: Cambridge University Press, 2014.
Jomier, Augustin. *Islam, Réforme et Colonisation: Une Histoire de L'Ibadisme En Algérie (1882–1962)*. Paris: Bibliothèque Historique des Pays d'Islam, 2020.
———. "Les lettrés étendus d'un Archipel Saharien. Les circulations de lettrés Ibadites (XVIIe siècle-années 1950)," *Revue d'histoire Moderne & Contemporaine 2*, no. 63-2 (2016): 14–39.
Jones, Linda Gale. *The Power of Oratory in the Medieval Muslim World*. Cambridge: Cambridge Studies in Islamic Civilization, 2012.
Kane, Ousmane Oumar. *Non-Europhone Intellectuals*. Dakar, CODESRIA, 2016.
———. *The Homeland Is the Arena Religion, Transnationalism, and the Integration of Senegalese Immigrants in America*. New York; Oxford University Press, 2011. Print.
Katiba (Dar es Salaam: Jumuiya ya Kiislamu ya Istiqaama Tanzania, n.d.), http://istiqaamatz.org/tz/images/documents/katibaenglish.pdf.
Katz, Marion. *Prayer in Islamic Thought and Practice* (Themes in Islamic History; 6.). Cambridge and New York: Cambridge University Press, 2013.
Keshodkar, Akbar. "Marriage as the Means to Preserve 'Asian-Ness': The Post-Revolutionary Experience of the Asians of Zanzibar." *Journal of Asian and African Studies 45*, no. 2 (2010): 226–40.
Keshodkar, Akbar. "Who Needs China When You Have Dubai? The Role of Networks and the Engagement of Zanzibars in Transnational Indian Ocean Trade." *Urban Anthropology and Studies of Cultural Systems and World Economic Development 43*, no. ½/3 (2014): 105–41.
Kharusi, Nafla. "The Ethnic Label Zinjibari: Politics and Language Choice Implications among Swahili Speakers in Oman." *Ethnicities 12*, no. 3 (2012): 302–18.
Koenings, Nathalie Arnold. "For Us It's What Came After: Locating Pemba in Revolutionary Zanzibar." In *Social Memory, Silenced Voices, and Political Struggle: Remembering the Revolution in Zanzibar*, edited by William Cunningham Bissel and Marie-Aude Fouéré, 145–90. Dar es Salaam: Mkuki na Nyota, 2018.
Laing, Stuart. *Ivory, Slavery and Discovery in the Scramble for Africa*. Dar es Salaam: Mkuki na Nyota, 2017.
Lang, Gottfried O., and Martha B. Lang. "Problems of Social and Economic Change in Sukumaland, Tanganyika." *Anthropological Quarterly 35*, no. 2 (1962): 86–101.
Lauzière, Henri. *The Making of Salafism: Islamic Reform in the Twentieth Century*. New York: Columbia University Press, 1983.

Leichtman, Mara A. *Shi'I Cosmopolitanisms in Africa: Lebanese Migration and Religious Conversion in Senegal*. Bloomington: Indiana University Press, 2015.

Leurs, Robert, Peter Tumaini-Mungi, and Abu Mvungi. "Mapping the Development of Faith-Based Organizations in Tanzania." *UK Aid. International Development Department*, University of Birmingham, January 2011.

Limbert, Mandana E. "Caste, Ethnicity, and the Politics of Arabness in Southern Arabia." *Comparative Studies of South Asia, Africa, and the Middle East* 34, no. 3 (2014): 590–98.

———. "Oman: Cultivating Good Citizens and Religious Virtue." In *Teaching Islam: Textbooks and Religion in the Middle East*. Boulder, CO: Lynne Rienner, 2007, 103–24.

Lincoln, Bruce. *Discourse and the Construction of Society: Comparative Studies of Myth, Ritual, and Classification*. New York: Oxford University Press, 1989.

Locke, John, and William Popple. *A Letter Concerning Toleration*. Blacksburg, VA: Virginia Tech, 2001.

Loimeier, Roman. *Between Social Skills and Marketable Skills: The Politics of Islamic Education in 20th Century Zanzibar*. Leiden, Netherlands: Brill, 2009.

———. "Perceptions of Marginalization: Muslims in Contemporary Tanzania." In *Islam and Muslim Politics in Africa*, edited by Benjamin Soares and René Otayek. 137–56. London: Palgrave MacMillan, 2007.

Love Jr., Paul M. *Ibadi Muslims of North Africa: Manuscripts, Mobilization, and the Making of a Written Tradition*. Cambridge: Cambridge University Press, 2018.

Mahmood, Saba. *Politics of Piety: The Islamic Revival and the Feminist Subject*. Princeton, NJ: Princeton University Press, 2004.

———. "Religious Freedom, Minority Rights, and Geopolitics." In *Politics of Religious Freedom*, 142–48. Chicago: University of Chicago Press, 2015, 143.

Mamdani, Mahmood. *Citizen and Subject: Contemporary Africa and the Legacy of Late Colonialism*. Princeton, NJ: Princeton University Press, 1996.

———. *Neither Settler nor Native*. Cambridge: The Belknap Press of Harvard University Press, 2020.

Martin, B. G. "Notes on Some Members of the Learned Classes of Zanzibar and East Africa in the Nineteenth Century." *African Historical Studies* 4, no. 3 (1971): 525–45.

Martin, Richard C. "Createdness of the Qur'ān." In *Encyclopaedia of Islam, THREE*, edited by Kate Fleet, Gudrun Krämer, Denis Matringe, John Nawas, Devin J. Stewart. Leiden: Brill, 2015.

Masquelier, Adeline. *Women and Islamic Revival in a West African Town*. Bloomington: Indiana University Press, 2009.

Masuzawa, Tomoko. *The Invention of World Religions, or, How European Universalism Was Preserved in the Language of Pluralism*. Chicago: The University of Chicago Press, 2005.

Mathews, Nathaniel. "Imagining Arab Communities: Colonialism, Islamic Reform, and Arab Identity in Mombasa, Kenya, 1897–1933." *Islamic Africa* 4, no. 2 (2013): 135–63.

———. Nathaniel Mathews. *Zanzibar Was a Country: Exile and Citizenship between East Africa and the Gulf.* (Oakland: University of California Press, 2024).

McCants, Will. "Oman, the Land of No Jihad." *Jihadica.* July 18, 2008. http://www.jihadica.com/oman-the-land-of-no-jihad/.

McCutcheon, Russell T. *Religion and the Domestication of Dissent or, How to Live in a Less Than Perfect Nation.* London: Equinox, 2005.

McDow, Thomas E. *Buying Time: Debt and Mobility in the Western Indian Ocean.* Athens: Ohio University Press, 2018.

McIntosh, Janet. *The Edge of Islam: Power, Personhood, and Ethnoreligious Boundaries on the Kenya Coast.* Durham: Duke University Press, 2009.

McMahon, Elisabeth. *Slavery and Emancipation in Islamic East Africa: From Honor to Respectability.* Cambridge: Cambridge University Press, 2013.

Médard, Henri, and Shane Doyle. *Slavery in the Great Lakes Region of East Africa.* Rochester, NY: Boydell & Brewer, 2007.

Mehta, Nanji Kalidas. *Dream Half-Expressed, an Autobiography.* Bombay: Vakils, Feffer and Simons Private LTD., 1966.

Middleton, John. *The World of the Swahili: An African Mercantile Civilization.* New Haven, CT: Yale University Press, 1992.

Mittermaier, Amira. *Giving to God: Islamic Charity in Revolutionary Times.* Oakland: University of California Press, 2019.

Muʻammar, ʻAlī Yaḥyá. *al-Ibāḍīyah bayna al-firaq al-Islāmīyah ʻinda kuttāb al-maqālāt fī al-qadīm wa-al-ḥadīth* (al-Ṭabʻah 3.). Wizārat al-Turāth al-Qawmī wa-al-Thaqāfah, 2000.

Muchira, Njiraini. "China Pushes for Implementation of Tanzania's Bagamoyo Port." *Maritime Executive.* April 29, 2022. Accessed March 15, 2024. https://www.maritime-executive.com/article/china-pushing-for-implementation-of-tanzania-s-bagamoyo-port.

Muhammed, Mahmud Mukhtar, and Umar Wahab Sina. "Faith in National Development: A Review of the Activities of the Istiqaama Muslim Organisation of Ghana," in 3rd Int'l Conference on Science and Technology. International Conference on Religion and National Development, Kumasi: Kwame Nkrumah University of Science and Technology (KNUST), 2018.

No Author. "Chinese 'Ivory Queen' Yang Fenglan Jailed in Tanzania." *BBC News*, February 19, 2019. Accessed March 30, 2024. https://www.bbc.com/news/world-africa-47294715.

Nurse, Derek, and Thomas Spear. *The Swahili: Reconstructing History and Language of an African Society, 800–1500.* Philadelphia: University of Pennsylvania, 1985.

Nye, Joseph S. "Public Diplomacy and Soft Power." *The Annals of the American Academy of Political and Social Science* 616 (2008): 94–109.

Oduor, Michael. "Tanzania Still in Denial about Covid-19 Existence Despite Surge in Cases." *Africa News*. February 18, 2021. https://www.africanews.com/2021/02/18/tanzania-still-in-denial-about-covid-19-existance-despite-surge-in-cases/.

"Organization Chart" (Ministry of Endowment and Religious Affairs, Sultanate of Oman). Accessed March 16, 2017. www.MERA.om/MERA/organization-chart/.

Orsi, Robert A. *The Madonna of 115th Street: Faith and Community in Italian Harlem, 1880–1950*. Second edition. New Haven; Yale University Press, 2002.

Ott, Jessica. "Umoja: A Swahili Feminist Ethic for Negotiating Justice in Zanzibar." *Feminist Anthropology*, 2022: 389–403.

Petersen, Derek R. "Introduction: Heritage Management in Colonial and Contemporary Africa." In *The Politics of Heritage in Africa: Economies, Histories, and Infrastructures*, edited by Derek Peterson, Kodzo Gavua, Ciraj Rassool, 1–36. Cambridge: Cambridge University Press, 2015.

Peutz, Nathalie. *Islands of Heritage: Conservation and Transformation in Yemen*. Stanford: Stanford University Press, 2018.

Rizvi, Kishwar. *The Transnational Mosque: Architecture and Historical Memory in the Contemporary Middle East*. Chapel Hill: University of North Carolina Press, 2015.

Ruette, Emilie. *Memoirs of an Arabian Princess from Zanzibar*. Mineola, NY: Dover, 2009.

Sachedina, Amal. "Nizwa Fort: Transforming Ibadi Religion through Heritage Discourse in Oman." *Comparative Studies of South Asia, Africa and the Middle East* 39, no. 2 (2019): 328–43.

Sachedina, Amal. *Cultivating the Past, Living the Modern: The Politics of Time in the Sultanate of Oman*. Ithaca, NY: Cornell University Press, 2021.

Said, Edward W. *Orientalism*. New York: Vintage, 1979.

Sālimī, ʿAbd Allāh ibn Ḥumayyid, Yaḥmadī, Khalīlī, Yaḥmadī, Hilāl ibn Zāhir, and Khalīlī, Saʿīd ibn Khalafān. *Talqīn al-ṣibyān mā yalzamu al-insān*. Al-Ṭabʿah 23. Masqaṭ: Maktabat al-Istiqāmah, 2003.

Saskia Sassen. *Territory, Authority, Rights from Medieval to Global Assemblages*. Updated ed. Princeton, N.J: Princeton University Press, 2006.

"Scholarships Tenable in Algeria for the Academic Year 2017/2018." Dreamjobz-STZ. Accessed October 9, 2020. https://dreamjobtz.blogspot.com/2017/06/tcu-scholarships-tenable-in-algeria-for.html.

Shahab, Ahmad. *What Is Islam? The Importance of Being Islamic*. Princeton and Oxford: Princeton University Press, 2016.

Shankar, Shobana. *An Uneasy Embrace: Africa, India and the Spectre of Race*. Oxford: Oxford University Press, 2021.

Shariff, Ibrahim Noor. *Tanzania Na Propaganda Za Udini*. Self-published: 2014.

Sheriff, Abdul. "Mosques, Merchants, & Landowners in Zanzibar Stone Town." In *The History and Conservation of Zanzibar Stone Town*, edited by Abdul Sheriff, 46–66. Zanzibar: Dept. of Archives, Museums & Antiquities, 1995.

———. "Race and Class in the Politics of Zanzibar." *Africa Spectrum* 36, no. 3 (2001): 301–18.

Shivji, I. G. *Pan-Africanism or Pragmatism?* (1st ed.). Mkuki na Nyota: 2008.

Skounti, Ahmed. "The Authentic Illusion: Humanity's Intangible Cultural Heritage, the Moroccan Experience." In *Intangible Heritage*, edited by Natauko Akagawa and Laurajane Smith, 88–106. New York: Routledge, 2009.

Spear, Thomas. "Neo-Traditionalism and the Limits of Invention in British Colonial Africa." *Journal of African History* 44, no. 1 (2003): 3–27.

Strobel, Margaret. *Muslim Women in Mombasa, 1890–1975*. New Haven, CT: Yale University Press, 1979.

Sultan, Ali. "Leaders of Islamist Group in Tanzania Freed, Charges Dropped." *Associated Press*. June 16, 2021.

"Tanganyika Si Guantanamo Ya Kutesa Masheikh (Tanzania Is Not a Guantanamo Where Shaykhs Can Be Tortured)," An-Nuur, September 11, 2015, sec. Headline and pp. 2–3.

Tiwani, Khalfan S. *Qamusi-Ssalaa*. Publication rights are reserved for the author, 2008.

Tolmacheva, Marina. "Toward a Definition of the Term Zanj." *Azania: Archaeological Research in Africa* 21, no. 1 (1986): 105–13.

Toronto, James A., and Muhammad S. Eissa. "Egypt: Promoting Tolerance, Defending against Islamism." In *Teaching Islam: Textbooks and Religion in the Middle East*, edited by Eleanor Abdella Doumato and Gregory Starrett, 27–51. Boulder, CO: Lynne Rienner, 2007.

Trimingham, J. Spencer. *Islam in East Africa*. Oxford: Clarendon, 1964.

Trouillot, Michel-Rolph. *Silencing the Past: Power and the Production of History*. Boston: Beacon, 1995.

Troutt-Powell, Eve. *A Different Shade of Colonialism: Egypt, Great Britain, and the Mastery of the Sudan*. Berkeley: University of California Press, 2003.

Turner, Simon. "'These Young Men Show No Respect for Local Customs'—Globalization and Islamic Revival in Zanzibar." *Journal of Religion in Africa* 39, no. 3 (2009): 237–61.

UNESCO World Heritage List. "M'Zab Valley." Accessed October 27, 2020. https://whc.unesco.org/en/list/188/.

"United Republic of Tanzania Situation." WHO (COVID-19) Homepage (World Health Organization). Accessed September 25, 2023. https://covid19.who.int/region/afro/country/tz.

U.S. Department of State: Office of International Religious Freedom. 2021 Report on International Religious Freedom: Oman, June 2, 2022. Accessed March 15, 2024. https://www.state.gov/reports/2021-report-on-international-religious-freedom/.

Valeri, Marc. "Ibadism and Omani Nation-Building Since 1970." In *On Ibadism*, edited by Angeliki Ziaka, 165–76. Hildesheim, Germany: Georg Olms, 2013.

Vocational Education and Training Authority. "About Us" (United Republic of Tanzania: Ministry of Education Science and Technology). Accessed May 25, 2022. https://www.veta.go.tz/about-us.

Wahab, Saada Omar. "Emancipation and Post-Emancipation in Zanzibar." In *Transition from Slavery in Zanzibar and Mauritius*, edited by Vijayalakshmi Teelock and Satyendra Peerthum, 45–68. Dakar: CODESRIA, 2016.

Ware, Rudolph T. *The Walking Qur'an: Islamic Education, Embodied Knowledge, and History in West Africa*. 1st ed. Chapel Hill: The University of North Carolina Press, 2014.

Westerlund, David. *Ujamaa Na Dini: A Study of Some Aspects of Society and Religion in Tanzania, 1961–1977*. Stockholm: Almqvist & Wiksell International, 1980.

Wilkinson, John C. "On Being an Ibāḍī." *The Muslim World* 105, no. 2 (2015): 142–56.

———. *The Imamate Tradition of Oman*. Cambridge: Cambridge University Press, 1987.

Williams, Julius Onome. "Ties of the Past, Deals of the Future: Oman's Contemporary Economic Relationship with East Africa." Undergraduate thesis. Harvard College, 2018.

Wortmann, Kimberly T. "Daʿwa at the Sultan's Mosque: An Example of Ibāḍī Women's Activism in Muscat." In *Local and Global Ibadi Identities*, edited by Yohei Kondo and Angeliki Ziaka, 367–73. Hildesheim, Germany: Georg Olms, 2020.

———. "Ibadi Muslim Schools in Post-Revolutionary Zanzibar." *Africa: Journal of the International African Institute* 92 (2022): 249–64.

———. "Omani Religious Networks in Contemporary Tanzania and Beyond," PhD diss., Harvard University, 2018.

———. "Reading Ibāḍī Women's Legacies through Stone Town's Built Environment." *Islamic Africa* 12, no. 1 (2021): 1–28.

El Zein, Abdul Hamid M. *The Sacred Meadows: A Structural Analysis of Religious Symbolism in an East African Town*. Evanston, IL: Northwestern University Press, 1974.

# LIST OF INTERVIEWS

Al-Hayat students and graduates (notes from group meeting), interview with author, Ilala Mosque, Dar es Salaam, June 3, 2019.
Anas (representative of the grand mufti's office), interview with author, Chake Chake, Pemba, February 4, 2016.
Ayman (Istiqaama leader), interview with author, Stone Town, Zanzibar, February 24, 2016.
Bi Aida (Ma'had Istiqaama administrator), interview with author, Tungu, Zanzibar, May 29, 2019.
Fahmy (Al-Hayat student), interview with author, Dar es Salaam, June 3, 2019.
Haidar (Istiqaama graduate and Al-Hayat student), interview with author, Zanzibar, July 5, 2019.
Ibrahim (Sunni teacher and imam), interview with author, Stone Town, Zanzibar, March 15, 2016.
Istiqaama Women's Group, group interview with author, Mwanza, April 26, 2016.
Jalali (former Istiqaama student), interview with author, Skype, August 15, 2017.
Juma (representative of Jambo Juice factory), interview with author, Shinyanga, June 18, 2019.
Maher (representative of Jabir ibn Zayd Mosque), interview with author, Kitumbini, Dar es Salaam, May 15, 2019.
Mariam (young Ibadi woman and interlocutor), interview with author, Arusha, Tanzania, March 29, 2016.
Mona (leader of Khairia Sunni Women's Group), personal interview, Mwanza, December 6, 2019.
Muhammad (former student at Al-Hayat), interview with author, Dar es Salaam, July 3, 2019.

Mzee Bakari (Ibadhi elder and Istiqaama representative), interview with author, Ziwani, Pemba, February 2, 2016.

Mzee Idris (Ibadhi Mosque caretaker), interview with author, Lalago, June 17, 2019.

Nuhu (former Istiqaama student), interview with author, Zanzibar, May 31, 2018.

Rachid (Arabic and Islamic Studies teacher at Istiqaama), interview with author, Tungu, Zanzibar, January 15, 2016.

Salim (former Istiqaama teacher), interview with author, Stone Town, Zanzibar, May 31, 2018.

Sara (founder of Women's Ma'had), interview with author, Mwanza Region, June 15, 2019.

Shireen (president of the Istiqama Women's Group), interview with author, Mwanza, April 25, 2016.

Yasser (senior BAKWATA official), interview with author, Kinondoni, Dar es Salaam, June 21, 2017.

Zayd (Shi'i community leader), interview with author, Stone Town, Zanzibar, March 16, 2016.

# INDEX

Page numbers in italics indicate illustrations.

Abd Allah b. Ibad, 48
Abd Allah bin Ba Kathir Al-Kindy, 56
Abdullah b. Baz, 40–41
Abdurrahman bin Rustam, 48–49
Abeid Amani Karume
   (r. 1964–1972), 12
Abu 'Ubayda bin Muslim bin Abi
   Karima al-Tamimi, 48–50, 68
Africa Outlook, 185
African National Congress
   (ANC), 154
African-Muslim indigeneity, 49–50,
   68
Afro-Shirazi Party (ASP), 12, 141
Aga Khan, 100
Ahlul Bayt Foundation (ABF), 46,
   62–63
Ahmad bin Sumayt, 56, 59
Aillet, Cyrille, 5
Akhtar, Iqbal, 60, 70n20
Algeria: Ibadhism in, 71n37, 133–36;
   Tanzania and, 154–55
Al-Hayat (Life Institute) (Algeria):
   employment opportunities and,
   142, 147; history and curriculum of,
   134–37; relationship with Istiqaama
   and, 131–33, 137–40, 142–44,
   154–55; Swahili (language) and,
   145; Tanzanian students at, 142–49
Ali b. Abi Talib, 31n10, 47
Al-Shabaab, 66
Anas (representative of the Grand
   Mufti's Office), 103
Anderson, Benedict, 35n46
Anglo-German Agreement
   (1866), 167
*An-Nuur* (newspaper), 102
Ansar Sunna, 74n96
Arab Spring, 92, 152
Arab Women's Institute (Mombasa),
   215n11
Arabic (language): in Algerian
   schools, 134, 148; Al-Hayat (Life
   Institute) (Algeria) and, 136, 144,
   145, 148–49; Istiqaama schools
   and, 111–12, 113–15, 117, 118–20,
   123–26, 151
Arusha Declaration (1967), 172

Association of Tanzanian Students in Algeria (ATSA), 145
Atfayyish, Abu Ishaq, 81
Atia, Mona, 80
Ayman (Istiqaama leader): on funding, 95, 100–101; on Ibadhi fiqh and ritual practice, 55–59; on intra-Muslim relations and history of Ibadhism, 45–46, 47–52, 61, 63, 65, 85–87; as source, 23
Azri, Khaled al-, 33n27
'azzāba, 133–34

Ba Kathir, 56, 59
Badri, Ahmed al-, 150
Bakhresa Group, 193–95n74
BAKWATA (National Muslim Council of Tanzania), 98, 100–104, 206, 208–10, 212–13
Balhaj, Muhammad al-Sheikh, 149
Balhaj, Qasim bin Ahmad al-Sheikh, 149–51
Bang, Anne, 54, 59
Baraza Kuu (Supreme Council of Islamic Organizations and Institutions in Tanzania), 101
Barghash bin Said (r. 1870–1888), 11, 18, 34n35, 63–64, 132
Bayyud, Ibrahim bin 'Umar, 134–36
Becker, Felicitas, 97–98
Ben Ali, Zine al Abidine, 152
Benabdallah, Lina, 37n70
Berber (language), 148
Bi Aida (Ma'had Istiqaama administrator), 124
Bilal b. Rabah, 50
Bilal Muslim Mission of Tanzania (BMMT), 50
Boko Haram, 52–53
Boumediene, Houari, 154
Bourguiba, Habib, 152

Boym, Svetlana, 217
Buffalo Agency (Cairo), 133
Busaidi dynasty, 11–12

calendars (Istiqaama), 195–97, *196*
Campbell, Gwyn, 32n18
Canning, Charles, 11
Canning Award, 11
Chama cha Mapinduzi (CCM; Party of the Revolution), 15–16, 141
China, 36n63, 37n70
Christianity, 66, 179–82
Confucius Institutes, 36n63
Cooper, Frederick, 34n35
cotton industry, 168–71, 182–83, 184–89
Coulson, Andrew, 191n26
COVID-19 global pandemic, 217
Curtis, Edward E., 50, 72n48
Custers, M. H., 158n73

Desplat, Patrick, 107n46
Dolezal, Luna, 86

East African Muslim Welfare Society (EAMWS), 100
East India Company, 11
education. *See* Istiqaama schools
Eickelman, Dale F., 40, 83
El-Gheithy, Said, 20–21, 23
extra-marital affairs, 56–57

Fahmy (Al-Hayat student), 145
Farai, Nassor al-, 195
Foucault, Michel, 42
French (language), 134, 144, 145, 147, 148
Friday prayer movement, 66–67, 80–81, 88–93, 176–77

# INDEX

Gaiser, Adam R., 71n29
Geertz, Clifford, 4, 93
Geimar, Hady, 16
Ghadafi, Muammar, 152
Ghana: Istiqaama schools in, 157n38
Ghazal, Amal, 12, 88, 133
Ghazali, Al-, 58
Glassman, Jonathan, 12
GMO (Grand Mufti's Office; Zanzibar), 98, 100, 101, 103–4
Gooding, Phillip, 32n18
Goshey, Emily, 52
Great Lakes Construction Company, 195
Gülen movement, 36n63

Haefali, Evan, 5
Haidar (Istiqaama graduate and Al-Hayat student), 145, 146–49, 154
Haidar, Najam, 74n81
Haitham bin Tarik (r. 2020–), 10, 31n2
*hajj* pilgrimage, 55
Hall, Stuart, 8, 42, 127
Harthi, Thani bin Amir al-, 166
Hoffman, Valerie, 24, 47, 68–69, 90, 91
hospitality, 41–42, 51, 54, 62, 68, 94. *See also* tolerance
Hurd, Elizabeth, 5

Ibadhi women: dress and, 114, 199–200; education and, 151, 203, 205–11; exclusion from public life of, 176, 196–97, 201–3, 213–14; in Lalago, 176, 178; piety and, 198. *See also* Istiqaama Women's Group
Ibadhi-Omani diaspora in Tanzania: characteristics of, 19–20, 171–72; in Lalago and Great Lakes region, 172–79, *174*, 182–92; migration flows and, 10–11, 141–42, 161–66, 171–72, 189–90; religious competition and, 179–82; women and, 197; Zanzibar Revolution and, 62. *See also* Istiqaama Muslim Community of Tanzania
Ibadhism: in Algeria, 71n37, 133–36; cultural heritage of Omanis and, 17–18; European Christian perspectives on, 53–54; fiqh and ritual practice of, 44–45, 55–59; Friday prayer movement and, 80–81, 88–93, 176–77; in Ghana, 157n38; *khawārij* (Kharijites) and, 4–5, 47–48, 51, 137; in Libya, 72n50; nonviolence and, 51–53; in Oman, 49, 64–65; origins and history of, 4–5, 47–51; other Muslims perspectives on, 39–41, 50–51, 56–59, 69; Qaboos bin Said and, 1; racial identities and, 59–63; selection of imams in, 48–49; study of Islam and, 25–27, 219–20. *See also* Istiqaama Muslim Community of Tanzania; tolerance
Ibrahim (Sunni teacher and imam), 45–46, 56–57, 59–60, 66–68
Ilala, Dar es Salaam, 131–32, *132*, 142
imagined communities, 35n46, 83
indigeneity, 49–50, 68
Ingrams, W. H., 53–54, 57
international terror networks, 52–53
Islam Noir, 153
Islamic extremist organizations, 52–53, 66
Islamic State (ISIS/ISIL), 52–53
Islamophobia, 66, 98
Ismailis, 20, 70n23, 100
Ismailiy, Ahmad al-, 43

Istiqaama Institute (Tungu): Arabic (language) and, 111–12, 113–15, 117, 118–20, 123–26; history and aims of, 74n87, 113–16; Omani textbooks in, 111–12, 115, 116–23, 126–28; sources and methodology on, 23; Swahili (language) and, 111–12, 117–20. *See also* Ayman (Istiqaama leader)
Istiqaama Muslim Community of Tanzania: branches of, 6, 7; calendars of, 195–97, *196*; diplomacy and soft power of Oman and, 1–4, 6, 9, 16–17, 26, 67, 78–81, 112, 145, 155, 219; exclusion of women from public life and, 176, 196–97, 201–3, 213–14; funding of, 95–98, 99, 100–101, 175, 178–79, 187–88; history and aims of, 5–10, 20, 30, 65, 77–78, 79–81, 85–88, 94–95, 99, 104–5 (*see also* Istiqaama schools); nostalgia and, 18–19, 22, 217; relationship with Oman and, 3–6, 95, 195 (*see also* textbooks); socioeconomic development and, 80, 96, 127, 144, 154–55, 187–89, 207; sources and methodology on, 4, 20–26; study of Islam and, 25–27; Tanzanian state Islamic authorities and, 98–99, 102
Istiqaama schools: Algerian teachers and, 149–54; Arabic (language) and, 111–12, 113–15, 117, 118–20, 123–26, 151; COVID-19 global pandemic and, 217; in Ghana, 157n38; history and aims of, 59, 65, 78, 80, 95, 113–16, 140, 217–18; in Lalago, 173–75, 186–89, *187*; Omani textbooks in, 104–5, 111–12, 115, 116–23, 126–28; opportunities for study abroad and, 99 (*see also*

Al-Hayat (Life Institute) (Algeria)); Swahili (language) and, 111–12, 117–20, 150, 151–52; women and, 203, 205–11
Istiqaama Women's Group (Mwanza): collaborations with Sunni and Shi'a Muslim charities, 205–13; role and activities of, 199–205, 214
Istiqaama Youth Organization, 137, *138*
Itandala, Buluda, 168, 180
ivory trade and smuggling, 164, 168, 182

Jābir b. Zayd, 48
Jabir bin Zayd Mosque (Dar es Salaam), 77, 78
Jalali (former Istiqaama student), 118–23
Jambo Food Products Ltd, *184*, 185–86
Jāmi'i Zinjibār (Stone Town), 1–4, 3, 17
Jamshid bin Abdullah (r. 1963–1964), 43
Jomier, Augustin, 133, 135
Jones, Linda Gale, 91–92
Juma (Jambo factory CEO), 183–89
*jumuiya* (community, association), 5. *See also* Istiqaama Muslim Community of Tanzania

Kabawi, 'Abdul bin Mas'ud al-, 152
*kafa'a*, 33n27
Kane, Ousmane, 19
Katz, Marion, 91
Kaunda, Kenneth, 191n33
Kenya-Uganda Railway, 168
Khairia Sunni Women's Group, 210–13

# INDEX

Khalili, Ahmad bin Hamad al-:
Abdullah b. Baz and, 40–41;
Ayman (Istiqaama leader) and,
45; biography of, 18, 78–82;
on createdness/uncreatedness
of Qur'an, 57; Friday prayer
movement and, 66–67, 80–81,
176–77; Ibadhism in Oman and, 65;
Istiqaama and, 5, 15, 77, 78, 86, 104,
117; Mwanza mosque and, 200; M.
Tiwani and, 137–39, *138*
Kharusi, Nafla S., 32n20
*khawārij* (Kharijites), 4–5, 47–48,
51, 137
Khoja caste, 60–61
Kikwete, Jakaya, 35n49
Kishwar, Rivzi, 1–2
Knut, Vikør, 54
Koenings, Nathalie Arnold, 141,
156n32

Lake Province Growers
Association, 170
Lang, Christian, 58
Lang, Gottfried, 170
Lang, Martha, 170
Libya, 71n37, 72n50, 134, 152, 158n73
Limbert, Mandana, 116
Lint and Seed Marketing Board, 170

Maher (representative of Jabir bin
Zayd Mosque), 77–78, 79, 92,
113, 149
Maji Maji rebellion, 169
Majid bin Said, 11
Maktabat Istiqaama (publishing
house), 22
Mariam (young Ibadi woman and
interlocutor), 39–41, 50–51, 57–58,
68, 161
Martin, B. G., 54

Martin, Richard C., 57
Masauni, Hamad, 195
Mazrui, Juma Muhammad al-, 137
McCutcheon, Russell T., 16–17
McDow, Thomas, 162, 166
Mehta, Nanji, 169
Metcalf, Barbara, 92
Middleton, John, 54
migration. *See* Ibadhi-Omani diaspora
in Tanzania
*Min al-Sawāhil* (TV series), 163
Ministry of Endowments and
Religious Affairs (MERA; Oman),
82, 83–85
Mittermaier, Amirah, 96
Mona (leader of Khairia Sunni
Women's Group), 210, 211–12
Mozambique Liberation Front
(FRELIMO), 154
Muʿammar, ʿAli Yahya, 152
Muʿawiyya b. Abi Sufyan, 47
Muhammad (former student at Al-
Hayat), 145
Muhammad bin Yūsuf Atfiyyash, 135
Muhieddine, Abdelkader bin, 158n71
Mzee Bakari (Ibadhi elder and
Istiqaama representative), 94,
99, 100
Mzee Idris (Ibadhi Mosque caretaker),
173–75, 177–78, 179, 182–83

Nahrawan, Battle of (658 CE), 4
neoliberalism, 4, 10, 68, 80, 96, 218
nonviolence, 51–53
nostalgia, 18–19, 22, 217
Nuhu (former Istiqaama student),
123–24
Nur al-Din al-Salimi, 136
Nurse, Derek, 125
Nyamanaro, 205–10
Nyerere, Julius, 154, 170, 172, 191n33

oil industry, 154
Oman: heritage regime in, 16–17; Ibadhi women in, 202; Ibadhism in, 49, 64–65; identity and nationalism in, 82–85; Istiqaama and, 3–6, 195 (*see also* textbooks); Jāmiʿi Zinjibār (Stone Town) and, 1–4, 3; *nahda* in, 13; population of, 24; role in Tanzania of, 1–4, 82–83, 218 (*see also* Istiqaama Muslim Community of Tanzania); tolerance in, 43, 218. *See also specific sultans*
Orsi, Robert, 38n75
Ott, Jessica, 204

pan-Africanism, 127, 154–55
pan-Islamism, 22, 100, 132
Pearson, Michael, 32n18
Pemba, 131, 137–42, *139*
Petroleum Development Organization (PDO), 162
Peutz, Nathalie, 3
Pew Templeton Religious Futures Project, 24
piety, 198
pious neoliberalism, 80
Pouwels, Randall L., 63, 75–76n100

Qaboos bin Said (r. 1970–2020): coup d'état (1970) and, 13; Friday prayer movement and, 88–89; Jāmiʿi Zinjibār and, 1–4; al-Khalili and, 82; Omani identity and, 83; *tasamuh* and, 64–65; tolerance and, 43
Qur'an: createdness/uncreatedness of, 57; Friday prayer movement and, 92; Istiqaama and, 99; al-Khalili and, 57, 81, 82; study of, 18, 49, 66, 87, 119, 125, 134, 151, 174–75, 178, 207, 211
Qutb, Sayyid, 87, 99

Rachid (Arabic and Islamic Studies teacher at Istiqaama), 151–54
racial identities, 59–63
Rashidi, Mubarak bin ʿAbd Allah al-, 72n44
Registration Insolvency and Trusteeship Act (RITA), 102
religious freedom, 5. *See also* tolerance
Religious Freedom Report, 24
religious transnationalism, 19–20
representation, theory of, 127
Revolutionary Government of Zanzibar or Serikali ya Mapinduzi Zanzibar (SMZ), 2
righteousness: exclusion of women from public life and, 196–97; Istiqaama as defined by, 5, 9, 20, 43, 52, 85–86, 100; Jāmiʿi Zinjibār (Stone Town) and, 17
Riyami, Habib al-, 2
Riyami, Nasser Abdulla al-, 81–83
Roman Catholic Church, 180, 181–82
Rustamid dynasty, 133
*ruya*, 40–41, 57

Sachedina, Amal, 16, 23
Safar (travel prayer), 176–77
Said bin Taimur (r. 1932–1970), 13
Salafism: Ansar Sunna and, 75n96; Friday prayer movement and, 90; Ibadhism and, 17, 52; reformist movements and, 49; study of Islam and, 27, 198; textbooks and, 121
*salat al-safar* (travel prayer), 176–77
Salim (former Istiqaama teacher), 125, 126
Sālimī, Nūr al-Dīn ʿAbd Allāh bin Humayyid al-, 81, 176
Salme, Princess, 20
Sara (founder of Women's Ma'had), 206–10

Sartre, Jean-Paul, 86
Sayyid Said bin Sultan, 11, 21, 54, 63
self-reliance (Sw., *kujitegemea*), 154, 198, 204
Shafi'i Islam: Friday prayer movement and, 80–81, 91–92; Istiqaama schools and, 150–51, 186; al-Khalili and, 79; racial identities and, 59–60; under sultanate rule, 64–65; tolerance and, 45, 54, 56–57, 64–65
Shankar, Shobana, 14
Sheriff, Abdul, 11
Shi'a Islam: Ibadhis mistaken for, 40, 50–51; racial identities and, 60–61, 62–63; tolerance and, 43, 46, 60–61, 65–66, 68–69
Shireen (president of the Istiqama Women's Group), 39, 199–200, 201–5, 213
Shivji, Issa, 97
Siffin, Battle of (657 CE), 4, 47
Siyabi, Ahmad ibn al-, 89–90
Skounti, Ahmed, 17
slavery and slave trade, 11, 43, 164
Societies Act (1954), 102
Sonatrach, 154
South Africa, 154
Spear, Thomas, 125, 182
Strobel, Margaret, 215n11
Sufism: Friday prayer movement and, 90; Ibadhism and, 53, 64, 85, 192n49; study of Islam and, 27, 198; *tariqa* and, 44
Sukuma Land Development Scheme, 169
Suleiman (Istiqaama Youth Organization leader), 131, 142
Suleman, Alhaji Umar Adam, 157n38
Sunni Islam: Khairia Sunni Women's Group and, 210–13; racial identities and, 60–61; tolerance and, 45–46, 54, 56–57, 59–60, 66–69; in Zanzibar, 2. *See also* Shafi'i Islam
SuperDoll, 195
Swahili (language): Al-Hayat (Life Institute) (Algeria) and, 145; vs. Arabic (language), 123–26; Ibadhi-Omani diaspora in Tanzania and, 15, 67, 81, 86, 189; Istiqaama schools and, 111–12, 117–20, 150, 151–52; Tanzanian students in Algeria and, 145

Table and Desk Foundation (TDCF), 206
*Tafahum* (magazine), 106n25
Tanganyika, 12, 14, 100, 162, 168–70. *See also* Tanzania (United Republic of Tanzania)
Tanganyika African National Union (TANU), 100
TANU (Tanganyika African National Union), 204
Tanzania (United Republic of Tanzania): Algeria and, 154–55; Christianity in, 66, 179–82; cotton industry in, 169–71, 182–83, 185–89; history of, 12; Islamophobia in, 66, 98; neoliberal institutions in, 4, 10, 68, 80, 96; neoliberal reforms in, 218; Oman and, 1–4, 82–83 (*see also* Istiqaama Muslim Community of Tanzania); population of, 24; state Islamic authorities in, 98–104 (*see also* BAKWATA (National Muslim Council of Tanzania); GMO (Grand Mufti's Office)); transnational diaspora organizations in, 36n63. *See also* Ibadhi-Omani diaspora in Tanzania; Zanzibar
Tanzanian Cotton Authority, 170
*taqiyya*, 49, 61

*Tarbiyya* (textbook), 116–17, 121
*tasamuh*, 64–65
*tawhid*, 46, 55
textbooks, 22, 104–5, 111–12, 115, 116–23, 126–28
Thuwaini bin Said, 11
Tiwani, Khalfan, 86, 137, 139–40, 177
Tiwani, Muhammad, 86, 137–40, *138*, 142–43, 149, 177
tolerance: discourses on difference and, 45–55; in Oman, 43, 218; racial identities and, 59–63; role in Ibadhi discourse of, 5–6, 42, 64–69, 83, 219; role of women and, 197; under sultanate rule, 63–64; in Zanzibar, 41–43, 44, 218
Tolmacheva, Marina, 72n45
transnational mosques, 1–2
Trouillot, Michel-Rolph, 15
Troutt-Powell, Eve, 14
Tungu. *See* Istiqaama Institute (Tungu)
Turkey, 36n63
Turner, Simon, 113

Uamsho, 62, 75n97
Uganda, 168–69
Uganda Company Ltd., 169
Ujamaa, 100, 170–71, *171*, 172–73, 204
*umoja* (unity), 204
United Arab Emirates (UAE), 39–40
United Republic of Tanzania. *See* Tanzania
*ustaarabu*, 45, 112
'Uthman b. Affan, 47

Valeri, Marc, 83, 84

Wahab, Saada Omar, 11
Wahhabism, 47, 51, 79, 83, 121

*wamanga*, 8–9
*waqf* (religious endowments), 134, 174, 200
Wilkinson, John C., 37n72
women. *See* Ibadhi women

Xi Jinping, 37n70

Yang Fenglan (Ivory Queen), 191n17
Yasser (senior BAKWATA official), 102

*zakat*, 55
*zanj*, 49–50
Zanzibar: Busaidi dynasty and British colonial rule in, 11–12, 63–64; government and population of, 23–24; heritage regime in, 16–17; Islamic education in, 112–13 (*see also* Istiqaama schools); Islamophobia in, 98; tolerance in, 41–43, 44, 218. *See also* Zanzibar Revolution (1964)
Zanzibar Muslim Academy, 1
Zanzibar National Archives (ZNA), 36n62
Zanzibar National Party (ZNP), 12
Zanzibar Revolution (1964): history and collective memory of, 12–16, 59–60, 62; Ibadhism and, 18; al-Khalili and, 79, 82; Pemba and, 141; religious life and, 43, 93–94; secularization of society and, 87
Zayd (Shi'i community leader), 46, 62–63, 65–66
Zein, Abdul Hamid El-, 42
Zinjibāris (Swahili-speaking diaspora in Oman), 8, 22

**Kimberly T. Wortmann** is Assistant Professor and a scholar of religion at Wake Forest University in North Carolina. Her research and writing are centered around transnational Muslim communities, religious institutions, Islamic education, and Swahili-speaking societies in East Africa and the Arab Gulf region.

*For Indiana University Press*

Lesley Bolton, Project Manager/Editor

Anna Garnai, Editorial Assistant

Sophia Hebert, Assistant Acquisitions Editor

Samantha Heffner, Marketing and Publicity Manager

Brenna Hosman, Production Coordinator

Katie Huggins, Production Manager

Bethany Mowry, Acquisitions Editor

Dan Pyle, Online Publishing Manager

Pamela Rude, Senior Artist and Book Designer

www.ingramcontent.com/pod-product-compliance
Lightning Source LLC
Chambersburg PA
CBHW020106020526
44112CB00033B/1046